SOCIAL CHANGE and the LIFE COURSE

Edited by GAYNOR COHEN

TAVISTOCK PUBLICATIONS
London and New York

First published in 1987
by Tavistock Publications Ltd
11 New Fetter Lane,
London, EC4P 4EE

Published in the USA by
Tavistock Publications
in association with Methuen, Inc.
29 West 35th Street,
New York NY, 10001

Printed in Great Britain at
the University Press, Cambridge

British Library Cataloguing in Publication Data

Social change and the life course. ——
(Social science paperback)
1. Family 2. Family—Political aspects
I. Cohen, Gaynor
306.8′5 HQ728

ISBN 0–422–79920–3
ISBN 0–422–79940–8 Pbk

Library of Congress Cataloging in Publication Data

Social change and the life course.
(Social science paperbacks; 354)
Bibliography: p.
Includes index.
1. Life cycle, Human. 2. Social change. 3. Family—Great Britain.
I. Cohen, Gaynor. II. Series.
HQ799.97.G7S65 1986 303.4
86–23848
ISBN 0–422–79920–3
ISBN 0–422–79940–8 (pbk.)

Contents

Preface

This book has its origins in a series of one-day seminars on social change organized at the Civil Service College. The purpose of these seminars was to enable senior civil servants to be brought up to date with the policy implications of recent research on specific themes. In organizing two of these seminars on the theme of the family and the life cycle I realized the dearth of research by sociologists and anthropologists in Britain which explores the life course implications of social change. This volume attempts to begin to fill that gap.

I am grateful to the contributors, most of whom participated in the original seminars, for being prepared to reformulate their data within a life course framework. I also appreciate their flexibility in adapting to suggested shifts in emphasis while the manuscripts were being written.

As our objective was to prepare a book which could be readily understood by a wide readership we discuss concepts which are popularly used in different and imprecise ways. The concept of 'life course' is used by all contributors in place of 'life cycle' as it has greater potential for the discussion of social change. All contributors also focus on 'the family' although aware of the fact that it is frequently used in misleading ways. The significance of the family, however, in modifying individual life course experiences could not be ignored. It is, moreover, a social institution which exists as an entity in its own right and as such intervenes in the process of social change.

The book is organized so that two chapters give an overview of particular aspects of social change across the life course. Other chapters discuss particular life stages. The emphasis throughout is on the interrelation between the family and social and economic changes. Most contributors take account of social class and gender differences across the life course. Within a book of this length, however, it has not been possible to give an exhaustive account of social change. The life course experiences of ethnic minority groups living in Britain or of the very rich or very poor are hardly discussed. While some authors refer to the social policy implications of the changes they discuss, there is still need for far more extensive work to be done on this aspect.

Anyone writing on the life course in Britain would need to acknowledge the inspiration provided by Rhona and Robert Rapoport who, through their own work, have encouraged social scientists and policy-makers to adopt a life course or life cycle perspective. I would particularly like to record my thanks for the personal advice they gave me in organizing this volume. I would also like to thank Rosemary Firth. The most important debt I need to acknowledge is that which I owe to Abner Cohen for his professional support and advice especially with the introduction.

1
Introduction: the economy, the family, and the life course

GAYNOR COHEN

This book attempts to explore the nature of recent changes in the life course in contemporary British society. The term 'life course' is used here rather than the more familiar 'life cycle', as the latter implies fixed categories in the life of the individual and assumes a stable social system, whereas the former allows of more flexible biographical patterns within a continually changing social system. There is an extensive literature on the use of these and similar terms emanating particularly from the USA (see for example Riley, Foner, and Johnson 1972; Elder 1978). With a few outstanding exceptions, British social scientists have only recently shown interest in a life course approach to social change.

Between them, the contributors to this volume relate biographical and subjective perceptual processes to broader structural changes in the society. In particular, they explore the dynamic relations between the individual and other members of the family and the household, and the relation between the household and the changing economy within the wider society.

A variety of approaches to social change is followed. Nissel (Chapter 9) focuses on demographic processes, but in the course of doing so she also discusses the impact of economic changes upon family structure, functions, relationships, and values across the life course. Most contributors use the past as a reference point from which to chart shifts in experience and in attitudes, such as Clark's comparison between Victorian and modern expectations of marriage (Chapter 5).

Biography and subjective experience are treated in different ways. Nissel sets her own personal biography within the context of demographic and structural changes. She compares certain aspects of her own life with those of her mother and daughter. Burgoyne (Chapter 2) discusses the relations between subjective experience and changing structural factors as they affect the lives of men and women through their life courses. Other authors deal with the problems and beliefs at particular life-crisis points such as leaving home or getting married and in this way analyse changes in personal identity, social status, and family relationships, which cover divergent life experiences of men and women. Throughout the life course men's time is structured by their jobs, women's by their domestic roles.

Clark (Chapter 5) alerts both academics and practitioners concerned with the problem of divorce not to lose sight of both its private and its public aspects. He argues that marital breakdown and remarriage can be fully understood only if the emotional and personal experiences of the couple are set within the context of structural changes, such as unemployment or poverty. Furthermore an understanding of the problems must be built on knowledge of preceding life course stages and on the relationship between a married couple and their wider family network.

In everyday life we are consistently using biography to judge individuals or to analyse their behaviour. Doctors and counsellors use it to guide them in offering advice on health or family problems. Employers use it to assess an applicant's suitability for a particular post. Biography offers insight into continuities with an individual's past which can be used to explain current and to predict future behaviour. Some chapters in this volume give indications of the way in which such characteristics as social class background, job patterns, and gender may have a consistent influence upon individuals throughout the life course.

THE SOCIAL CONSTRUCTION OF THE LIFE COURSE

The life course is like a bus journey punctuated by stages, with boarding and embarkation points. Authors in this book stress that these stages are not fixed, have changed in length in response to wider social change, and that new stages have emerged. The boarding and embarkation points for childhood, youth, and mid life have either lengthened or shortened over time and vary according to region or culture.

Childhood, as Busfield (Chapter 3) reminds us, is an historical novelty. Our notion of childhood has been shaped by changes in the socio-economic and political structure. Busfield traces the implication of these changes in shifting research attention from fertility, to child-rearing patterns, to the more recent emphasis on parenting. The latter again reinforces the link between the economy, career timetables, and the different parenting experiences of mothers and fathers respectively.

The extent and experience of youth, that period of metamorphosis from childhood to adulthood, has also varied both regionally and historically. In rural Wales in 1940 the youth group, collectively referred to by Alwyn Rees (1950) as *'y bechgyn'* (the boys), ranged in age from sixteen to thirty-five. Marriage brought association with the group to an end; confirmed bachelors gradually left the group as they approached middle age.

The boundaries and conceptualization of youth, as Coffield shows (Chapter 4), have fluctuated markedly even in recent times. The imagery associated with the affluent creativity of youth in 1960 contrasts starkly with that used to describe the demoralized young unemployed of the 1980s. Coffield argues that changes in the economy are the source of these fluctuations, although not all youth will be equally affected. He notes the potential gulf between a generation of unskilled working-class young people who risk remaining unemployed and unemployable throughout their lives and younger members of their family with better training to secure new jobs generated by the economy.

Unemployment in the north-east is extending the period of youth and dependency, as without a job young men and women have to remain living at home with their parents.

Adulthood is often depicted as a single stage in life's journey, undifferentiated by further boarding or embarkation points. This stage, which occupies the longest time span in the life course, is popularly perceived as a plateau between growing up and growing old (Burgoyne, Chapter 2). It does in fact incorporate numerous substages such as leaving home, getting married, setting up house, moving home, becoming a parent, parenting, maintaining a household or career. Further differentiation has been introduced by divorce, remarriage, cohabitation, and changes in the labour market structure, such as redundancy and early retirement.

From the popular literature and mass media Hepworth (Chapter 6) identifies the recent growth of yet another stage: mid life. His argument is that shifts in the timing of life phases may well be accompanied by changes in commonly held perceptions of individual capacities and abilities associated with that phase. Parents of today are likely to experience the 'empty nest' stage at a much earlier point in the life course than previous generations. They will both look and be perceived as younger than the preceding generation and because of the extension of life they will have more of their life course to live through (Nissel, Chapter 9). Assumptions of growth, development, and creativity have been associated with the early stages of the life course. Mid and late stages have been seen as heralding decline, decay and dependence. Hepworth argues that a growing emphasis on self-development and individual growth accompanying an extension of the retirement period has shifted traditional attitudes to ageing and has generated a new mid-life phase associated with creativity and growth. The extent to which the capacity for individual development can actually be realized, however, is likely to be limited by the personal and material resources which individuals have acquired over the life course.

Discussions of mid life and retirement (Chapters 6 and 7) offer clear indicators of the potential quality of life in the post-retirement period. These indicators have their roots in labour market careers. Jobs offer resources (both financial and personal) and the potential for individual development which will continue to influence individual life courses beyond the career stage itself. Similarly, as Phillipson (Chapter 7) has pointed out, tensions in the immediate pre-retirement period, such as those created by recent economic upheavals like unemployment or redundancy, may well have an adverse effect on the experience of retirement itself.

Although this book does not examine old age through the eyes of the elderly themselves, recent studies are stressing the need to shift from a perception of old people that emphasizes their frailty and dependence to one which recognizes the continued capacity for individual growth and development throughout life (Wenger 1984). Certainly the old people who speak through the pages of Blythe's (1979) account of the *View in Winter* give every indication of continued activity.

Any change in one stage of the life course has implications for subsequent stages. The emerging imagery of mid life as a period of growth and development is affecting popular perceptions of post-retirement and even of old age. Personal problems and experiences too can be fully understood only with reference to the preceding life course stage. Phillipson (Chapter 7) argues that the experience of retirement needs to be analysed as part of the life course and as a sequence of interrelated stages rather than as a single stage. The quality of life in retirement will reflect continuities with working life: the level of income, or the degree of personal development. It will also reflect the quality of conjugal relationships developed earlier in life. A crisis such as redundancy or enforced early retirement experienced in the pre-retirement phase may well have a debilitating impact upon retirement itself.

The impact of extreme material inequalities influences experience throughout the life course. Burgoyne (Chapter 2) points to the contrasting life course experiences of the very rich and the very poor, while Coffield's sample is made up of young unqualified unemployed. Although it is beyond the scope of this book to trace the impact of disadvantage through the life course other studies offer evidence that extreme deprivation and discord experienced in early home life can retard later educational and social development (Rutter and Madge 1976).

It would be misleading to see each change in life experience as automatically determined by changes in preceding life course stages. The process of change is dynamic and, especially within the family, may be affected by the relationship between generations. This relationship need not be one of conflict. The emphasis on conflict in much of the social science literature masks the significance of the two-way learning process. Parents may respond differently to each of their children because of the reaction and behaviour of the children themselves (Riley *et al.* 1969).

Different types of exchanges take place between generations of the same family. Because of the extension of life children are no longer likely to inherit wealth at the time when they most need it (Nissel, Chapter 9). Grandchildren are now more likely to benefit from money inherited from grandparents.

The notion of reciprocity between different generations of family members, however, goes beyond exchanges of goods or even services and is based on deep-rooted gender-related norms and values. Otherwise why should the predominantly female carers in Ungerson's survey (Chapter 8), given the increased availability of labour market jobs for women, voluntarily undertake the burden of caring for the dependent elderly? Leonard's study (1980: 9) of marriage in a South Wales town, suggested that notions of obligation and reciprocal exchanges were sown early in life. Mothers 'spoiled' their adolescent daughters because they were 'anticipating some return on parental investment by giving care or companionship in parents' old age'. Their attitudes reflect those of the Gonja people who see care of children as an investment in care by children in parents' old age: 'in infancy your mother and father fed you and cleared up your messes; when they grow old you must feed them and keep them clean' (Goody 1983: 13). It is a notion which some might perceive as more appropriate for a simple agrarian than a complex industrial economy with its demands for rationality in employment practices.

Ungerson (Chapter 8) reminds us that this view of a reciprocal exchange is more unequal than ever before. The extension of life means that services to the elderly may stretch out over a very much longer period than services to children. Moreover it is women who almost always care for older dependent relatives. The four male carers in her sample were all caring for spouses.

Another significant gender difference was that, for women, caring was often an alternative to paid employment while the men carers had not interrupted their employment by caring activities. Wenger's survey (1984) of old people in north Wales found that primary care still came from the family and reflected mutual expectations although changes in the life course had meant that the children of the dependent elderly might themselves have been retired and in need of support and thus unable to provide consistent care for the over-seventy-fives.

At the same time other changes currently taking place in the life course may well extend the potential pool of carers. Recent evidence from the USA indicates that the increase in the divorce rate has encouraged greater involvement between grandparents and their grandchildren. Contact between grandparents and children whose parents are divorced is greater than with children still living with both parents. Children are often cared for by grandparents immediately following their parents' divorce. In some cases US courts have awarded custody of the children to grandparents even when neither natural parent is claimed to be unfit to care for the child. Certainly other factors such as the age of the grandparents are likely to influence the degree of contact between generations, with younger grandparents being more involved than older ones (Aldous 1985). Further research may indicate whether increasing involvement as a result of parents' divorce is likely to encourage an increase in the number of grandparents being cared for by their grandchildren at a later stage in the life course.

THE DYNAMICS OF FAMILY CONTINUITIES AND ECONOMIC CHANGE

Thus grandparents are acting as a countervailing force against the disruptive effects of divorce upon children. Indeed at every point the processes of change are resisted by basic family relations and values and their impact is thereby modified. This is why the notion of the family is so often used, particularly by politicians, to represent a support for and a haven from the destructive forces of change.

This assertion is made even in the face of such contradictory evidence as rising divorce rates and the disappearance of the stigma of illegitimate birth. There are now different family forms and the model of 'two parents – two children' can no longer be claimed to be the norm. But whatever the form, the family continues to have real as well as symbolic significance. It remains as a stubborn, complex, biological, psychological, economic, and cultural entity that exists in its own right and intervenes in the process of social change in a powerful way.

It is through the family that we gain an identity and continuity with the past: a name, physical characteristics, a 'place' in the community, and a reference point against which we are measured or can measure others. There are 'good' families offering support and comfort and 'bad' families where the weak, who are usually female and conditioned to be unaggressive (Heidensohn 1985) may be abused by the strong. Whatever its quality, the total family complex will influence the choices and experiences of its members throughout the life course.

Individual members of the same family may have very different life course experiences. Most chapters stress the impact of gender differences upon: young people struggling for independence; parenting; personal development; and caring for elderly dependants. Women are still constrained by their commitment to their families and are therefore prevented from achieving equality with men in the labour market.

Nevertheless, as Nissel points out, the changing status of women is possibly *the* major change in our society. Evidence of the rise in women's economic activity rates (Martin and Roberts 1984) shows that the period of women's confinement to the private world of the family is now over.

The family is not merely the passive recipient of wider economic change; it is an active agent capable of modifying or even initiating changes in the labour market. Personal careers and individual timetables often conflict with the timetables set by the labour market. At times family obligations may take priority over labour market demands for rationality and efficiency and either hinder or block the process of economic change.

The family then may be important for continuity both within an individual life course and in the relation between that life course and the wider economy. It is this interrelation between the forces for changes which stem from the economy and the family's countervailing pressures for continuity and stability which will be examined below. The structural changes discussed cover unemployment, redundancy, women's increased labour market activity, and the changing structure of the labour market. The impact of personal labour market career changes on the family throughout the life course will also be discussed.

WOMEN IN THE LABOUR MARKET

Life course experiences today must be affected by the remarkable increase in married women's labour market activity over the past thirty years. Yet there is little evidence that this has weakened women's allegiance to their traditional family responsibilities. Motherhood is still as vital for the gender identity of most women as paid employment is for men (Busfield, Chapter 3). Women's paid employment may well affect their decision of when to have a child but only for a minority of couples will it determine whether they have children at all.

The drop in the birth-rate since the beginning of this century is explained more by the reduced numbers of children per family than by the lack of desire for children (see Nissel, Chapter 9, *Table* 5). Surveys among young women in the USA show that fewer than 10 per cent enter adulthood with no desire for children (Rossi 1984) and Nissel's chapter shows that in Britain only one in ten married couples are without children.

Childbirth certainly disrupts women's careers although, as Burgoyne points out (Chapter 2), those who have built up some 'career capital' before the arrival of children will be in a stronger position than others when they return to the labour market. Some biographies of women in senior posts indicate that the decision whether and when to have children is related to a carefully developed personal career programme (Fogarty, Allen, and Watters 1981). Although such individuals are rare we need more evidence on the impact which current increases in the educational and training 'capital' of girls, higher levels of economic activity, and some extension of job opportunities at higher grades have had on family decisions on procreation by those affected.

It is the presence of a child under the age of five at home which has the greatest impact on whether or not women are economically active. A recent survey of women's employment found that significantly more women with children aged five to ten were working than those with children under five (Martin and Roberts 1984). Furthermore, although women are more likely to return to the labour market as their children get older, their continued caring responsibility for their children will influence the place, timing, and conditions of their employment. Despite the upward trend in the numbers of mothers returning to the labour market (Martin and Roberts 1984) the choice of jobs open to them is likely to be limited. Suburban residential areas, for instance, chosen in the interests of children in particular, offer a limited range of jobs for women. Similarly child-care timetables will encourage mothers to seek part-time rather than full-time employment. The most common child-care arrangements favoured by working mothers are family-based with fathers and grandmother providing the most frequent source of child-care (Martin and Roberts 1984). The lack of good, affordable day-care facilities again restricts the job opportunities of women who lack family support.

Motherhood is likely to limit women's labour market choices mostly when children are young. The responsibilities of parenthood however will be felt throughout the course of mothers' labour market careers. Part-time jobs are more likely than others to be in work areas exclusive to women, low paid, and offering fewer opportunities for training or promotion (Martin and Roberts 1984). Yet the convenience and flexibility of part-time work for women with young children is often more important than the career opportunities offered by the job. There is however a strong association between part-time employment status and downward job mobility (Martin and Roberts 1984). The effect of this pattern upon women's own career aspirations and achievements across the life course needs to be further explored. Current labour market trends indicating a further growth in demand for part-time unskilled, non-manual workers (Parsons 1985) suggest that women may continue to occupy peripheral, low-paid jobs which offer little potential for career advancement because their domestic responsibilities are likely to encourage mothers to select such jobs.

It is not surprising therefore that a majority of full-time female employees and a significant minority of part-time employees should claim that they are working primarily not because of personal career aspirations but in order to contribute to the household income (Martin and Roberts 1984). Currently wives, even in families with children, contribute about 25 per cent of household income (Nissel, Chapter 9). Some commentators have argued that increased female labour force activity has led to the development of more symmetrical relationships between husbands and wives within the household (Young and Willmott 1973). Others have qualified this claim with the argument that the sharing of household activities varies with the life course with greater parity between the sexes being apparent in later stages when women will have returned to the world of paid employment after child-rearing. Undoubtedly a shift in attitudes has taken place and men are now more willing to assist with domestic burdens especially with working wives (Kamerman 1980) but the main responsibility for care of home and children still rests with the wife.

It is not surprising therefore that despite the change in women's social status, recent studies of redundant workers (Morris 1983) have shown that even in families where there has been a shift in power, where females not males are the wage-earners, the notion that authority rests in the adult male has been slow to shift. To illustrate the priority given by women to the domestic sphere, some studies of women in employment have shown the various ways in which they attempt to make their work-place an extension of their home. The bright decor of the typing pool with its colourful posters and trailing plants is often reminiscent of the lounge of a modern house (Kanter 1977).

The high percentages of women employed in caring or service occupations reflect attempts to gain an easy alliance between domestic private and labour market public worlds. In Ungerson's study of carers, the caring activity was, for some of the women, an alternative to paid employment while for men, at a similar life course stage, this would not have been conceivable (Ungerson, Chapter 8). Many women clearly accept caring as a 'natural' and possibly lifelong task. Many in Ungerson's sample had apparently chosen to undertake the care of an elderly relative while still caring for dependent young people. Others, unable to find employment congruent with the social status they had acquired through their husbands' employment because of their lack of qualifications and skills, were using caring as a socially legitimate escape from the labour market. Similarly I found that younger women, wives of upwardly mobile young executives, who lacked the qualifications to find anything other than a low-status local job, would often choose pregnancy and the extension of the caring phase rather than face re-entry into the labour market (Cohen 1977).

We need more information than is currently available on older women's working lives, their domestic activities, and relationships. Since the 1960s there has been a rise in the level of married women's labour market participation especially in the older age groups (Martin and Roberts 1984). Women who do return to the labour force after taking time off to care for young children may not choose to retire at the same time as their husbands who will have experienced a longer and unbroken career. Some large employers, such as the Civil Service, in removing age barriers to recruitment to particular grades have shown an awareness that women's career timetables do not match those of men. Nevertheless given the current scarcity of jobs, both women and men are likely to experience pressure to retire even before rather than after the statutory age for retirement. There is also some evidence that women with retired husbands tend to choose early retirement. Although the decision may be taken voluntarily (Nissel, Chapter 9) there may also be informal pressures which force women to do so.

Further information is needed on the implication of women's employment for the quality of their domestic life especially in the later stages in the life course. The extensive study of Martin and Roberts (1984) paid less attention to older than to younger working women. There are indications for instance that female unemployment has a far greater impact upon the degree of social isolation experienced by older than by younger working women (Martin and Wallace 1985).

Given the extension of life, many more families are likely to be faced with the task of caring for elderly, possibly dependent relatives. Eversley (1982), taking account of trends in ageing, has stressed the interrelations between the changing occupational structure, in particular the increase in the number of women in paid employment, the decline in numbers of economically inactive people of pre-pensionable age (married women and single, unmarried daughters), and the increase in the absolute numbers of elderly. The overall effect, he argues, is bound to be a reduced capacity of the family to care for the elderly population.

It is obvious from Ungerson's contribution (Chapter 8) that some families are still attempting to cope with the care of elderly relatives. It is also obvious that women are most likely to be carers although the pool available for caring may well diminish in future years. Unlike men in her sample, women carers were spread at varying positions on the lifespan. Men in contrast had chosen to care (in each case for their wives) only on retirement. Phillipson (Chapter 7) too indicates that the men who took early retirement in order to care for sick wives were already near to retirement age and caring did not disrupt their careers. For some women caring was an alternative to paid employment but others had attempted to undertake both tasks. More research is needed on the impact of caring for the elderly upon women's labour market careers. Martin and Roberts (1984) claim that caring for a sick, elderly relative had less of an impact on womens' jobs than caring for younger dependants. But their study could not reflect the effect that caring has upon 'voluntary' retirement from the labour force and upon the quality of life experienced by such carers upon retirement. Any further study should take account of life course factors, of the extent to which willingness to care has stemmed from values and attitudes developed earlier in life, and of the relationships between carers, the dependent elderly, and younger family members. Studies of families' experiences of retirement have so far concentrated attention upon the impact of the husbands' not the wives' job experiences upon the quality of life after retirement.

CHANGES IN MEN'S INDIVIDUAL CAREER PATTERNS

In accepting that their family responsibilities take precedence over their labour market activities, most women are also accepting that for their husbands these priorities will be reversed, although it may take them some time to become aware of the implications. The impact is likely to be acute when the demanding periods in career timetables conflict with the most demanding phases in the family life course. The first experience of such conflict is likely to be when men's career patterns coincide with child-care demands and lead to an unequal distribution of the burden of care. It is at this time that women are likely to be particularly vulnerable and dependent on their husbands for material and emotional support. The widely accepted ideology and rhetoric of conjugal sharing and equality between spouses has provided justification for such dependence (Bujra and Caplan 1978). In reality this ideal cannot always be met. It may be this conflict between expectations and reality which causes some mothers to suffer severe depression after childbirth (Chapters 2 and 3).

Both Burgoyne (Chapter 2) and Busfield (Chapter 3) note the peripheral status of the father at the birth of a child. The extent to which fathers continue to remain peripheral within the household may well depend upon the way mothers cope with child-rearing problems, especially in the early stages. In a study of households on a suburban housing estate which were experiencing a common problem of conflict between husband's job and family demands, wives coped through developing a close network of reciprocal supportive relationships with neighbours which freed husbands from many family chores and obligations. Yet some husbands complained later of feeling excluded and marginal within their own home as their wives no longer needed their assistance (Cohen 1981).

Career patterns change over the life course. Men between the ages of forty-five and retirement have been described as being at a stable 'career maintenance stage' (Glenn 1980). Those already in high-status jobs with successful careers are likely to be at their peak career stage and will maintain a high level of involvement with their work. Those already thwarted in their career ambitions may be less involved (Kanter 1977). There are indications that the latter, together with others, realizing the reduced potential for further advancement in their current occupations, are likely to turn to other sources such as family leisure or community for fulfilment (Levinson *et al.* 1978; Hall 1976; Rapoport and Rapoport 1975). Yet changes in career experience over the life course will continue to have an effect on retirement. Reactions to retirement are likely to be affected by such factors as the manner of retirement, the type of job, and the prospective quality of life ahead. Psychological adjustments to the absence of a rigid daily routine for instance may pose problems, especially for non-voluntary retirees. Given the pervasive influence of the 'occupational clock' upon domestic routines it is no accident that a gold watch is the traditional reward for faithful service offered by employers at retirement rituals. Some who are choosing to retire early, and these include individuals in high-status jobs, may not need to make dramatic timetable adjustments on retirement. Those who are in occupations currently in demand, such as accountants, may have the opportunity of extending their careers through early retirement given that current major changes in the structure of employment have brought with them a proliferation of consultancies.

The type of job will also significantly affect life course experiences. A man's job is likely to influence where and how the family will live, the way the children are reared, the type of school attended, the way children develop, and even their achievements in adult life (McKinley 1964).

Some jobs are more likely than others to inhibit men's involvement with their families. 'Greedy' occupations such as mining or fishing (Coser 1974) or job categories such as senior management executives (Young and Wilmott 1973; Pahl and Pahl 1971) may physically remove men from home for substantial periods of time. Frequent housing moves, a characteristic of the early careers stages in many occupations, will limit the employment possibilities open to men's wives (Cohen 1977). The strain on wives today is likely to be disproportionately higher than in earlier times as the child-rearing period is now shorter, more concentrated, and more likely to coincide with that period of their husbands' working lives when they are least free to offer assistance.

It should also be pointed out that sometimes strains in domestic relationships may be experienced because of lack of separation between home and work (Finch 1983). Small business provides an example of employment which may utilize the labour of all family members (Scase and Goffe 1980). Another source of strain, as noted above, stems from the fact that the ideology of equality in conjugal relations is unlikely to be met in reality especially in the early parenting period. Yet even before childbirth the differential expectations which men and women bring to marriage are negotiated within the framework set by the world of employment and lay the foundations for the structure of domestic relationships throughout the life course (Burgoyne, Chapter 2).

It has been suggested that, to avoid conflict between the expectations and reality of marriage, some men allow their labour market careers to influence when and even who they marry. Studies of highly mobile executives for instance showed that some men ascertained whether or not a chosen partner would be prepared to be geographically mobile before proposing marriage (Pahl and Pahl 1971; Cohen 1977). We do not know the extent of such conscious attempts to plan and manipulate marriage. However, as it is more likely that most people marry for reasons totally unconnected with working life, couples will have to adjust to the tensions likely to result from the conflict between men's career and family demands.

Wives are likely to adapt to the pressures in different ways. Whatever the coping pattern selected, it may well influence family and conjugal relations at subsequent life course stages. Some women for instance may not have the social skills or resources needed to consistently rebuild a network of friends whenever they are required, by their husband's work, to move home. Clark's third case study (Chapter 5) showed that for at least one wife the only way to cope was through assistance from alcohol, a pattern which led ultimately to divorce. Wives of company men in my study (Cohen 1977) had certainly developed sufficient personal resources to cope with many residential moves and to consistently negotiate new friendships and reciprocal exchanges of services based on intensive social interaction with neighbours. Yet even these satisfactory arrangements did not fully resolve tension between spouses. Within but a few years the satisfaction which husbands had initially expressed at the way their wives were coping had turned to unease. Wives had coped so well that husbands felt that their relationships with their children and spouses had been threatened. Had my research continued on a longitudinal basis it would have been possible to see whether the influence of this particular coping pattern lasted beyond children's primary school years.

It is young middle-class men who are most likely to be occupationally and geographically mobile. The elderly are likely to make a limited number of moves. The result may be a separation between generations which leaves families incapable of caring for elderly dependants. It may also affect the quality of life experienced by some old people, especially the elderly poor who remain isolated from other members of their family within such areas as the inner cities (Eversley and Bonnerjea 1980). A recent study on relations between spatial factors and social relationships between the elderly and their children (Warnes, Howes, and Took 1985: 245) found 'neither the high incidence of unconcern or neglect towards elderly parents that is sometimes alleged' but that the spatial separation of children from parents was likely to reduce the frequency of visits exchanged. Even short-distance moves often led to less frequent contact. The job or the job status of a child or that child's spouse will affect their likelihood of moving away from parents. In general higher status jobs mean more moves and greater separation from parents.

On the other hand some studies have shown that proximity between parents and children may well increase with old age. Loss of a partner may encourage an individual to move nearer to his or her children. A study of old people in eight rural communities in north Wales showed that many old people experienced greater proximity and increased contact with the younger generation (Wenger 1984). This study included those elderly who had retired to the country from urban districts who were less likely to have contact with their children than were those who had always lived in the locality. Distance was particularly likely to affect the degree of contact and hence the relationship between these new country-dwellers and their grandchildren.

Certain types of employment are also more likely than others to foster the development of skills and human resources which can be redeployed within the life course. From his survey of different categories of workers in retirement, Phillipson (Chapter 7) distinguishes between categories of work which foster skills that are of use only during the period of employment and those which have value for retirement. The bank of 'skill capital' which architects had accumulated in the course of their careers had a significant impact upon the quality of their lives at pre- and post-retirement stages. The trend towards greater autonomy and personal control which has been encouraged to develop within all areas of working life (Rapoport and Sierakowski 1982) had done much to facilitate the development of human resources which foster self-development throughout the life course.

Small businessmen are more likely than others to stress their lack of social skills regardless of their financial gains and to emphasize the social problems arising from the socially isolated and home-centred nature of their work activities. For them the approach of retirement brings a tendency for self-appraisal and a reassessment of the rewards of making money (Scase and Goffe 1980).

The type of employment may influence or even determine housing styles. Sometimes housing comes 'with the job' although its size and location may vary over the life course. A bishop's palace will be the last and not the first home of a successful cleric. Where housing is tied to the job the post-retirement phase may bring with it uncertainties and pressures as households may not have built up housing capital over the life course. Housing patterns in traditional communities may be dominated by one employer and are a powerful inducement to work-force loyalty.

I have illustrated already the way in which family demands inhibit women's career development. There are countless other examples of the ways in which family pressures may also inhibit men from responding to career demands. As Chester (1971) has shown, the experience of divorce for example is likely to create stress which in turn will affect the work efficiency of both male and female employees. Occupational welfare is an employer strategy which recognizes the potential hazard of these tensions upon the effectiveness of the work-force. The work-load of occupational welfare workers reflects the impact of life course pressures and of changes in the wider economy upon the private lives of individuals.

CHANGES IN LABOUR MARKET DEMANDS

Since the last war there has been considerable change in the occupational division of labour. The main structural change has been the shift from manufacturing and heavy industry to the service sector. Even with the production industries, however, there has been a growth in 'white collar' including higher managerial and professional jobs (Parsons 1985). Changes in patterns of technology are a major feature underlying these occupational trends with the more recent growth in micro-electronics technology.

It is not possible to stereotype the qualities which will be needed for 'new' technology professions as these will vary with the type of work or the nature of the employing organization. A recent study suggested however that they are more likely to demand, amongst other things: a broader range of skills, higher educational levels, a greater degree of initiative, and individual discretion (Parsons 1985). These are not necessarily the qualities needed in the older or 'traditional' jobs and professions (Bernstein 1974). They will, therefore, need to be developed within the family and the school, through child-rearing, education, and training geared to *changing* employment needs.

There is evidence of a direct relationship between father's occupation and child-rearing patterns. Some writers have focused exclusively upon this relationship while adopting different criteria for analysing work patterns. Kohn (1959, 1969) used the blue-collar/white-collar dichotomy as a way of characterizing basic differences in parental values. Miller and Swanson (1958), using the two main categories of entrepreneurial and bureaucratic argued that the structure of the work context was more important than occupational status in influencing a mother's child-rearing styles. The stress on individualism within middle-class work areas in particular has had the effect of encouraging families to adopt child-rearing practices designed to further internalize contraints and control. Working-class child-rearing patterns, as longitudinal studies in Britain have shown, still stress external constraints and discipline while middle-class patterns are more likely to emphasize moral responsibility and postponement of immediate gratification (Newson and Newson 1965, 1968, 1976).

In Bernstein's view, however, broad social-class categories are too crude to take account of occupational and family differences. He applied the dichotomy of 'traditional' and 'non-traditional' to both working- and middle-class families, maintaining that in both the traditional roles are formalized according to age and sex rather than according to personal qualities as is the case in non-traditional working- and middle-class families (Bernstein 1974: 178). Families from the 'old' middle class are most likely to send their children to public school or schools which have a structured curriculum and pedagogy leading to established professions, while the 'new' middle class are most likely to send their children to schools with an unstructured curriculum and 'invisible' pedagogy which prepare children for the 'new' professions (Bernstein 1975).

In British society there has been a high degree of short-range social mobility (Goldthorpe *et al.* 1980), which has meant that many people have moved away from their community of origin and from the jobs available in those communities. Many have moved into the newer categories of managerial or professional jobs; this was the case with families included in my study of a south London housing estate (Cohen 1977). These families and others like them, who were experiencing the insecurity of a shift in their social and occupational status, needed to ensure that their children's status would be more secure than their own. One way that children would achieve subsequent security would be through gaining credentials; another would be through the acquisition of cultural capital (Bernstein 1975). Some studies have identified the mother's role as particularly significant in families of the 'new' middle class in fostering the appropriate values, qualities, and skills in their children (Bernstein 1975).

Fathers in my housing estate study were mostly young, upwardly mobile executives, with a higher social and economic status than that of their own parents. The task of ensuring that children maintained the status and advantages acquired through men's jobs was delegated to their wives who attempted to bring up their offspring in a way which matched their husbands' rising job status even if this meant a conflict with their own background and style of upbringing. A visit from grandmother often created a minor revolution in household routine: 'It's like stepping back into the old world. I have given up telling Mum that our pattern is different. ... I just allow myself to slip back into the old ways: a big dinner at midday, a heavy tea at four, supper at nine and the boys down with us for the whole evening.'

In addition, believing that fathers could stimulate children's, especially sons', occupational achievements by providing them with role models, these mothers developed a variety of strategies to maintain a positive relationship between fathers and children. In their absence, the fathers' image was frequently bolstered by mothers in a number of ways (Cohen 1981). Mothers were the link through which men sustained their involvement with their children.

It should be noted however that the close relationships between mothers and young children which had developed in fathers' absences from home could be made to work either for or against men's interests. Close relations with children sometimes provided women with convenient wedges through which they might exclude their husbands from close familial relationships, further emphasize men's marginal status within the household, and set a pattern for domestic relations which might have implications for subsequent life course stages.

It was important to the estate mothers to forge close links with the primary school in order to achieve a close correspondence between their own child-rearing style and the pedagogy of the school. Estate parents had been instrumental in pressuring the education authority to set up a school almost exclusively for estate children. The close correspondence between school and neighbourhood enabled mothers to communicate effectively with teachers and to participate in a number of school functions. The continuity achieved between home and school education and training allowed mothers to manipulate the school towards a pedagogy which was in the educational and occupational interests of the children.

There are known class differences in parents' ability to achieve any continuity between home and school. Working-class families are often bewildered when faced with 'invisible' school pedagogies and new teaching styles. It is not that these parents are uninterested in their children's schooling, they simply do not know how to tackle either the school staff or the teaching techniques.

Even middle-class parents find access to and involvement in primary schools easier than in secondary schools where the school curriculum is dominated by an examination system which encourages a more formal pedagogy. The invisible pedagogy of the estate school in my study therefore served an important function for families for only a limited period of time. Parents manipulated the school into developing a more formalized approach when it was clear that their children would need to be equipped with skills appropriate for the secondary stage of their educational careers (Cohen 1981).

Family, school, and work

Investment in education in the 1950s and 1960s, far from achieving its aim of developing more effective use of human resources and an efficient labour force (Karabel and Halsey 1977) and of equalizing opportunity, may in fact have reproduced class relationships. Some theorists have argued that non-cognitive, class-based personality factors acquired through the family and reinforced through the schools are far more important in allocating economic and social rewards than are cognitive factors (Bowles and Gintis 1972). A full analysis of this relationship between social class and education should, but rarely does, take account of the developmental processes involved within school, family, and community.

The main areas where demand for labour has increased (apart from the less skilled, non-manual occupations dominated by female workers) have been in jobs requiring higher rather than lower skill levels. Currently Britain's labour force is unable to provide enough skilled labour to meet this demand. International comparisons of skills and qualifications profiles have shown that in Britain more young people are likely to leave school without experience of some form of full-time further education or training than in countries such as Germany, Japan, or the USA (Institute of Manpower Studies 1984). The two-year Youth Training Scheme (YTS) launched in 1986 is an attempt to reduce the skill deficit. But one of the problems it faces is that as a post-school training initiative it needs to correct or modify attitudes inimical to any further education or training which young people may have developed at school (Watts 1983).

Yet school-based attempts to change education and training provision to match changing labour market needs may encounter opposition both from educationalists and parents. The

Technical and Vocational Education Initiative (TVEI) for instance was launched in 1983 as an attempt to develop more vocational and technical training for students of all levels of ability. Although preliminary evidence suggests that it is succeeding in attracting students of mixed abilities, the task is not easy. Parents of middle- or higher-ability-level children are likely to respond to rising youth unemployment figures by clinging even more firmly to the tried and tested O- and A-level routes to higher education. Reduced job opportunities do not encourage risk-taking, especially as in the past, vocational education has been perceived as appropriate only for the socially inferior.

TVEI may encounter even more difficulty with another of its aims which is to change attitudes to curriculum areas or jobs traditionally considered appropriate or 'natural' for a particular sex. Traditionally girls have not opted for vocational and technological training. The seeds of this gender stereotyping of curriculum areas stem from attitudes planted in early childhood. By adolescence most girls expect that marriage and motherhood will be their main careers, supplemented by some peripheral labour market activity. Coffield's data show that unemployment is having little impact on traditional attitudes to gender.

Despite evidence of significant gains made by girls in O- and A-level examinations, these qualifications are primarily in the arts rather than science or technology. The evidence from TVEI is that as yet there is still significant sex imbalance within those curriculum areas most likely to lead girls to the acquisition of scarce labour market skills. Schools are recognizing that at fourteen it is already too late to change well-entrenched gender-related attitudes to particular subjects or to particular jobs. It is worth noting that although Nissel recalls her own educational route, through a girl's public school to university at a time when few girls were offered that opportunity, the curriculum offerings even at that academically oriented school did not stretch sufficiently to include mathematics.

A major feature of the shift in the occupational structure described above has been an increased emphasis on individualism and initiative. The child-rearing patterns of the socially mobile families to which I have already referred reflected this emphasis on personal development based on internalized rather than externalized constraints. Currently educationalists, faced with changes in patterns of employment and in the qualities needed from the labour force, are rethinking the possible future scenarios and are attempting to adapt the curriculum accordingly (Watts 1983). New vocational training programmes are encouraging the development of personal resources, flexible skills, individual motivation, and the ability to apply knowledge to a range of jobs and life course situations.

With the extension of life the period available for individual growth is now longer (Hepworth, Chapter 6). People are more concerned with the quality of the extended life period ahead. Hepworth identifies the development of a new model or concept of mid life based on a drive towards self-fulfilment and personal growth which is dependent upon the greater affluence of households at this stage in the life course. The growth of this new concept is in turn likely to affect and generate a range of attitudes and behaviour patterns.

Within a marriage this struggle for an independent identity has to co-exist with the need for mutual compromise between spouses in order to achieve marital stability. The conflict between these forces may be one explanation of the rise in the divorce rate. Another is the extended length of marriages. A recent article in *The Times* (Clough 1986) pointed out that marital separations of 'younger' or 'older' elderly couples which may not feature in the statistics because they conflict with popular perceptions of the elderly as asexual are increasing because of the greater investment in personal relationships, the development of individuality, and retirement problems.

Occupational changes affect some neighbourhoods more than others. Stable or 'traditional' communities dominated by one (or more) large employer are often associated with specific cultures or life styles. Community studies have documented the association between such neighbourhoods and types of conjugal role relationships (Bott 1957). Men's work often offered them a segregated masculine culture and community. Wives were able to turn to female relatives for support with home and children. The close relation between women, especially mothers and daughters, dominated domestic relationships (Young and Willmott 1957).

Housing patterns in traditional communities may be

dominated by one employer. Often in such areas employers, through 'co-opting' employees' families (Kanter 1978) have maintained a close correspondence between the values and attitudes of work and home. Work-force loyalty – which can be won in a number of different ways – ought, in theory, to generate greater responsiveness to changes in the organization, conditions, and content of work.

I grew up in a village in which a large proportion of the population was employed in a local oil refinery owned by BP. Recruitment patterns had often been through informal, family, and community networks. The influence of the company permeated social and family as well as work relationships. The phrase 'It's just like one large happy family' was often used by management and re-invoked through their regular monthly magazine which gave personal information on a cross-section of their local employees. 'The company has been so good to us', was a familiar local remark and company benefits were bestowed on family members throughout the life course: exchange holidays abroad, adventure holidays, scholarship and student loan schemes for children of employees, access to high-standard leisure facilities for all, post-retirement organizations, newsletters, and company-subsidized social activities.

Even in the most rationally organized and bureaucratic organizations it is possible to find regional pockets where family and organizational interests are so intertwined that job information and selection tend to be confined to the neighbourhood and the work-force comprises networks of members of the same families. This pattern of interrelations tends to mitigate potential conflicts likely to arise between men's careers and other family demands. But on the other hand the investment by family members in a particular employer over time inhibits the work-force from responding flexibly to major changes in the structure of the labour market. Employees are likely to choose to remain in the area they have known all their lives rather than to move in search of jobs. Unemployment leads to a tightening of connections between local firms and family networks (Coffield, Chapter 4; Harris, Lee, and Morris 1985).

The most complete example of correspondence between jobs and family life occurs within family-run small businesses where there is no rigid demarcation between home and work and female family members may well be incorporated within the one family enterprise. Such organizations may impose a different pattern of life course differentiation as business control may be determined by inheritance rather than by age or gender.

Small businesses are also a feature of some sections of ethnic minority communities in Britain. Asians, for example, who have migrated from the towns and cities of India and East Africa, have frequently set up a family business in British towns and cities. They often rely on a clientele drawn from the same ethnic (or geographical) origin. The effect on the one hand may be to protect family members, especially women and young girls from exposure to what may be perceived as the negative disruptive influences of the more permissive majority culture. On the other hand this form of protection may result in this sector of the economy being less responsive to changes and planning processes such as employment protection or health and safety regulation initiated by the wider national economy.

UNEMPLOYMENT AND REDUNDANCY

The main current crises created by economic changes are unemployment and redundancy. The impact of unemployment is most keenly felt by those at the very early or very late stages of their careers. Unemployment for instance is changing the timing and experience of youth. The lack of work and the wage, the keys to a separate adult identity, will affect young people's ability to marry and set up a separate household and for some, the scars of long-term unemployment will remain throughout the life course (Coffield, Chapter 3).

The dramatic rise in unemployment in the 1970s sharply magnified the failure of schools in Britain to provide for pupils in the lower ranges of ability. Too many students left full-time education with few or no qualifications, as the sixteen-plus examination system was designed to cater only for the top 60 per cent of the ability range.

Government-sponsored programmes set up to alleviate the problem have not always taken into account family influences or the regional context. The Youth Opportunities Programme (YOP) and the one-year Youth Training Scheme (YTS) offered some training and work experience but were not up to the task of counteracting the shattering impact of the collapse of an entire regional industrial base. Nor have such schemes succeeded in encouraging young people to seek different types of employment in other parts of the country.

Coffield's chapter highlights the significance of the family, especially in some regions, in maintaining continuity in attitudes to employment despite the traumatic change in employment opportunities. The fact that Whitehall officials or residents in the south-east may perceive certain responses to changes in the structure of the labour market as 'rational' does not necessarily make them rational to people living in areas of high unemployment. In such areas the family and community support system may well be more reliable than that provided by the state. Moreover, the closer connections between family networks and local firms fostered by unemployment will be more likely to lie in the area where other family members are employed in local firms (Harris, Lee, and Morris 1985). Studies of young blacks have shown that their over-reliance on 'formal' recruitment procedures such as job centres has *increased* their chances of remaining unemployed (Gaskell and Smith 1981; Dex 1978).

The overall effect of changes in the economy both through extended periods of unemployment or through the vocational training referred to above is that young people may remain dependent upon their parents for a longer period of time. The potential implication of an extended period of dependency for subsequent life course stages, such as marriage and child-rearing, will need further exploration. Individuals in the pre-retirement stage are another social category likely to be affected by unemployment and redundancy. The closure of heavy industries in particular is having a severe impact on employees at pre-retirement. The pre-retirement phase (late forties to fifties) may well become a retirement reality for many as a result of the increasing redundancy rate. Whatever their causes redundancies will have differential effects, depending upon life course stage, community networks, and types of employment. Recent research has focused upon the impact of redundancy within local labour markets; upon the effects of changes in industrial structure upon communities. A study in a South Wales steel company showed that redundancy has led to employers gaining tighter control over recruitment patterns and over terms and conditions of employment (Harris, Lee, and Morris 1985). Access to jobs, now provided by private contractors, has led to increased dependence upon informal labour market recruitment. Individuals need to be part of the 'right' local network in order to be acceptable to the recruiting agency. The most striking finding of this study and one common to other studies of redundancy (for example, Walker, Noble, and Westergaard 1985) is that one-third of redundants were likely to withdraw altogether from the labour market. Those who are over fifty are especially likely to be discouraged by a range of subtle and informal social pressures from applying for jobs.

This enforced and extended period of retirement, which is likely to affect some areas of employment more than others, may cause social and financial worries. Conjugal relations may also be adversely affected, especially by enforced early retirements. Some women may well resent a husband's unaccustomed presence within the house. A study of the impact of male unemployment amongst redundant steel workers upon their family relationships (Morris 1985) offers little evidence of increased activity by those men within the household, but does note a corresponding reluctance on the part of wives to agree to what they perceive as an invasion of their personal domain.

CONCLUSION

The problems created by rising unemployment and increased redundancy are so dramatic that they tend to overshadow the impact of other types of economic change upon the domestic lives of individuals. The career of the main family wage-earner for instance will continue to change throughout the life course, creating problems of adjustment for other family members. There have been significant changes in the employment activity rates of married women and in the availability of part-time employment which attracts mothers into the labour-market. There has even been a growth in demand for labour in specialist professional areas.

Family demands, relationships, and attitudes may well inhibit individuals from making a 'rational' response to these changes. Women's domestic responsibilities continue to take priority over their labour market activity. Family stress such as divorce or death may affect the work performance of employees of both sexes. Family values and relationships are particularly likely to inhibit change in areas dominated by one or more 'traditional' industries which are also likely to be areas experiencing high levels of unemployment.

Some of the contributors have discussed the implication of some of these life course changes for social policies. Clearly there is a need for policy-makers to take account of life course processes when setting up new social initiatives. A thorough discussion of this aspect is beyond the scope of this introduction but deserves to be the focus of a separate volume.

REFERENCES

Aldous, J. (1985) Parent–Adult Child Relations as Affected by the Grandparent Status. In V.L. Bengston and J.F. Robertson (eds) *Grandparenthood*. Beverley Hills, Calif.: Sage.

Bernstein, B. (1974) *Class, Codes and Control*. (Vol. 1, revised edn) London: Routledge & Kegan Paul.

Bernstein, B. (1975) *Class, Codes and Control*. (Vol. 3) London: Routledge & Kegan Paul.

Blythe, R. (1979) *The View in Winter*. Harmondsworth: Penguin.

Bone, M. (1977) *Pre-School Children and the Need for Day Care*. London: HMSO.

Bott, E. (1957) *Family and Social Network*. London: Tavistock.

Bowles, S. and Gintis, H. (1972) *Schooling in Capitalist America*. London: Routledge & Kegan Paul.

Bujra, J. and Caplan, P. (1978) *Women United, Women Divided*. London: Tavistock.

Chester, R. (1971) Health and Marriage Breakdown. *British Journal of Preventive and Social Medicine* 25: 231–35.

Clough, E. (1986) *The Times* 7 March.

Cohen, G. (1977) Absentee Husbands in Spiralist Families. *Journal of Marriage and the Family* 39: 595–604.

Cohen, G. (1978) Women's Solidarity and the Preservation of Privilege. In J. Bujra and P. Caplan (eds) *Women United, Women Divided*. London: Tavistock.

Cohen, G. (1981) Culture and Educational Achievement. *Harvard Educational Review* 51 (2): 270–85.

Coser, L.A. (1974) *Greedy Institutions*. New York: Free Press.
Dex, S. (1978) Job Search Methods and Ethnic Discrimination. *New Community* VII 1, winter 1978–79.
Elder, G.H. jun. (1978) Approaches to Social Change and the Family. In J. Demos and S. Boocock (eds) *Ageing and the Life Course*. London: Tavistock.
Eversley, D. (1984) New Aspects of Ageing in Britain. In T. Hareven and K. Adams (eds) *Ageing and Life Course Transitions*. London: Tavistock.
Eversley, D. and Bonnerjea, L. (1980) *Changes in the Size and Structure of the Resident Population of Inner Areas*. London: SSRC.
Finch, J. (1983) *Married to the Job: Wives' Incorporation in Men's Work*. London: Allen & Unwin.
Fletcher, R. (1977) *The Family and Marriage in Britain*. Harmondsworth: Penguin.
Fogarty, M., Allen, I., and Watters, P. (1981) *Women in Top Jobs: Twelve Years After*. London: Heinemann.
Gaskell, G. and Smith, P. (1981) Alienated Black Youth: An Investigation of 'Conventional Wisdom' Explanations. *New Community* IX 2.
Glenn, N.D. (1980) Values, Attitudes and Beliefs. In O.G. Brim and J. Kagan (eds) *Constancy and Change in Human Development*. Cambridge, Mass.: Harvard University Press.
Goldthorpe, J.H., Llewelyn, C., and Payne, C. (1980) *Social Mobility: Class Structure in Modern Britain*. Oxford: Oxford University Press.
Goldthorpe, J.H., Lockwood, D., Bechhofer, F., and Platt, J. (1969) *The Affluent Worker in the Class Structure*. London: Cambridge University Press.
Goody, E. (1983) *Parenthood and Social Reproduction*. Cambridge: Cambridge University Press.
Hall, D.T. (1976) *Careers in Organisations*. Santa Monica, Calif.: C.A. Goodyear.
Harris, C.C., Lee, R.M., and Morris, L.D. (1985) Redundancy in Steel: Labour Market Behaviour, Local Social Networks and Domestic Organisation. In R. Finnegan, D. Gallie, and B. Roberts (eds) *New Approaches to Economic Life*. Manchester: Manchester University Press.
Heidensohn, F. (1985) *Women and Crime*. London: Macmillan.
Institute of Manpower Studies (1984) *Competence and Competition*. London: National Economic Development Office.
Kamerman, S.B. (1980) *Parenting in an Unresponsive Society*. New York: Free Press.
Kanter, R. Moss (1977) *Men and Women of the Corporation*. New York: Basic Books.
Kanter, R. Moss (1978) Families, Family Processes and Economic Life.

In J. Demos and S. Boocock (eds) *Turning Points*. Chicago, Ill.: University of Chicago Press.
Karabel, J. and Halsey, A. H. (eds) (1977) *Power and Ideology in Education*. Oxford: Oxford University Press.
Kohn, M.L. (1959) Social Class and Parental Values. *American Journal of Sociology* 64: 337–51.
Kohn, M.L. (1969) *Class and Conformity: a Study in Values*. Homewood, Ill.: Dorsey Press.
Leonard, D. (1980) *Sex and Generation*. London: Tavistock.
Levinson, D.J., Darrow, C.N., Levinson, M.B., and McKee, B. (1978) *The Seasons of a Man's Life*. New York: Knopf.
McKinley, D.G. (1964) *Social Class and Family Life*. Glencoe, Ill.:
Martin, J. and Roberts, C. (1984) *Women and Employment Survey*. London: HMSO.
Martin, R. and Wallace, J. (1985) Women and Unemployment. In R. Finnegan, D. Gallie, and B. Roberts (eds) *New Approaches to Economic Life*. Manchester: Manchester University Press.
Miller, D.R. and Swanson, G.E. (1958) *The Changing American Parent*. New York: Wiley.
Morris, L.D. (1983) Renegotiation of the Domestic Division of Labour in the Context of Male Redundancy. Paper presented at 1983 British Sociological Association Conference.
Morris, L.D. (1985) Patterns of Social Activity and Post Redundancy Labour Market Experience. *Sociology* 18: 339–52.
Newson, J. and Newson, E. (1965) *Patterns of Infant Care in an Urban Community*. Harmondsworth: Penguin.
Newson, J. and Newson, E. (1968) *Four Years Old in an Urban Community*. Harmondsworth: Penguin.
Newson, J. and Newson, E. (1976) *Seven Years Old in the Home Environment*. London: Allen & Unwin.
Pahl, J. and Pahl, R.E. (1971) *Managers and their Wives*. London: Allen Lane Press.
Pahl, R.E. (1984) *Divisions of Labour*. Oxford: Blackwell.
Parsons, D. (1985) *Changing Patterns of Employment in Great Britain*. Sheffield: Manpower Services Commission.
Rapoport, R. and Rapoport, R. (1975) *Leisure and the Family Life Cycle*. London and Boston, Mass.: Routledge & Kegan Paul.
Rapoport, R. and Rapoport, R. (1976) *Dual Career Families Re-examined*. London: Martin Robertson.
Rapoport, R. and Rapoport, R. (1980) The Impact of Work on the Family. In P. Moss and N. Fonda (eds) *Work and the Family*. London: Temple Smith.
Rapoport, R., Rapoport, R., and Strelitz, Z. (1977) *Fathers, Mothers and Others*. London: Routledge & Kegan Paul.

Rapoport, R. and Sierakowski, M. (1982) *Recent Social Trends in Family and Work in Britain*. London: Policy Studies Institute.

Rees, A. (1950) *Life in the Welsh Countryside*. Aberystwyth: University of Wales Press.

Riley, M.W., Foner, A., Hess B., and Toby, M.L. (1969) Socialization for the Middle and Late Years. In D.A. Goslin (ed.) *Handbook of Socialization Theory and Research*. Chicago, Ill.: Rand McNally.

Riley, M.W., Foner, A., and Johnson, M. (1972) *Aging and Society*. (Vol. 3) New York: Russell Sage.

Rossi, A. (1984) Gender and Parenthood. *American Sociological Review* 49: 1–18.

Rutter, M. and Madge, N. (1976) *Cycles of Disadvantage*. London: Heinemann Educational.

Scase, R. and Goffe, R. (1980) *The Real World of the Small Business Owner*. London: Croom Helm.

Walker, A., Noble, I., and Westergaard, J. (1985) From Secure Employment to Labour Market Insecurity: The Impact of Redundancy on Older Workers in the Steel Industry. In R. Finnegan, D. Gallie, and B. Roberts (eds) *New Approaches to Economic Life*. Manchester: Manchester University Press.

Warnes, A.M., Howes, D.R., and Took, L. (1985) Residential Locations and Inter-generational Visiting in Retirement. *Quarterly Journal of Social Affairs*, 1(3).

Watts, A.G. (1983) *Education, Unemployment and the Future of Work*. Milton Keynes: Open University Press.

Wenger, C. (1984) *The Supportive Network*. London: Allen & Unwin.

Willis, P. (1984) Youth Unemployment: A New Social State. *New Society* 29 March: 475–77.

Wilson, H. (1970) The Socialisation of Children. In R. Holman (ed.) *Socially Deprived Families in Britain*. London: Bedford Square Press.

Young, M. and Willmott, P. (1957) *Family and Kinship in East London*. London: Routledge & Kegan Paul.

Young, M. and Willmott, P. (1973) *The Symmetrical Family*. London: Institute of Community Studies.

2
Change, gender, and the life course

Jacqueline Burgoyne

INTRODUCTION

The rituals and customary enquiries which surround the arrival of a new baby act as powerful reminders of the overwhelming significance of gender in shaping the infant's destiny and future life. Almost invariably the first question relates to sex: 'Boy or girl?' As parents and others begin to rehearse the likely future course of the new arrival's life, gender differences are so much taken for granted that the apparent naturalness and inevitability of the divisions and inequalities which will flow from them are rarely questioned (Oakley 1972). Our belief that to be born male or female confers entirely different personal heritages is powerfully reinforced both in our own experience of being of one gender and our observations and indirect knowledge of what it might be like to be the other. This 'taken-for-granted' quality of our beliefs about sex and gender is but one of the many reasons why it is often such a difficult area to write about.[1] Not only are we limited by – even, at times, imprisoned within – our own gender but the legitimacy of any observations we might make about 'the opposite sex' is undermined when the basis of our knowledge is called into question. It is not surprising, therefore, that so much personal conversation, public discussion, or academic debate of what we have learnt to call 'gender issues' eventually degenerate into the ritualized exchange of a variety of stereotyped views which themselves testify to deep and apparently unbridgeable divisions between woman and man.

In this chapter we are concerned principally with the ways in which gender – being either male or female – affects the life patterns of individuals. There are, however, other intersecting factors to be taken into account, in particular class, regional, and ethnic differences as well as, of course, the effects of belonging to a particular historical generation. As a result some biographical 'turning-points' or stages of life appear to affect both sexes in very similar ways so that, for example, class-related factors may be much more important in explaining divisions and diversity of experience in some instances than others. It is also important to incorporate a time dimension into our analysis. On the one hand, the realization that men's and women's lives generally turn out very differently undoubtedly affects the way each sex visualizes the future with its particular hopes and fears. Again, as I hope to show, gender differences are likely to be more significant at some stages in the life course than at others. Similarly women and men 'explain' and make sense of their past biography in rather different ways. Thus, in both prospect and recollection, their significant biographical 'milestones' are often very different.

In the summer of 1985 I asked one class of fifteen-year-olds to imagine they were at the end of their lives and to write their autobiographies in a preliminary attempt to replicate Veness's earlier study (Veness 1962). In both studies young people were startlingly realistic about their own futures. It was hard to believe that they had not been consumers of contemporary government publications on employment and social trends, so closely did their projected futures match what would be most likely to happen to them. Although there are important differences between the two generations, gender itself provides a critical source of continuity. Amongst both groups the aspirations, preoccupations, and anxieties of girls and boys differed markedly. Boys generally outlined stories in which occupational goals and achievements ran parallel with family events and domestic changes. Most girls still saw marriage as a critical turning-point tipping the balance of their lives inexorably towards domesticity and motherhood. Although today's sixteen-year-old girls were much more likely to include references to returning to work after having children or to describe the difficulties of combining motherhood with a career, the expected pattern of their lives in the future was still very different from that of their male contemporaries.

Such differences are also echoed in the accounts of their past lives offered by older women and men. In the context of research interviews in which participants are encouraged to tell their stories with the minimum of direct questioning, or when specific questions are asked about past events, there are clear gender differences.[2] The 'headlines' or 'mileposts' used by women generally focus on personal relationships and family events, with the exception of those who might be described, and see themselves, as 'career' women who often use the time framework of job changes to locate the dates or sequences of particular events in their lives.

By contrast the milestones of their earlier life used by men are primarily occupational. This is confirmed by other research findings which indicate that, although their family life may be equally important to them in some respects, taking responsibility for charting its history, marking its anniversaries is not normally seen as a man's job. An earlier study of kinship in Britain illustrates how women act as 'bridges' between their husbands and the wider kin group (Firth, Hubert, and Forge 1970).

GENDER AND CHANGE IN THE POST-WAR PERIOD

Although the principal landmarks in the political and public emancipation of women preceded the Second World War, their personal and domestic consequences – for women *and* men – really only became apparent in the post-war period. For at least two generations, those who married and had children at the end of or immediately after the war, and their children who grew up in the 1950s, such changes have created their own particular uncertainties, hostilities, and potential for liberation. Very few people could have remained entirely unaffected by these changes, even if only at secondhand, but the level and pace of change have been very uneven. This is partly because Britain is still a deeply divided society whose local and occupational communities, class, and status groupings remain largely insulated and differentiated from one another and most of us occupy relatively watertight social worlds which reinforce our values and assumptions on matters such as gender. Although the majority of British women now use the same kinds of sanitary towels, and Marks and Spencer's underpants provide the final line of defence against nakedness for men from all social classes, the range of taken-for-granted beliefs and common-sense assumptions about the differences between women and men is very large indeed.

Consider, by way of example, the obvious contrasts between the covert and implicit assumptions about gender differences conveyed to the readers of the *Sun* and the *Guardian* or the angry clashes between old-fashioned paternalistic trade union leaders and women delegates witnessed at recent Labour Party Conferences. On the one hand what we read or extract from our observations of the social worlds closest to us tends to reinforce our existing assumptions but we also experience occasions when we are forcibly reminded that those who live very different lives from our own do not necessarily think or act like us. Chance encounters, personal crises or changes, or even exposure to an explicitly 'evangelistic' social and political analysis of the origins and consequences of continued inequalities between the sexes are all capable of undermining previously held views. As a result many women, and some men, speak of their adoption of what are generally called 'feminist' beliefs and practices in terms redolent of a religious or political conversion. Such shifts in consciousness have also been accompanied by attempts to alter those aspects of the language which describe the everyday relationships of men and women, which bear testimony to continuing gender inequalities as well as social behaviour itself. Jokes about the inclusive language of 'persons', for example, draw attention to the confusion which surrounds so many aspects of female–male relationships and are indirect evidence of a mutual hostility which often lies just below the surface.

It is for this reason that the complexities of my commission – to review and summarize the available evidence on gender differences in life patterns and personal biography – with all its problems about the nature and limitations of the available evidence, pale into insignificance in comparison with the challenge of confronting the unconscious hopes and fears, alliances and hostilities, both individual and collective, which we, persons – female and male – each bring to such a subject. Our most important asset in this task is the cultivation of a 'sociological imagination' in the sense which C. Wright Mills first described it:

> 'The sociological imagination enables its possessor to understand the larger historical scene in terms of its meaning for the inner life and the external career of a variety of individuals. It enables him [or her! JB] to take into account how individuals, in the welter of their daily experience, often become falsely conscious of their social positions.'
>
> (Mills 1970: 11)

He argues that a social scientific analysis of contemporary issues and problems should enable individuals to understand how their biographical circumstances have been shaped by particular historical events and social changes. Furthermore this imagination should help its possessor to appreciate that 'By the fact of his living he contributes, however minutely, to the shaping of this society and to the course of its history, as he is made by society and by its historical push or shove' (Mills 1970: 12).[3]

APPROACH, TERMINOLOGY, AND SOURCES OF EVIDENCE

As other chapters indicate, the terms 'life cycle' and 'life course' have themselves been subject to a great deal of criticism and reformulation. Nevertheless they remain useful analytical categories, not least because they make sense to and – without the often unnecessarily obscure terminology – are used by ordinary people when they wish to explain their lives to others (see Salmon 1985: Chapter 2). Developing comprehensive and exclusive categorizations of typical life cycle stages does, however, pose more problems. In this chapter I intend to use five:

1 Childhood: preparing to grow up.
2 Adolescence: becoming an adult.
3 Getting married and becoming a parent.
4 The changes and transitions of adult life.
5 Losses and endings.

As the titles imply I intend to focus primarily on the turning-points involved, considering in each case:

1 The changes in formal status or personal identity which are related to each stage.
2 The changes in living arrangements and/or household composition involved.
3 The changes in patterns of close relationships and, in particular, shifts in loyalties such as who is expected to and does come 'first' in their lives at each stage.

I have already made several references to the significance of class inequalities in explaining differences in the life patterns of individuals. Other studies have reviewed central elements of recent sociological debates on class (Giddens 1973; Giddens and Held 1982; Giddens and Mackenzie 1982).

In this analysis of differences in life patterns and biographical experiences I intend to distinguish between:

Upper class	Members of households financed primarily by unearned income, although one or more of them may work, often on a 'part-time' basis as directors, consultants, or managers of their own wealth.
Middle class	Members of households where the majority of financial resources come from income carried in non-manual occupations.
Working class	Members of households which are financed primarily through wages from manual occupations and/or state benefits.

Although the contribution of the very small proportion of the population who by my definition might be classified as 'upper class' may have a minimal effect on our notions of 'average' standards in most areas of domestic life, they are in some respects still significant opinion setters in relation to family and domestic life, not least because of the part played by the British Royal Family in the embodiment of what are essentially middle-class family values. They also mix extensively with those at the upper frontier of the middle class who occupy powerful positions in government, at a policy-making level in the Civil Service, and those members of the ecclesiastical, judicial, and medical élite whose expertise influences public discussion of many issues in which assumptions about the proper roles of women and men are discussed. (See Rex 1974; Burgoyne, Ormrod, and Richards 1986: Chapter 3.)

The blurring which takes place at the lower frontier of the middle class is of a rather different kind. In the 1950s it was commonly argued that an erosion in manual and routine non-manual wage differentials and the apparent adoption, at least by some manual workers, of a middle class 'privatized' domestic life style had undermined the significance of the traditionally made distinction between the middle and working class. Such arguments have been powerfully countered in a range of empirical and analytical studies (Goldthorpe *et al.* 1969; Westergaard and Resler 1975).

The problem about where to 'place' women in relation to the class structure has theoretical, methodological, and very practical, political implications. It is not surprising therefore that the whole issue has been the subject of a long-running debate (Oakley 1981).[4] For our purposes it is impossible to rely exclusively on any one of the three possible viewpoints Oakley summarizes: women as a distinct class, woman's class defined by her family, or dependent on her own occupation. Each may be significant at different stages in the life course or offer some explanatory power over particular issues. For example, when we are concerned with the kinds of views a woman may hold about gender issues, her upbringing and thus the class of her family of origin, her own educational experience and former occupations may be much more significant than her husband's occupation. On the other hand women's general standard of health and life expectancy are greatly affected by their husbands' class position (Graham 1984).

The material reviewed in the remainder of this chapter is

diverse in intention and methodology and most was collected in a period in which, as I have already stressed, customs and mores were changing rapidly. Piecing together a picture from these ill-fitting jigsaw pieces has been difficult but very illuminating, not least because I now know much more clearly where the obvious 'gaps' are. The first of these concerns the family and personal lives of men, particularly adult working-class men. In the last decade what Oakley has described as 'an eruption of feminism inside academic disciplines and government departments' (Oakley 1981: 284) has stimulated an enormous range of research into women's lives, inside and outside the family, but with some exceptions there has been little parallel exploration of the male species in his domestic environment.[5]

CHILDHOOD: PREPARING TO GROW UP

Social scientific understanding of childhood as a stage in the life course has been greatly increased through study of the experience of children in widely divergent cultures and earlier periods of history. Work of this kind reminds us that our definitions of its boundaries, our assumptions and expectations of children of different ages are specific to particular cultures and historical periods (Busfield, Chapter 3). Contemporary western societies place particular emphasis upon their 'not-yet-adult' qualities and portray childhood as a 'place of waiting'.

Although we sometimes idealize childhood as a time of innocence, suggesting by our sentimental reminiscences that its pleasures flew past all too quickly, we have little tolerance for life's permanent children, the 'childish' adult, or those whose handicaps or infirmities prevent them from achieving 'normal' developmental milestones. This sense of preparing to move forward, past the age-related stages which characterize childhood and adolescence into adult life itself, helps us to understand many aspects of intergenerational behaviour. Parents in particular, but also other adult relatives, friends, and those whose job it is to care for and educate them, all play their parts in leading, encouraging – even, on occasion, coercing – children towards adulthood. From the outset preparation for the eventual assumption of the capabilities, roles, and responsibilities of adulthood begins to divide the sexes from one another. The effects of structured social inequality based on class, ethnic origin, and region also become apparent even in the earliest months of life (Reid 1981: 126, 129). By the age of five the lives of those children born in 1970 who were part of the Child Health and Education Study bore testimony to the potential long-term consequences of such inequality (Osborn, Butler, and Morris 1984). Other studies bear testimony to the way disadvantage is transmitted from one generation to the next (Madge 1983; Mack and Lansley 1985).

Explanations of the origins of gender differences in rates and levels of child development have, for obvious reasons, been a matter for considerable debate amongst developmental psychologists and other interested social scientists. Although the arguments are sometimes crudely simplified with an action replay of earlier 'nature versus nurture' debates, recent writers argue for the development of a model which would take due account of the complex patterns of interaction between biological and social factors over time (Archer and Lloyd 1982: Chapter 9).

Although psychoanalytic accounts of development have always recognized that gender differences were significant, recent work by feminist psychotherapists in particular has begun to shed light on the ways these differences eventually affect the relationships of women and men in adult life (Chodorow 1978; Eichenbaum and Orbach 1984). At first very small babies are unaware that they are in any way differentiated from their mothers but the growth of a sense of separate self, though a source of frustration and anger, is an essential aspect of 'growing up'. Boys begin this 'growing up' process by acting out their developing sense of autonomy and independence from their mothers. As a result some writers have argued that girls often find it particularly difficult to separate from their mothers, especially if, for whatever reason, their mothers are reluctant to let them go. This is the reason why girls often feel ambivalent about their own attempts to gain a measure of independence and autonomy from their mothers, with whom they must continue to identify on gender grounds. Mothers who find their daughters' potential for independence and autonomy particularly threatening often use signs of their own vulnerability to encourage their daughters to begin to 'look after' them (Eichenbaum and Orbach 1983: 56).

Although boys may receive greater encouragement to make this journey of separation, other writers point to some of the difficulties which occur in adult life as a result. One psychotherapist writes:

> 'In my own clinical practice I would say that most, if not all, the men I meet exhibit some fear of closeness or intimacy with women. Sometimes this is manifested by complete exclusion of the woman from their lives or in less extreme cases the man may behave in ways to curtail, control or distance himself within a relationship.'
>
> (Ryan 1985: 22)

Richards uses object-relations theory in a similar way to Chodorow to describe how boys' experience of being fathered affects the development of masculine identity. From birth fathers represent separateness and detachment, acting chiefly as representatives of the outside world. As boys begin to move away from their mothers emotionally they see their masculinity as being essentially different from, even opposed to, their mothers' femininity. Richards argues that this may lead to

> 'a blunting and suppression of their nurturing and emotional side and our emphasis on the external attributes of power, economic position. . . . They are growing into a world of work where their status will be defined by their occupation, and their emotional and family life will be seen as secondary and an "extra" part of their life.'
>
> (Richards 1982: 69)

The growth of independence and autonomy also encourages the development of a sense of self which evolves as children imitate and identify with members of their own sex and is confirmed and reinforced whenever those around them react and relate to them differently because of their sex. By the age of five there are clear and obvious differences between the sexes which affect, for example, their preferred toys and types of play activity (Davie *et al*. 1984: Chapter 4).

By the age of seven, another study found that parents of girls had begun to supervise them more closely because they believed they were more vulnerable and needed greater protection than boys (Newson and Newson 1976).

Although many of the effects of class inequality become apparent at an early age they do not generally affect one sex *more* than the other. However class-based differences in child-rearing and educational patterns are likely to deepen gender divisions in some instances. For example upper-class children educated in the private school system are still much more likely to be educated in single-sex groups from the age of seven onwards (Lambert 1975). Certainty and confidence about their future destiny is not limited to those boys who grow up knowing that they will follow in their fathers' footsteps in the most obvious sense of inheriting a title, estate, or place at the head of a family business. Sons of senior civil servants, military or church leaders, leading members of the scientific, medical, or legal professions 'following their father' into the same public school and Oxbridge college gain confidence from this continuity, aware that they are destined for very similar positions of power to their fathers.

Potential role-models for upper-class girls are more diverse, depending in part on family tradition and the kind of education they receive. Some have mothers who pursue their own professions or business interests, others work virtually full time in various forms of voluntary public service while others are 'full-time' wives whose lives are organized round their husbands' position and responsibilities (Finch 1983). Those girls who attend one of the 'top' girls' public schools, perhaps transferring into the sixth form of one of the former boys-only schools at sixteen, certainly acquire the necessary qualifications and educational capital to become part of the still small minority of women who enter traditional élite occupations. At the other extreme, others, most recently caricatured as 'Sloanes', appear to have changed very little from Mitford's autobiographical heroines of an earlier generation as they pass their time together waiting for marriage (Mitford 1970).

At the other end of the social scale many of the adversities experienced by children growing up in poverty are linked with family disruption or belonging to a typical household group. However, it is important to recognize that in the long run it is most often poverty itself, with all its associated deprivations rather than the fact of separation, divorce, or illegitimacy, which makes it difficult to create domestic security and continuity for children (Coffield *et al.* 1980; Smart 1984). Although there is, as yet, insufficient research-based evidence, some studies such as those examining the impact of divorce upon children (Wallerstein and Kelly 1980) suggest that the long-term adverse consequences of family stress are more obvious in boys than girls (Rutter 1970).

ADOLESCENCE: BECOMING AN ADULT

Despite the range and variety of perspectives on this period of life separating the child from the definitely adult, there is considerable convergence in the way adolescent goals and preoccupations are portrayed. As we have already seen childhood includes strong elements of preparation for adulthood, but it is during this neither-truly-child-nor-completely-adult phase in between that teenagers begin to lay claim to independence from their parents in both an emotional and material sense. It is significant, therefore, that each of the four interrelated transitions associated with this period are very closely linked with independence from parents. They are completing full-time education; starting work; leaving home; forming a cohabiting partnership, most often, but not always, through marriage.

In each case external changes in their economic and social status and the circumstances of their daily lives also run parallel with inner, psychological changes in which new aspects of self and identity are negotiated and internalized. The uncertainties of the passage to full adult status provoke questions about both past and future, the answers to which help to shape many facets of their present behaviour and sense of self. Gender differences are, of course, crucial aspects of this transformation. Not only do adolescents become increasingly aware that their sex confers its own destiny, but also preparation for their very different futures continues the separation of the sexes begun in childhood. For example, although teenage girls and boys are both preoccupied with gaining an increasing measure of separation from home and family and share the same sense of belonging to a different generation to that of their parents, with its own conflict, negotiation, compromises, and occasional acts of defiance (Kitwood 1980: 125), the issues in dispute are frequently different.

Much of the domestic friction between adolescents and their parents is focused on issues of control and supervision: doing homework, domestic chores, informing parents where they are going, and being back on time. But girls and boys are generally treated differently. Middle-class parents may limit their teenage boys' leisure activities because they are concerned about progress at school. Their working-class counterparts may be anxious about boys 'getting into trouble'. Teenage girls however – especially those from middle-class homes – have 'the additional problem of convincing their parents that they will not have an opportunity to engage in sexual activity' (Kitwood 1980: 128). This is confirmed in a recent Home Office study of parental supervision (Riley and Shaw 1985). Home life also provides another potential arena of conflict for girls because they spend more time at home and are generally expected to do more domestic work than their brothers (Kitwood 1980: 148; Riley and Shaw 1985: 20).

As adolescents move towards adulthood their perceptions of what the future holds for them become increasingly influential determinants of both their daily preoccupations and activities as well as of the critical educational and occupational decisions made in the late teens. For example, while the majority of young women realistically expect that marriage and motherhood will be their main 'career', their male peers look forward to a life in which their working and domestic lives unfold side by side. As a result young women find it much more difficult to reconcile those aspects of their identity which are based on academic achievement and career ambitions with conventional assumptions about the centrality of marriage and motherhood for women as well as their own varying levels of preoccupation with finding 'Mr Right' and 'settling down'. Thus while schools and later on institutions of further and higher education follow contemporary orthodoxies by attempting to treat young women and men as if there were no significant differences in their future destinies, young women themselves know otherwise. Whether they have grown up in traditional working class communities in which employment opportunities for young women are now declining so that an early marriage and motherhood are accepted as inevitable (Leonard 1980; Westwood 1984), or are, by contrast, encouraged to follow their brothers into further education or occupational training which will lead to a 'career', they are aware that motherhood, if not marriage, however long postponed will fundamentally alter the pattern of their lives.

The linked pairs of transitions involved in growing up: completing full-time education–starting work; leaving home–forming a cohabiting partnership, may each include a preliminary period of 'part-time' rehearsal before the final transition is accomplished. Thus for example, sixth form and further education college students are normally allowed greater freedom over attendance than younger students; many teenagers' first experience of work is part-time employment in a 'Saturday' or 'holiday' job; parents may permit teenagers to go away on holiday with their boy or girlfriends or to stay at each other's homes occasionally. Leaving home begins early for a minority of the wealthiest teenagers who attend private boarding schools, while a thankfully smaller proportion of the least privileged spend their teenage years in the care of the local authority. At eighteen-plus roughly one in ten of the age group leave home 'part-time' for higher education or vocational training (Central Statistical Office 1986: Table 3.15).

Free time spent on leisure activities is also an important means of preparing for adulthood. While many of the interests and activities of late childhood for boys such as hobbies, sports, and simply hanging around with friends persist through adolescence into adult life, girls seem much more likely to describe a time when they put away 'childish' things, exchanging the pre-occupations of childhood for a growing-up world in which romance and boyfriends became an increasingly dominant focus. This is reflected in friendship patterns. Boys generally have a larger circle of friends whom they 'knock around with' as well as networks based on particular interests or groupings (Kitwood 1980; Willis 1977). Girls are more likely to have one or two close or 'best' friends who act as confidantes and collaborators in their pursuit of the boyfriends on whom their status increasingly depends.

Differences in expectations about what the future holds for them also help us to understand some of the main gender differences in courting behaviour and attitudes towards dating and romance more generally. Girls unlike their boyfriends are generally more preoccupied by the relationship itself (Sarsby

1983: 129), already aware that marriage and more significantly motherhood will sooner or later transform their lives completely. Not only do young women devote more of their leisure time to finding, maintaining, and discussing their relationships with potential partners (McRobbie 1978; Brake 1980), but also the newly married women studied by Mansfield generally portrayed their courtship as one where they had been more eager to get married than their husband (Mansfield 1985).

However these studies also help us to understand why *both* partners may feel ambivalent about the process of 'settling down' inevitably associated with marriage. The customs of courtship, engagement, and marriage, the jokes about 'tying the knot', the rituals signifying reluctance at the loss of 'freedom' involved, all illustrate a collective and personal recognition of the inevitable costs of accepting the adult status afforded by marriage (Leonard 1980; Westwood 1984). Thus the idealism of romance and being in love is tempered by a realistic understanding of the responsibilities which will follow when falling in love is seen as the first step in a courtship 'career' which will eventually lead to marriage. Perhaps this is the reason why Sarsby found that middle-class adolescents, and girls in particular, held loftier views about romantic attachments, as something which could be enjoyed without immediate consideration of the domestic dependencies which would follow. By contrast the recently married young women in Mansfield's study were glad to be able to say that they had married the first or second person with whom they had had a serious relationship and also displayed considerable enthusiasm for married life.

The majority of these couples, like those in Leonard's earlier study, were living at home until they married so that for them, getting married and leaving home go hand in hand as it does for the majority of the population (Kiernan 1985). For some at least the need to leave home because of family problems or the desire to assert their independence from their parents was a consciously recognized reason for choosing to marry at that time. Others spoke more generally of the benefits of marriage because it gave them the privacy and autonomy of a place of their own. Thus, in so far that the particular stage at which a dating relationship is transformed into a potential marriage partnership is linked with a desire for and access to independent housing, students and young adults in relatively well-paid occupations and others whose work involves travel will tend to marry later than average. For them setting up some sort of independent living base, which might vary from job-based residential accommodation through shared, rented flats to buying a home as a single person also offers the opportunity of entering into some kind of cohabiting partnership away from the watchful eyes of parents and this makes marriage itself a less urgent consideration.[6]

GETTING MARRIED AND BECOMING A PARENT

The physical relocation which follows marriage for the majority of newly wed couples provides a symbolic reminder of the profound changes in status and identity involved when they move out of their parents' home into a 'place of their own'. Formalized changes in address, next of kin and, for women, their name itself, betoken other more private but pervasive alterations in their lives. Although they are likely to have discussed their new roles and even rehearsed them on a part-time basis, Mansfield found that it was during the early months of marriage that the framework of their future life together as a married couple was established. Thus the practical activities of 'making a home' – decorating and furnishing – run parallel with the creation of domestic rituals and routines which are matched by alterations in the pattern and significance of their contacts with family and friends. Such changes are also reflected in the inner, emotional aspects of their relationship with one another. Albeit unconsciously, newly weds begin to surrender certain aspects of their identity as separate individuals in favour of those which celebrate and reinforce their new identity as one of a pair and thus, in some senses, now incomplete without the other.[7]

Gender differences remain significant as the inner, private worlds of face-to-face, intimate relationships which are constructed, maintained, and on occasion renegotiated on a personal, 'individual' basis are also partially shaped by the public worlds in which they are located (Burgoyne and Clark 1984). Thus couples who begin their life together with the expectation that he would be the main breadwinner while she ran their home and cared for their children begin to lay the foundations of their domestic partnerships accordingly (Mansfield 1985).

Early in marriage, even before motherhood takes wives out of paid employment, couples may become enmeshed in a web of interlocking dependencies which generally circumscribe the daily lives of wives more than those of their husbands.[8]

The transitions encompassed first by marriage and then parenthood are closely interrelated. In the first place, popular conceptions and images of the ways in which an individual's life is expected to unfold designate them as parallel, highly valued personal goals so that sympathy and a degree of curiosity are often directed at those who fail to achieve them in a conventional sequence (Busfield 1974). Paradoxically, as unmarried cohabitation has become increasingly popular and widely accepted (Brown and Kiernan 1981; Burgoyne 1985a), marriage is now even more closely associated with the intention to have children. As a result cohabiting couples may begin to consider the idea of getting married seriously only if they wish to start a family (Burgoyne 1985a; Clark, Chapter 5). Those who postpone parenthood or make a definite decision *not* to have children generally have responsibilities, interests, sources of personal investment, or anxieties which deflect them from this normative pattern. These might include career commitments, especially for women, mutual enjoyment of the fruits of the high standard of living afforded when both partners have well-paid jobs, or absorbing leisure interests or non-work commitments which they are reluctant to forego. Anxieties about the future, either in world political or ecological terms, or because of job insecurities or more personal misgivings about being able to become satisfactory parents may also deter couples from starting a family (Campbell 1985).

The decision to have children has been portrayed as a joint matter but it is important to recognize that in this, as in other areas of married life, wives and husbands may hold divergent and potentially conflicting views and behave in quite different ways (Bernard 1982). Thus many publicly portrayed 'joint' decisions to start a family may be seen in a different light in private as one partner is aware that he or she has put pressure on the spouse to 'try for' a baby or to welcome and redefine an apparently unplanned pregnancy (Simms and Smith 1982).

Given the generally greater significance of motherhood it is more often women who persuade their husbands that they both 'want' a baby. However, there is some evidence that men in partnership with highly career-oriented women,[9] childless men who marry women who already have children from an earlier partnership, or those who wish to use commitment to parenthood as a means of cementing a potentialy insecure relationship find that they are much more anxious to become parents than their partners (Burgoyne and Clark 1984: Chapter 5; Burgoyne 1985a).

If marriage signifies the assumption of full adult status, parenthood confers its greatest responsibility although its impact is experienced rather differently by each sex. There is now a wealth of social scientific research which highlights the personal and social changes which follow when the arrival of a first baby turns 'two into three' (Clulow 1982: 24). Not only are the rituals and economics of daily domestic life fundamentally altered but also new parents' anxieties and uncertainties are often compounded by the unexpected intense feelings about their own experiences of childhood and the reordering of their close relationships which accompany the transition.

In prospect as Busfield (Chapter 3) argues, becoming a mother is often portrayed as the key to personal fulfilment and provides, for many women, an unparalleled means of ensuring that they will 'count' by occupying a role in which they will at last be taken seriously by family, friends, and the world at large. Consequently it is not surprising that women who have experienced a great deal of pain, conflict, and uncertainty in their own family relationships in the past as well as those designated 'failures' at school or unable to find satisfactory employment look first to motherhood as a source of identity, personal satisfaction, and a means of giving and receiving love. Such women are particularly ill prepared for the realities of motherhood as the normal stresses which accompany this fundamental change in their lives are often exacerbated by other problems generated by poverty, poor housing, and social isolation.

The negative impact which many women experience after childbirth is discussed by Busfield. But it should not be forgotten that husbands also experience a significant life transition when they become fathers, albeit in the context of a daily life in which their roles and identities as workers usually act as the important source of continuity and stability. Busfield (Chapter 3) refers to studies of men's experiences of pregnancy and childbirth which illustrate both their sense of marginality in the birth process itself and what Richman (1982) calls 'the hidden side of masculinity'. Thus the dramatic experience of the birth itself, with its build up of tension and anxiety, and the relief and celebration which follow the arrival of a new person in their life, who is in a unique sense 'their own', arouse and encourage the expression of strong emotions. As Richards suggests these contrast sharply with most cultural images of fatherhood and, in most cases, their own experience of being fathered, so that becoming a father engenders its own contradictions and confusions (Richards 1982). These are generally resolved, or at least recede, when they return to work; daily life resumes its customary timetable and the job-based aspects of their identity as men reassert themselves, while awareness of their new responsibilities as fathers often increases their commitment to work (Simms and Smith 1982: 145–47).

THE CHANGES AND TRANSITIONS OF ADULT LIFE

In one sense the achievement of adulthood confers a sense of having 'arrived' so that we do not expect the journey through the middle years of adult life to be marked by the sense of development, progress, and above all change which characterized childhood and adolescence. The very phrase 'settling down', so often used in association with the decision to marry and have children, suggests that once its constraints are accepted, the period of life which follows marks a plateau between growing up and growing old. Such images are strong and pervasive. As a result we are liable to underestimate how much change individuals, households, and family groups are exposed to during this phase of the life course, so that popular stereotypes of adults in families, as of family life itself, are frozen at the stage when the newly created family unit most closely resembles Leach's 'cornflakes packet norm' (Leach 1967).

While many commentators of different political and ideological persuasions have rightly drawn attention to the need to recognize the increasing diversity of family and household patterns (Rapoport, Rapoport, and Stretlitz 1977; Gittins 1985) exploration of the sources of change to which members of typical, or as Chester has labelled them, 'neo-conventional' families (Chester 1985), are exposed is an equally important undertaking. In particular it is important to examine the sources of variation in both sexes' attitudes towards and experience of marriage, parenthood, and paid employment as they journey through the years which follow the arrival of children.

While women are conscious that the arrival of further children will initially increase their responsibilities, they also look forward to a time – often when their youngest child starts school – when they can regain a measure of autonomy often, though not always, through paid employment (Nicholson 1980: Chapter 4). Men, by contrast, often see the *responsibilities* of fatherhood primarily in material terms, so that they look forward to twenty years or so in which defending or improving their family's standard of living will be a central preoccupation. Their home and family life, as well as to varying degrees leisure and outside interests, provide a sense of purpose as well as a contrast and counterbalance to the demands of their working life.

There are, of course, important class-based sources of variation in this pattern. For example the living arrangements and child-rearing patterns of both the most and least privileged families in our society deviate, albeit for different reasons, from conventional norms. While poverty prevents some parents from providing their children with an independent home or even a settled address and remains one of the most important reasons why children are admitted into local authority care, many upper-class parents have several 'homes' and also make use of substitute child-care in the form of nannies, domestic servants, and boarding schools.

The experiences of women who obtain professional qualifications or who follow other occupations which offer a career structure and a strong sense of occupational identity before their marriage are very different from the majority of women whose experience of paid employment before marriage serves only to confirm the wisdom of choosing marriage and motherhood as their main career. Not only are married women who have had 'careers' more likely to return to work full time and earlier than other married women of the same generation (Martin and

Roberts 1984) but their intention to do so will have affected their own – and, to varying degrees, their husbands' – expectations for the future even while they were at home bringing up children full time. They are therefore much more likely to plan their return to work carefully and even if the ever-diminishing supply of jobs thwarts these plans, their identity as individuals includes an element of potential autonomy which women who do not build up any career 'capital' before having children may well lack.

Any analysis of the springs of action which set in motion the most common changes and transitions of adult life needs to pay particularly close attention to the intermeshing of work- and family-related factors (Burgoyne 1985c). It is clear that historical changes in women's *and* men's patterns of employment as well as the work biographies of particular couples have affected prevailing assumptions about what *ought* to happen as well as to what actually goes on in practice. Thus public awareness that many more married women now work outside the home has generated beliefs that men 'ought' now to take a greater share in domestic work and to be more actively involved in bringing up their children (see Martin and Roberts 1984: Chapter 12; Jowell and Witherspoon 1985). Men and women, like one of the couples cited in Clark's case studies (Chapter 5) frequently seem apologetic about their essentially traditional domestic practices. However, what happens in practice is likely to be influenced by local community or peer group patterns, biographical contingencies, and the negotiations and compromises of individual couples. The weight of evidence from 'snapshot' studies of couples at various stages in the married life course suggests that even amongst middle-class couples who might be expected to espouse the new orthodoxies of domestic partnership (Edgell 1980) there is little sign of a significant redistribution of responsibility. These findings should, however, be considered alongside other evidence which suggests that significant changes in the way couples organize their domestic lives do take place over the life course, in response to illness and marital difficulties (George and Wilding 1972; Burgoyne and Clark 1983) as well as their economic circumstances (Pahl 1984). There are, unfortunately, no reliable studies of the ways in which marriages alter over the course of a lifetime so that it is possible to speculate only very tentatively about the kinds of factors which encourage or deter couples from renegotiating the balance of their domestic tasks and responsibilities in response to changing needs and circumstances.

Early studies of 'dual-career' couples (Rapoport and Rapoport 1976) were perhaps over-optimistic. The job opportunities for most young mothers are very limited and in any event their belief that they 'ought' to be at home with their children is usually matched only by their breadwinner husbands' desire to see them remain there. Studies of the experiences of families in which the husband is unemployed (Bell, McKee, and Priestley 1983; Morris 1985; Burgoyne 1985b) underline this point very forcibly. There is very little evidence that high levels of male unemployment and, in some areas, increased part-time job opportunities for women, are encouraging role 'swaps' or alterations in traditional domestic divisions of labour. The more closely the husband's masculinity and sense of self-worth is based upon identity as worker and breadwinner, the more difficult it is for his wife to take over that role or to suggest that he should do more around the home.

While it would be misleading to suggest that the range and diversity of styles of parenting found amongst 'dual-career' couples is entirely the result of their labour-market advantages or that the high levels of stress experienced by unemployed families is solely the result of their poverty, it is possible to trace connections between the two. In each case their earlier experiences, going right back to childhood and adolescence, help to determine their response to the need for change. These early experiences are reinforced throughout the life course by family, friends, and community with whom they have discussed their plans over many years, modifying them in response to changed circumstances. They are also far less likely to hold the kinds of unyielding images of gender differences which would undermine their confidence in their own and their partners' capacity to take on 'each other's' responsibilities. In addition they are more likely to have had access to a range of potential role models amongst their friends and kin, whose married lives may portray the potential for diversity and change, a potential confirmed at every turn by their favourable and relatively secure economic position.

Thus studies of the effects of living in poverty bear testimony to the ways in which it affects women, men, and children at different stages in the life course (see Townsend 1979; Mack and Lansley 1985) and is transmitted from generation to generation (Rutter and Madge 1976; Madge 1983). For those in the middle years of life who have grown up in poverty and whose early years of marriage and bringing up children have been characterized by periods of unemployment, frequent changes of accommodation, and perhaps homelessness, 'planning ahead' and the conscious anticipation of change have little relevance. Between these extremes lie the majority of married couples whose capacity to adapt to either changed external circumstances – job changes, the departure of grown-up children – or the changes in their relationship which may follow is affected by a multitude of personal and structural factors. However it is clear that, regardless of the nature of the work, having a job of some sort is still crucial for both women and men, albeit in somewhat different ways. For most men their sense of self-worth as husbands and fathers remains firmly attached to their role as breadwinners. Paid employment is also important for women, helping to insulate them from the depressive episodes often associated with the early years of child rearing (Brown and Harris 1978), as it brings a degree of financial autonomy, time away from the home, and a potential source of contact with other women. For an increasing number of women, part-time study also provides the beginnings of autonomy and is a first step in developing a working identity of their own once their child-care duties begin to diminish and, as the film *Educating Rita* showed so clearly, is often a very significant source of change in a marriage.

Women also derive a great deal of emotional support from the relationships of daily life. For those who marry and settle amongst a close-knit family group, family gatherings and the regular exchange of domestic and child-care services help to sustain a supportive network of social contacts which gives shape to their domestic routine and is an important source of help when difficulties occur. Other women who do not live near their families, or who do not feel 'close' to them, create their own social networks of friends from amongst neighbours, workmates, and others (Cohen 1977). They are most likely to be able to do so if they have already experienced close, confiding, and reciprocal relationships of this kind earlier in their lives as teenagers, or while at college or at work. Thus women who marry very young and have lost contact with their own families as the result of serious conflict which has not been resolved (Thornes and Collard 1979: 62–4), and who find themselves living in a new area where they do not know anyone, are much less likely to make friends than those with more positive earlier experiences of friendship. When problems occur they may find they have no one to turn to except their partner, so that if these difficulties lie in the marriage itself, they may feel entirely alone (Brannen and Collard 1982).

LOSSES AND ENDINGS

This final section is concerned with some of the most important personal and social changes which are associated with 'growing old'. Unlike earlier stages in the life course these are not as closely linked with particular chronological ages, except that official retirement ages signal a change in economic and social status.

Early intimations of the significance of the passage of time are often provided in the middle years by the physical ageing process itself, although, as Hepworth (Chapter 6) indicates, perceptions of the middle years are 'socially constructed'. For women the menopause is a clear signal that their child-bearing years are over, while men gradually become aware that their physical strength and stamina are diminishing. However, whereas certain aspects of ageing can serve to increase men's physical attractiveness, for example greying hair and 'firmer' features, female norms of attractiveness are strongly associated with youth. The buoyant market in beauty products and cosmetics for women designed to minimize or, at least, obscure the physical effects of growing older bear ample testimony to women's fears about the loss of this aspect of their identity. Men also report an increase in minor physical symptoms in the middle years (Open University 1985: 145–51). Again Hepworth indicates in Chapter 6 that one effect of social change is an increasing incidence in the 'male menopause' phenomenon.

Changes at work associated with growing older may also serve as reminders of the passage of time well before formal retirement age. Career disappointments which signify that the individual has gone as far as he – and, less frequently, she – can go often lead to a reappraisal of career goals (Sofer 1970; Cooper and Davidson 1982). While some manual workers find that their jobs begin to 'disappear' as a result of the advance of technology or industrial decline, others are forced into turning down overtime or into short-time working because of health problems (Townsend 1979: Chapter 19). Although, as we have already seen, women's working patterns are different, they too begin to reduce their hours of working or to leave the labour market altogether during their fifties (Martin and Roberts 1984: 11), often to care for sick or elderly dependants (Ungerson, Chapter 8).

Changes in the working lives of older women and men frequently run parallel with changes on the domestic front. Many parents find that bringing up teenagers is in itself a significant source of stress (Nicholson 1980: 182) and their eventual departure may be eagerly anticipated, but they are not necessarily prepared for the effect of the 'empty nest' on their own lives. In the same way that men in demanding or uncongenial jobs who look forward to retirement, even volunteering to 'go early', are shocked by the sense of loss and purposelessness which follows the holiday-euphoria of the first few months. In both instances couples have to adapt to significant changes in the rituals and tempo of their daily lives as well as to learn to accept that a stage in their life, formerly central to their sense of self-worth, is now over.

The very significant increase in the proportion of the population now over, or soon reaching, the age of retirement as well as general improvements in the health and well-being of this age group have led to a much greater emphasis on retirement – as Hepworth points out (Chapter 6) – as a positive and distinctive phase in the life course. Becoming a grandparent is perhaps the most common and significant transition which most people experience. To many it is an opportunity to offer their family their time and other available resources through such things as babysitting, supplying additional financial help where they can, and, if it was asked for, the benefit of their advice and experience (Cunningham-Burley 1985). This shift in priorities away from their own household towards their children's families often coincides with a growth in concern for their own elderly parents. In both instances it is generally, though not always, women's lives which are most directly affected by such responsibilities. As a result their experience of the transition to retirement when they, their husbands, or both, leave paid employment is much less abrupt. The daily pattern of domestic work and their contacts with friends and kin have already been set and have been a central element of their identity over many years; they are important sources of continuity and stability amidst other changes and uncertainties. Given that much contemporary wisdom about how to enjoy retirement and live to a ripe old age advocates 'keeping busy' it is not surprising therefore that women live longer and also cope better with the most significant loss faced at this time, the death of their spouse (Parkes, Benjamin, and Fitzgerald 1969). In this, as in earlier periods of life, women who have access to a supportive network of friends or kin as well as earlier experience of a meaningful working life of their own seem to cope better than those who do not (Elder 1982).

CONCLUSION

When people talk about the influences on their lives they often use the metaphor of a journey in which certain key decisions and experiences determine its route thereafter. The material presented in the final section of this chapter serves to remind us that despite cosy 'Darby and Joan' images of togetherness in old age, women and men reach this final stage of life by very different routes and that, in certain respects, their experience of the journey and their preoccupations *en route* have been quite different. It is therefore ironic that it is sometimes only as a result of the vicissitudes of growing old that stereotyped views of gender differences are undermined. For example, many retired men (Ungerson, Chapter 8; Blythe 1981) become 'handier' round the home than they have ever been before, where necessary taking on the nursing care of those in greater need than themselves. By the same token, distanced now from the dependent female stereotypes of early adult life, women are able to reveal the stamina and inner strength they may have acquired through a lifetime in which much of their labour and their most important struggles have been hidden behind the closed doors of the family home.

NOTES

1 Following Ann Oakley I intend to use the terms 'sex' and 'gender' as she does in *Sex, Gender and Society* (1972):

> *Sex* the two divisions of . . . human beings respectively designated as male or female.
> *Gender* . . . any of two or more sub-classes . . . that are purely arbitrary but also partly based on distinguishable characteristics such as . . . sex (as masculine, feminine . . .).
> (Webster's *Third New International Dictionary*)

As this and her later writing indicate, disentangling 'sex' from 'gender' in the 'many fields where the existence of natural differences between male and female has been proposed' and 'to separate value judgements from statements of fact' (Oakley 1972) are very difficult tasks.

2 Although we noticed these differences in our original analysis of the life histories of remarried couples, David Clark and I have subsequently become very conscious of our general lack of attention to gender issues in this study (see Burgoyne and Clark 1984). I hope that this imbalance has been redressed somewhat in a later study of unmarried cohabiting couples (Burgoyne 1985a). Both of these studies were financed with the aid of grants from the then Social Science Research Council (HR 6635 and G0020008).

3 For some readers, at least, certain aspects of my own biography may be useful background in interpreting the rest of this chapter. I was born in 1944 and was thus part of the first generation of women to benefit from the post-war increased educational opportunities and career expectations held out for women. Although my family enjoyed a high degree of material comfort, my childhood and adolescence were punctuated by the illness and death of both parents. I was educated as a boarder at a girls' public school which imbued its own particular pre-1960s version of feminism. After reading social science at Sheffield University, I have worked as a school teacher and lecturer ever since. Most of my teaching and research is now centrally concerned with gender issues and I have always lived the kind of life in which – sometimes with great difficulty – my working and personal life run in parallel. Though regarded as 'unsound' by feminists of what Jill Tweedie calls 'the separatist tendency', it is comforting to find that my apparently over-moderate stance on some issues creates the kinds of discomforts of which Mills might have approved, in many unconsciously chauvinist institutions and social circles long overdue for reform.

4 See, for example, the debate which has been taking place in recent issues of *Sociology*, the journal of the British Sociological Association. The opening shots were fired by Goldthorpe (1983). Replies from Stanworth (1984) and Heath and Britten (1984) followed. A recent contribution (Dale, Gilbert, and Arber 1985) proposes a theoretical framework and methodology which would integrate women into class theory through developing an occupational class schema which is based on different criteria from those used to classify men's occupations.
5 Although attention has been paid to the courtship patterns and hopes for the future of adolescent boys (Willis 1977; Brake 1980) and, more recently, men's roles as fathers (Beail and McGuire 1982; McKee and O'Brien 1982; Russell 1983; Jackson 1983), with the pioneering exception of Tolson (1976) relatively little attention was paid to male personal identity. Recently there has been a spate of widely publicized journalistic accounts (Hodson 1984; Roberts 1984; Ford 1984) and the beginnings of a psychological exploration of male sexuality (Metcalfe and Humphries 1985).
6 Amongst a small sample of cohabiting couples in Sheffield, now in their late twenties and early thirties, over a third had left their parental home at an unusually early age, mainly as a result of serious conflicts with parents and family break up. Others had formed cohabiting partnerships while they were students. (See Burgoyne 1985a.)
7 Janet Askham's study (1984) of the processes of communication between married couples highlights the potential tension between the maintenance of individual identity and ensuring the stability of the marriage, suggesting that it is managed through developing strong couple-based norms of customary behaviour and the maintenance of 'no-go' areas over issues with a potential for conflict.
8 Mansfield found that the social lives of the women in her study were far more restricted than those of their husbands, a finding confirmed in an ongoing study of women and leisure in Sheffield. (See Green, Hebron, and Woodward 1986.)
9 Cooper and Thompson's study (1984) of 'famous' women includes several examples of the potential conflict between career goals and constraints and the decision to start a family. This is also tragically illustrated in Sara Keays's account of her relationship with Cecil Parkinson (Keays 1985).

REFERENCES

Aitken, S. (1985) The Case of the Agoraphobic Miner's Wife. *Changes: The Psychology and Psychotherapy Journal* 3 (4): 110–13.

Ambrose, P., Harper, J., and Pemberton, R. (1983) *Surviving Divorce: Men beyond Marriage*. Brighton: Wheatsheaf.
Archer, J. and Lloyd, B. (1982) *Sex and Gender*. Harmondsworth: Penguin.
Askham, J. (1984) *Identity and Stability in Marriage*. London: Cambridge University Press.
Bagehot, W. (1963) *The English Constitution*. London: Fontana.
Beail, N. and McGuire, J. (eds) (1982) *Fathers: Psychological Perspectives*. London: Junction Books.
Bell, C. and McKee, L. (1983) Marital and Family Relations in Times of Male Unemployment. Paper given at SSRC Research Workshop.
Bell, C., McKee, L., and Priestley, K. (1983) *Fathers, Childbirth and Work*. Manchester: Equal Opportunities Commission.
Berger, P. L. (1963) *Invitation to Sociology: A Humanistic Perspective*. Harmondsworth: Penguin.
Bernard, J. (1982) *The Future of Marriage*. (2nd edn) New York: Yale University Press.
Blythe, R. (1981) *The View in Winter*. Harmondsworth: Penguin.
Boulton, M. G. (1983) *On Being a Mother: A Study of Women with Pre-School Children*. London: Tavistock.
Brake, M. (1980) *The Sociology of Youth Cultures and Youth Subcultures*. London: Routledge & Kegan Paul.
Brannen, J. and Collard, J. (1982) *Marriages in Trouble*. London: Tavistock.
Brown, A. (1982) Fathers in the Labour Ward: Medical and Lay Accounts. In L. McKee and M. O'Brien (eds) *The Father Figure*. London: Tavistock.
Brown, A. and Kiernan, K. (1981) Cohabitation in Great Britain: Evidence from the General Household Survey. *Population Trends* 25.
Brown, G. W. and Harris, T. (1978) *Social Origins of Depression*. London: Tavistock.
Burgoyne, J. (1985a) *Cohabitation and Contemporary Family Life*. End of Award Report to the Economic and Social Research Council.
Burgoyne, J. (1985b) Unemployment and Married Life. *Unemployment Unit Bulletin* November: 7–10.
Burgoyne, J. (1985c) Gender, Work and Marriage: Patterns of Continuity and Change. In *Relating to Marriage*. Rugby: National Marriage Guidance Council.
Burgoyne, J. and Clark, D. (1983) You are What You Eat: Food and Family Reconstitution. In A. Murcott (ed.) *The Sociology of Food and Eating*. London: Gower Press.

Burgoyne, J. and Clark, D. (1984) *Making a Go of It: A Study of Stepfamilies in Sheffield*. London: Routledge & Kegan Paul.

Burgoyne, J., Ormrod, R., and Richards, M. (1986) *Divorce Matters*. Harmondsworth: Penguin.

Busfield, J. (1974) Ideologies and Reproduction. In M. P. M. Richards *The Integration of a Child into a Social World*. Cambridge: Cambridge University Press.

Campbell, E. (1985) *The Childless Marriage*. London: Tavistock.

Cavendish, R. (1982) *Women on the Line*. London: Routledge & Kegan Paul.

Central Statistical Office (1986) *Social Trends 1986*. London: HMSO.

Chester, R. (1985) The Rise of the Neo-Conventional Family. *New Society* 9: May.

Chodorow, N. (1978) *The Reproduction of Mothering*. Berkeley, Calif.: University of California Press.

Clulow, C. (1982) *To Have and to Hold: Marriage, the First Baby and Preparing Couples for Parenthood*. Aberdeen: Aberdeen University Press.

Coffield, F., Robinson, P., and Salsby, J. (1980) *A Cycle of Deprivation? A Case Study of Four Families*. London: Heinemann Educational.

Cohen, G. (1977) Absentee Husbands in Spiralist Families. *Journal of Marriage and the Family* 39: 595–604.

Cooper, C. and Davidson, L. (1982) *High Pressure: Working Lives of Women Managers*. London: Fontana.

Cooper, C. and Thompson, L. (1984) *Public Faces, Private Lives*. London: Fontana.

Cunningham-Burley, S. (1985) Constructing Grandparenthood: Anticipating Appropriate Action. *Sociology* 19 (3): 421–36.

Dale, A., Gilbert, G. N., and Arber, S. (1985) Integrating Women with Class Theory. *Sociology* 19 (3): 384–409.

Davie, C. E., Hutt, S. J., Vincent, E., and Mason, M. (1984) *The Young Child at Home*. London: NFER–Nelson.

Dunnell, K. (1979) *Family Formation*. London: HMSO.

Edgell, S. (1980) *Middle-Class Couples: A Study of Segregation, Domination and Inequality in Marriage*. London: Allen & Unwin.

Eichenbaum, L. and Orbach, S. (1983) *What Do Women Want*? London: Fontana.

Eichenbaum, L. and Orbach, S. (1984) *Understanding Women*. Harmondsworth: Penguin.

Elder, G. H. (1982) Historical Experiences in Later Years. In T. Hareven and K. Adams (eds) *Ageing and Life Course Transitions*. London: Tavistock.

Evans, P. and Bartolome, F. (1980) *Must Success Cost so Much*? London: Grant McIntyre.

Finch, J. (1983) *Married to the Job: Wives' Incorporation in Men's Work*. London: Allen & Unwin.

Firth, R., Hubert, J., and Forge, A. (1970) *Families and their Relatives*. London: Routledge & Kegan Paul.

Ford, A. (1984) *Men*. London: Weidenfeld & Nicolson.

George, V. and Wilding, P. (1972) *Motherless Families*. London: Routledge & Kegan Paul.

Giddens, A. (1973) *The Class Structure of Advanced Societies*. London: Hutchinson.

Giddens, A. and Held, D. (1982) *Classes, Power and Conflict: Classical and Contemporary Debates*. London: Macmillan.

Giddens, A. and Mackenzie, G. (1982) *Social Class and the Division of Labour: Essays in Honour of Ilya Neustadt*. Cambridge: Cambridge University Press.

Gittins, D. (1985) *The Family in Question: Changing Households and Familiar Ideologies*. London: Macmillan.

Goldthorpe, J. H. (1980) *Social Mobility and Class Structure in Modern Britain*. London: Oxford University Press.

Goldthorpe, J.H. (1983) Women and Class Analysis: In Defence of the Conventional View. *Sociology* 19 (4): 465–88.

Goldthorpe, J.H., Lockwood, D., Bechhofer, F., and Platt, J. (1969) *The Affluent Worker in the Class Structure*. London: Cambridge University Press.

Graham, H. (1984) *Women, Health and the Family*. Brighton: Wheatsheaf.

Green, E., Hebron, S., and Woodward, D. (1986) Women, Leisure and Social Control. In J. Hamner and M. Maynard (eds) *Women and Violence*. London: Macmillan.

Hargreaves, D. J. *et al*. (1981) Psychological Androgyny and Ideational Fluency. *British Journal of Social Psychology* 20: 33–5.

Heath, A. and Britten, N. (1984) Women's Jobs Do Make a Difference. *Sociology* 18 (4): 475–90.

Hodson, P. (1984) *Men*. London: BBC Publications.

Howard, J. (1984) *Margaret Mead – A Life*. London: Harvill Press.

Hunt, A. (1978) *The Elderly at Home: A Study of People Age 65 and Over Living in the Community in England in 1976*. London: HMSO.

Jackson, B. (1983) *Fatherhood*. London: Allen & Unwin.

Jowell, R. and Witherspoon, S. (1985) *British Social Attitudes: The 1985 Report*. London: Gower Press.

Keays, S. (1985) *A Question of Judgement*. London: Quintessential Press.

Kiernan, K. (1985) The Departure of Children: The Timing of Leaving Home Over the Life-Cycles of Parents and Children. *Centre for Population Studies Research Paper* 85–3. University of London.

Kitwood, T. (1980) *Disclosures to a Stranger: Adolescent Values in an Advanced Industrial Society*. London: Routledge & Kegan Paul.

Lambert, R. (1975) *Chance of a Lifetime*. London: Weidenfeld & Nicolson.
Leach, E. (1967) *A Runaway World*? The Reith Lectures. London: British Broadcasting Corporation.
Leonard, D. (1980) *Sex and Generation*. London: Tavistock.
McFadyean, M. (1985) What Now for the Daughters of the Revolution? *Sunday Times* 1 September: 28–34.
McGuire, J. (1985) Mother–Daughter and Father–Son Relationships. Paper presented to the British Psychological Society Developmental Section. Annual Conference, Belfast.
Mack, J. and Lansley, S. (1985) *Poor Britain*. London: Allen & Unwin.
McKee, L. and O'Brien, M. (eds) (1982) *The Father Figure*. London: Tavistock.
McNally, F. (1979) *Women for Hire: A Study of the Female Office Worker*. London: Macmillan.
McRobbie, A. (1978) Working-Class Girls and the Culture of Femininity. In Women's Studies Group (eds) *Women Take Issue*. London: Hutchinson.
Madge, N. (1983) *Families at Risk*. London: Heinemann Educational.
Mansfield, P. (1985) *Young People and Marriage*. Occasional Paper 1. Edinburgh: Scottish Marriage Guidance Council.
Marris, P. (1974) *Loss and Change*. London: Routledge & Kegan Paul.
Martin, J. and Roberts, C. (1984) *Women and Employment: A Lifetime Perspective*. London: HMSO.
Mead, M. (1971) *Coming of Age in Samoa*. (first published 1928) Harmondsworth: Penguin.
Metcalfe, A. and Humphries, M. (1985) *The Sexuality of Men*. London: Pluto Press.
Mills, C. W. (1970) *The Sociological Imagination*. (first published 1959) Harmondsworth: Penguin.
Mitford, N. (1970a) *Love in a Cold Climate*. Harmondsworth: Penguin.
Mitford, N. (1970b) *The Pursuit of Love*. Harmondsworth: Penguin.
Monck, E. (1985) Affective Disorders and Problems in Eating Control in a Community Study of 15–19-year-old Girls. Paper presented to the British Psychological Society Development Section. Annual Conference, Belfast.
Morris, L. (1985) Redundancy and Patterns of Household Finance. *Sociological Review* 32: 492–523.
New, C. and David, M. (1985) *For the Children's Sake: Making Childcare More than Women's Business*. Harmondsworth: Penguin.
Newson, J. and Newson, E. (1970) *Four Years Old in an Urban Community*. Harmondsworth: Penguin.
Newson, J. and Newson, E. (1976) *Seven Years Old in the Home Environment*. Harmondsworth: Penguin.
Nicholson, J. (1980) *Seven Ages*. London: Fontana.

Oakley, A. (1972) *Sex, Gender and Society*. London: Temple-Smith.
Oakley, A. (1979) *Becoming a Mother*. Oxford: Martin Robertson.
Oakley, A. (1980) *Women Confined: Towards a Sociology of Childbirth*. Oxford: Martin Robertson.
Oakley, A. (1981) *Subject Women*. London: Martin Robertson.
Open University (1985) *Birth to Old Age: Health in Transition*. Book 5 for U205, Health and Disease. Milton Keynes: Open University Press.
Osborn, A.F., Butler, N., and Morris, A. (1984) *The Social Life of Britain's Five-Year-Olds: A Report of the Child Health and Development Study*. London: Routledge & Kegan Paul.
Pahl, J. (1984) The Allocation of Money within Households. In M.D.A. Freeman (ed.) *State, Law and the Family: Critical Perspectives*. London: Tavistock.
Parkes, C.M., Benjamin, B., and Fitzgerald, R.G. (1969) Broken Heart: A Statistical Study of Increased Mortality among Widowers. *British Journal of Psychiatry* 127: 204–10.
Pearlin, L.I. (1982) Discontinuities in the Study of Ageing. In T. K. Hareven and K. J. Adams (eds) *Ageing and Life Course Transitions*. London: Tavistock.
Pollert, A. (1981) *Girls, Wives, Factory Lives*. London: Macmillan.
Rapoport, R. and Rapoport, R. (1976) *Dual Career Families Re-examined*. London: Martin Robertson.
Rapoport, R., Rapoport, R., and Strelitz, Z. (1977) *Fathers, Mothers and Others*. London: Routledge & Kegan Paul.
Reid, I. (1981) *Social Class Differences in Britain*. (2nd edn) London: Grant McIntyre.
Rex, J. (1974) Capitalism, Elites and the Ruling Class. In P. Stanworth and A. Giddens (eds) *Elites and Power in British Society*. London: Cambridge University Press.
Richards, M.P.M. (1982) How Should We Approach the Study of Fathers? In L. McKee and M. O'Brien (eds) *The Father Figure*. London: Tavistock.
Richards, M.P.M. (forthcoming) *Marriage, Children and Divorce*. London: Cambridge University Press.
Richman, J. (1982) Men's Experience of Pregnancy and Childbirth. In L. McKee and M. O'Brien (eds) *The Father Figure*. London: Tavistock.
Richman, N. (1976) Depression in Mothers of Pre-School Children. *Journal of Child Psychology and Psychiatry* 17: 75–8.
Riley, D. and Shaw, M. (1985) *Parental Supervision and Juvenile Delinquency*. Home Office Research Study 83. London: HMSO.
Roberts, Y. (1984) *Man Enough*. London: Chatto & Windus.
Russell, G. (1983) *The Changing Role of Fathers*. Milton Keynes: Open University Press.

Rutter, M. (1970) Sex Differences in Children's Responses to Family Stress. In E. J. Anthony and C. M. Koupernik (eds) *The Child and his Family*. London: Wiley.

Rutter, M. and Madge, N. (1976) *Cycles of Disadvantage*. London: Heinemann Educational.

Ryan, T. (1985) Roots of Masculinity. In A. Metcalfe and M. Humphries (eds) *The Sexuality of Men*. London: Pluto Press.

Salmon, P. (1985) *Living in Time: A New Look at Personal Development*. London: Dent.

Sarsby, J. (1983) *Romantic Love and Society*. Harmondsworth: Penguin.

Simms, M. and Smith, C. (1982) Young Fathers: Attitudes to Marriage and Family Life. In L. McKee and M. O'Brien (eds) *The Father Figure*. London: Tavistock.

Smart, C. (1984) *The Ties That Bind*. London: Routledge & Kegan Paul.

Smith, C. and Lloyd, B. (1978) Maternal Behaviour and Perceived Sex of Infant Revised. *Child Development* 49: 1263–265.

Sofer, C. (1970) *Men in Mid Career*. London: Cambridge University Press.

Stanworth, M. (1984) Women and Class Analysis: A Reply to John Goldthorpe. *Sociology* 15 (2): 159–70.

Stoller, R. (1975) *The Transsexual Experiment*. London: Hogarth Press.

Thornes, B. and Collard, J. (1979) *Who Divorces*? London: Routledge & Kegan Paul.

Tolson, A. (1976) *The Limits of Masculinity*. London: Tavistock.

Townsend, P. (1979) *Poverty in the United Kingdom*. Harmondsworth: Penguin.

Townsend, S. (1983) *The Secret Diary of Adrian Mole aged 13¾*. London: Methuen.

Veness, T. (1962) *School Leavers*. London: Methuen.

Voysey, M. (1975) *A Constant Burden: The Reconstitution of Family Life*. London: Routledge & Kegan Paul.

Wallerstein, J.S. and Kelly, J.B. (1980) *Surviving the Break Up*. London: Grant McIntyre.

Westergaard, J. and Resler, H. (1975) *Class in a Capitalist Society*. London: Heinemann Educational.

Westwood, S. (1984) *All Day Every Day: Factory and Family in the Making of Women's Lives*. London: Pluto Press.

Willis, P. (1977) *Learning to Labour*. London: Saxon House.

Yeandle, S. (1984) *Women's Working Lives: Patterns and Strategies*. London: Tavistock.

Young, M. and Willmott, P. (1973) *The Symmetrical Family*. London: Routledge & Kegan Paul.

3
Parenting and parenthood

Joan Busfield

Parenting and parenthood if not considered in themselves a stage in the life cycle are, like marriage, commonly viewed as a mark of adulthood and for most people they are crucial components of the life cycle or life course. Becoming a parent is a major point of transition and the birth of a first child has an enormous impact on the individual's life in a range of ways: psychological, economic, and social (Oakley 1981; Breen 1975). This is true for both men and women, but the significance of parenthood is not the same for the two genders, a point which the recently fashionable term 'parenting' ignores and even hides. Within the ideological construction and *de facto* reality of the division of labour between men and women, having children and rearing them constitute the standard justification for and legitimizing of women's position in society (Firestone 1971; Oakley 1982). While, therefore, having children is a core component of a woman's identity to the extent that to have a child is often regarded as making her a 'real' woman, men's identity has been centred far more on their occupation in the labour market than on being a parent (Busfield 1974). Notions of parenting and parenthood gloss over such differences in the ideas and the reality of having and rearing children for men and women.

Two rather different sets of ideas and assumptions underlie the recent use in the social sciences of the gender-neutral terms of parenting and parenthood. First and most obviously there is an increasing interest in the parent as opposed to the child, whether viewed as a numerical addition to the population or as an individual whose behaviour and character are moulded by parental actions. As we shall see this is a marked change between work carried out prior to and after the beginning of the 1970s. Second, however, there is the controversial assumption that relations between men and women are becoming more symmetrical and egalitarian and that men are becoming more involved in the day-to-day care of their children, so making it seem more appropriate to talk in the gender-neutral term of parents rather than of mothers or, less commonly, fathers (Young and Willmott 1973). This assumption is commonly made in recent official discussions of the family and relations between parents and children, but it has been questioned in a range of feminist and sociological writing on the family which I discuss below (Morgan 1985: Chapter 1).

The use of the terms parenting and parenthood highlights, therefore, the way in which studies in these areas, like research in the social sciences more generally, reflect changing ideas and assumptions – ideas and assumptions which are themselves a product of the political and policy concerns of the historical period, as well as the theoretical and methodological fashions of the disciplines within whose framework they are carried out. The questions which have been asked about having and caring for children, the concepts used, and the assumptions on which research has been based, as well as the methods adopted, vary enormously. Our knowledge of parenting and parenthood, like other areas of knowledge, is socially constructed (Berger and Luckman 1966; Wright and Treacher 1982). Consequently if we are to examine the enormous literature which currently constitutes our knowledge of parenting and parenthood it is essential to identify the ideas and assumptions on which it is founded and to show the way in which knowledge is moulded by changing social, economic, and political forces. This is the task of this chapter.

Prior to the 1970s two aspects of parenting and parenthood received the bulk of the research attention. First, considerable attention was paid to the demographic features of parenting, in particular to the quantity and tempo of child-bearing, as well as to related patterns of marriage, illegitimacy, and birth control. Second, there was a considerable amount of research on what was usually referred to in the literature as child-training or child-rearing practices – a topic which sociologists conceptualized as childhood socialization.

THE DEMOGRAPHIC ASPECTS OF PARENTING

The demographic aspects of parenting have long attracted attention because of their obvious implications for state policies. Demography itself developed as a discipline in large part because of the state's interest in counting its subjects for both military and taxation purposes (Glass 1973). During this century the long-term decline in the birth-rate which began in the second half of the nineteenth century, as well as the continuing high levels of infant and maternal mortality of the early decades of the century, fuelled fears about the future military, political, and economic strength of the nation, while the smaller family sizes of the middle classes helped to generate eugenic concerns (Hobsbawm 1969; Fraser 1984; J. Lewis 1980). As the focus on maternal mortality indicated, women's child-bearing capacity was held to be crucial to the numerical strength of the population and in this context it is interesting to note that fertility is conventionally measured in relation to the female rather than the male population.

In the period after the war the immediate post-war baby boom, followed by the steady rise in the birth-rate between 1955 and 1964, helped to alleviate anxieties about population decline, but the impact of long-term changes in the demographic structure of the population became an increasingly dominant concern. In particular the long-term decline in child-bearing together with increased longevity were yielding an ageing population and a potentially greater burden of social and economic dependency, which even in the more affluent 1960s was a matter of some public concern (Phillipson 1982). The introduction and widespread use of the contraceptive pill in the mid-1960s, coinciding as it did with a return to declining birth-rates, only temporarily halted in the period 1977 to 1980, served, if anything, to strengthen this interest. Moreover, since the mid-1970s the desire to control and even reduce public expenditure, as well as the restriction of employment opportunities, have heightened the belief, contentious though it is, that caring for persons of pensionable age at existing levels of welfare constitutes an unmanageable burden for the public purse. As a result the demographic aspects of child-bearing have continued to attract attention throughout the post-war period.

But it is not only the tempo and quantity of child-bearing (or indeed mortality), with their implications for the age structure of the population, which are relevant to debates about the cost of welfare provisions. Changes in the household structure of the population, which result from changing patterns of family formation and dissolution, are also important as far as social policies are concerned. They have attracted considerable attention in the post-war period because of the marked changes in household structure which have occurred. On the one hand increased longevity and smaller family sizes have meant increases in the number of single-person households: from 12 per cent of households in 1961 to 23 per cent in 1982 (Central Statistical Office 1984: 31). On the other hand increases in illegitimacy and the growing resort to divorce have markedly increased the number of single-parent households (there were some 860,000 of these in 1977) as well as the number of step-families (Popay, Rimmer, and Rossiter 1983: 9; Burgoyne and Clark 1984).

The majority of single-parent families, around eight out of nine, are headed by a woman and for a number of reasons a high and increasing proportion (47 per cent in 1982) are dependent on social security payments (Popay, Rimmer, and Rossiter 1983: 47). The quality of parenting in these single-parent households has been a matter of debate as has the significance of the less frequent or non-existent contact between father and child. However a range of research indicates that the material poverty these families experience is a crucial factor in many of the problems they face (Marsden 1969; Ferri 1976; Ferri and Robinson 1976). There is, too, concern about the experiences of children brought up by step-parents, especially the reluctance to allow contact with the biological parent outside the new family – usually the father (Burgoyne and Clark 1984: 202–03). Since there is also an increasing number of couples living either with children who are economically independent or on their own, the supposedly normative family structure of two natural parents and one or more dependent children living together has become less common. The proportion of households corresponding to the normative structure of parents and dependent children (but not necessarily the children of both of them) fell from 38 per cent in 1961 to 29 per cent in 1982 (Central Statistical Office 1984: 31). Clearly being a member of one of these 'normal' families may be a common occurrence for most individuals at some point in the life course and may be considered the normative (desirable) family structure, but there are many other common household types.

CHILD-REARING PRACTICES

Much of the study of child-rearing practices in the post-war period has been similarly prompted by political and policy concerns. The common assumption underlying these studies is that adult social behaviour is largely determined by childhood upbringing. Consequently where some aspect of adult social behaviour becomes the focus of attention, usually because it is considered undesirable, the aim is to identify the features of child-rearing which account for its occurrence so that policy-makers can be in a position to suggest the kinds of social changes which could prevent its development in later generations.

The early ideas on which Bowlby's classic maternal deprivation thesis, later transformed into attachment theory, was founded were first formulated in a study of delinquents carried out just before the war and published as a book in 1946 entitled *Forty-four Juvenile Thieves*. Identifying a typical 'affectionless character' of these thieves, Bowlby sought to explain their delinquency and lack of concern for social norms in terms of separation from their mother, which he found to be more common in the biographies of the thieves than in his control sample of children with other types of problems. Some of Bowlby's ideas were reiterated and expanded in his war-time discussions of evacuation, and this early work on the effects of separation led to his selection by the World Health Organisation after the war to carry out a study of homeless children, first published as *Maternal Care and Mental Health* and later popularized as *Child Care and the Growth of Love* (Bowlby 1952, 1953). Subsequent research cast doubt on a number of Bowlby's conclusions, not least on the necessity he had suggested for the continuous care and love of one person, usually the mother (Rutter 1972). More recently feminists have suggested that it is no coincidence that Bowlby's ideas were developed and flourished at a time when government policy had required that women give up their paid employment and be content with staying at home as mothers (Oakley 1982; Wilson 1977). Although Riley regards this analysis as over simple, the way in which ideas like those of Bowlby are often used as components of ideologies of motherhood and domesticity to make women feel their place is in the home with their children cannot be in doubt, even though increasing proportions of married women with young children are now employed in the labour market, albeit largely in part-time jobs (Riley 1983; Mackie and Pattullo 1977).

Adorno's classic study *The Authoritarian Personality* similarly took as its starting-point another feature of behaviour considered socially and morally undesirable – in this case anti-Semitism – and sought to tie it first to a broader constellation of prejudicial attitudes, then to identify a more general authoritarian personality, and finally to show how this personality had its origins in a particular type of upbringing which was grounded both socially and psychologically (Adorno *et al.* 1964). The Adorno study, like Bowlby's, was strongly influenced by Freudian ideas and asserted the importance of early childhood experiences in accounting for subsequent behaviour. It is this Freudian assumption which undoubtedly accounts for the relative neglect of how parents treat their children in the later years of childhood and in adolescence, with the notable exception of some of the longitudinal studies of child-rearing (Douglas, Ross, and Simpson 1968).

Building on the same Freudian legacy and the assumption of the close connection between child-rearing practices and later behaviour, a range of studies carried out in the 1950s and 1960s examined the details of child-rearing (often those aspects such as breast-feeding and toilet-training which Freudian theory indicated were of especial importance), making comparisons between different societies, social groups, and individual families (Erikson 1965; Whiting and Child 1953; Miller and Swanson 1958; Whiting 1963; Bronfenbrenner 1959). While some studies, particularly the cross-cultural studies of anthropologists, tried to show the link between the child-training practices and a particular feature of adult social behaviour, many took the impact of the child-rearing on subsequent behaviour as given, implying that the observed difference in child-rearing must have some impact on later behaviour – an assumption which has since been called into question (Clarke and Clarke 1976). Adult behaviour may be determined as much by immediate or recent situational factors as by childhood upbringing, though the relative contribution of the two will depend on the behaviour at issue.

Although many sociologists have been influenced by Freudian ideas (Talcot Parsons is a notable example), they have often used different concepts and different theoretical frameworks when approaching questions of the relation between the social behaviour of one generation and the next (Parsons and Bales 1956). The concept of socialization is the standard sociological term in this area and much of the work has been carried out within a symbolic interactionist framework. This approach assumes that the process of socialization involves many different social others in addition to parents and continues throughout the individual's life. Consequently much of the sociological work on later socialization does not deal with parental behaviour (Clausen 1968; Brim and Wheeler 1966).

Methodologically the studies of child-rearing and child-socialization have been diverse. Whereas Bowlby's initial study was based on clinical biographies, in formulating and developing his ideas he also drew heavily on the animal studies carried out by ethologists (Blurton Jones 1974; Riley 1983: 92–108). Adorno's account of the psychological origins of anti-Semitism was also largely derived from retrospective clinical interviews, although a large-scale survey was used to obtain basic material on attitude structures, personality types, and social background (Adorno *et al.* 1964). The anthropologists' direct participant observation of child-rearing has seemed less feasible in western societies, given the private nature of family life, and to avoid the limitations of retrospective data some studies in the USA and Britain, such as those of the Newsons, have used longitudinal designs with structured survey interviews at different points in the life course (Newson and Newson 1965, 1968, 1976). Since many of the latter studies question parents about how they behave towards their children rather than directly observing their behaviour, they still leave open the problem of the relation between verbal accounts and actual behaviour (Thomas 1974). The use of child-training manuals as essentially prescriptive rather than descriptive texts raises even greater methodological problems. (Newson and Newson 1974). To avoid such problems some recent work uses direct observational techniques, yet even this does not circumvent all methodological problems, since the period of observation is inevitably restricted and there is evidence that the presence of the observer affects the behaviour of those observed (Lewis 1982).

FROM CHILD TO PARENT

The common feature of studies of the demographic aspects of parenting and of child-training practices has been the ultimate focus on the child, viewed either as a numerical addition to a demographically structured population or as a potential citizen of an existing social order to which it must be socialized, a process which can be accomplished with more or less success. From this point of view the quality of parenting has been assessed in terms of its consequences for the child, not for the parent. A comment in an early paper by Bowlby shows the way in which he judged mothering in terms of the child's behaviour:

> 'It seems probable that most mothers are reasonably good but that mothers of neurotic children are frequently bad, in the sense that they have very strong feelings of hatred and condemnation towards their children, or else make inordinate demands from them for affection . . . it would be sentimental to shut our eyes to their existence or to think that they do not have a damaging effect upon their children.'
>
> (Riley, 1983: 94)

A good (normal) child suggests a good mother; a bad child a bad mother.

Since the 1970s, however, although work on these two aspects of parenting has continued, there has been a basic shift of attention from child to parent. What individuals do as parents has become important not only because of what it does to the size and structure of the population or because of what it does to the child's later attitudes and behaviour, but also because of its implications for the parents themselves. Their needs as well as those of their children are brought into the picture. This shift of attention has meant a far greater concern with individuals' experiences as parents (with an attendant shift to qualitative methodology) – with what it is like to be a parent, not just with what parents do, though of course the two are intimately connected. And in the process a number of the assumptions underlying earlier studies of parenthood have been called into question. These assumptions concern the nature of the parent–child relationship and the context in which it occurs.

Earlier studies of parenting tended to assume that parenting is essentially a dyadic relationship between the individual parent and the individual child, or between the individual parent and the children viewed as a collective grouping; they tended to assume, especially studies of parenting in western societies, that the mother had the main responsibility for bringing up the child, a task for which she was assumed to be naturally suited by instinct and emotion; and they tended to assume that child-rearing occurred in a harmonious, conventional family unit, in which there was a clear and just division of labour and a complementarity of tasks and interests that was acceptable to all. Earlier studies generally operated, therefore, with a model of an idealized family unit which, not surprisingly, demographic and social changes as well as feminist ideas have called into question. More recent research on parenting has, in contrast, assumed that the family as a unit, even when it consists of two parents and one or more children, is not one in which the division of labour is necessarily equitable; that individual interests may well be in conflict so that the family is the site of potential tension and struggle rather than harmony; and that roles have to be learned and legitimized and are not instinctively based (Oakley 1976a, 1981; Dreitzel 1974). And in this process fatherhood as well as motherhood has begun to receive attention and the dynamics of husband–wife or partner interaction have come into view (McKee and O'Brien 1982; Backet 1982).

One further related and important feature of more recent studies of parenting has been the greater attention to the social, ideological, and political context in which parenting occurs. Far more emphasis has been given, for instance, to the cultural and ideological pressures on women to become mothers, to the links between motherhood and gender identity, to the constraints on women to stay at home while their children are young and so forth (Busfield 1974; Burgoyne and Clark 1984: 27).

The early 1970s produced a range of studies, both historical and contemporary, which examined the cultural and ideological context of child-bearing and motherhood. The inspiration for the burgeoning scholarship concerning parent–child relations came from Aries's *Centuries of Childhood*, first published in English in 1962. It argued for the historical novelty of the notion of childhood itself; it pointed to the way in which the child came to be removed from the realm of adult life into the increasingly private world of the family and school; and it asserted an increasing attachment of parent to child. Subsequent research developed and reiterated Aries's arguments, generally seeing the moment of transition as occurring in the eighteenth century (Anderson 1980). Although recently contested by one or two scholars who assert the basic constancy of our notions of childhood and our treatment of children over time, empirical data largely support the view of the changing character of ideas and practices *vis-à-vis* children over time as well as between different social groups (Pollock 1983).

Much of the new work which looks at parenting from the parent's rather than the child's point of view has been as much concerned with having children as with looking after them – with becoming a parent as much as being a parent – a subject which has yielded interesting and valuable data on the significance of an experience of parenthood in contemporary society.

PREGNANCY AND CHILDBIRTH

Several studies published in the early 1970s explored the close interconnection of ideas and expectations about marriage and having children, pointing to the way in which having children was normally viewed as a taken-for-granted and essential component of marriage, to the extent that unmarried women, if pregnant, were assumed to want the pregnancy terminated (Busfield 1974; MacIntyre 1976; Busfield and Paddon 1977). Research also explored the constellation of ideas about the positive value of children which sustains the belief that children are both necessary and desirable: ideas about the emotional satisfaction and sense of meaning and purpose children give, about their importance to women's gender identity and about the opportunity they provide to create a family of one's own and leave some mark on future generations (Busfield 1974).

Research which has focused on women's experiences of pregnancy and childbirth has generally been highly critical of current practices surrounding pregnancy and childbirth, especially those of the medical profession, and has emphasized the negative aspects of women's experiences of being pregnant and giving birth: their sense of alienation and distress when faced with the bureaucratic structures of the hospital and an impersonal, interventionist medical profession which makes frequent use of such strategies as inductions, caesareans, and episiotomies (Cartwright 1979; Brighton Women and Science Group 1980). Studies in this area, influenced and informed by feminist ideas, have developed and amplified sociological theorizing about professional power and the role of science to offer an analysis of pregnancy and childbirth which emphasizes the subjugation of women during pregnancy and childbirth to a male-dominated medical profession, whose power, status, and prestige encourage the use of interventionist procedures and increasingly sophisticated technologies in medical locations (Freidson 1970; Johnson 1972). The political and policy implications of the work are well developed and the difficulties of securing home deliveries and of avoiding medical interventions are well documented, as are the problems of maintaining an autonomous midwifery profession in the face of these trends, since over 90 per cent of births in Britain now take place in hospital (Donnison 1977: Oakley 1976b; Brighton Women and Science Group 1980).

Relatively few studies have examined fathers' feelings about childbirth itself. The occasional studies which have been carried out suggest that men find no clear place for themselves when they are present at the birth of their child in hospital, despite the trend towards encouraging fathers' greater involvement in antenatal classes and childbirth, feeling helpless in the face of their partners' labour, in the way of the hospital's routine, and redundant in the face of medication the women were given (Brown 1982).

The shift in the locus of childbirth from home to the hospital has created a further problem – that of ensuring a smooth and satisfactory transition from hospital to home. In hospital a woman who is giving birth is in a position of some dependence and many of her material and practical, if not her emotional, needs and those of her child are met. She then returns home to an environment in which the responsibility for the child's welfare is primarily hers. Yet ironically women, despite the positive ideology of motherhood, have little preparation for the actual work which is involved in caring for babies and young children (Richards 1975; Antonis 1981). Oakley suggests that these new responsibilities are an important factor in the profound anxiety many women (71 per cent of her sample) experience on returning home from hospital (Oakley 1981: 143). This anxiety is to be distinguished from the postnatal depression that occurs during the first few days after birth which was experienced by some 84 per cent of her sample (Oakley 1981: 125). For the majority this anxiety was only temporary. Nevertheless, it is the overriding responsibility for the child's welfare which many authors see as the basic problem of motherhood for women in present-day society, a society whose productive activity and familial relationships are organized in ways which separate domestic work and work in the labour market. It is these structural features which create a situation in which child-rearing is the sole responsibility of the mother and there is little real sharing with spouse or kin, or indeed little support in the form of public services. Let us look, therefore, at some of the recent studies of the experience of motherhood and fatherhood.

BEING A PARENT

Boulton, in her study *On Being a Mother* (1983), looks at variations in the experience of motherhood in a sample of married women, none of whom was working. She argues that if we are to examine these experiences more fully it is helpful to distinguish women's immediate response to looking after their children from the sense of meaning, value, and significance they experienced in thinking about their lives as mothers. The latter reflected the way women felt about children in their more contemplative moods and might well be submerged by the feelings generated by the more immediate demands of children. The two dimensions of their response generated four types of experience of motherhood: 'fulfilled', where women had a strong sense of meaning and purpose, and enjoyed the immediate situation of child-care; 'alienated', where the values were reversed, where there was a weak sense of meaning and purpose and the woman was irritated by the immediate situation of child-care; and two intermediate categories: 'satisfied', where the immediate response was one of enjoyment, but the sense of meaning and purpose was weak; and 'in conflict', where the immediate response was one of irritation, but the sense of meaning and purpose was strong. Of the total sample of fifty mothers (selected it should be noted from a group of married women living in 'good' social conditions) some nineteen fell into the 'fulfilled' category, five into the 'satisfied', ten were 'in conflict', and sixteen 'alienated' (Boulton 1983: 53–4).

Roughly half of the mothers enjoyed the immediate situation of child-care; roughly half were irritated by it. The sources of the women's irritation and satisfaction varied. More working-class women 'found it difficult and stressful to resolve the conflict between housework and child-care responsibilities'; more middle-class women felt that child-care monopolized their lives and made them feel a loss of individuality (Boulton 1983: 129). They felt children inhibited their freedom and autonomy 'and made them mothers rather than individuals' (Boulton 1983: 94).

Boulton considers the impact of the father's support and help on the mother's experience. In her sample only nine of the husbands gave extensive help, eighteen moderate help, and twenty-three (nearly half) minimal help – hardly evidence (*contra* Young and Willmott) that the sharing of child-care between parents is now widespread (Boulton 1983: 95). Here, too, class differences were apparent, though they were restricted to the 'extensive' and 'moderate' categories, with middle-class husbands being more likely to give extensive help, working-class husbands 'moderate' help (Boulton 1983: 145). The impact of the husband's help also varied by class. In the working class a husband's help made a substantial difference to a woman's immediate response to child-care, reducing the burden of her work in a context where the lower level of material resources made child-care more burdensome. In contrast, in the middle-class families, additional help from a husband had far less impact on a woman's immediate enjoyment or irritation, partly because the husband's help could do little to alleviate her sense of monopolization and loss of individuality which was at the core of her dissatisfaction with being a mother. A husband's involvement and support in domestic matters did not mean that he shared the basic responsibility for the children.

Another recent study of twenty-two middle-class families, carried out by Backet and published as *Mothers and Fathers* (1982), has its theoretical foundation in symbolic interactionism and emphasizes the ideas and beliefs surrounding parenthood and the process of negotiation between mothers and fathers. It points to the potential contradiction in the families she studied between the reality of the women's daily commitment to looking after their children and having the overall responsibility for child-care and the egalitarian ideology on which family organization and interaction is supposed to be based. Since the ideology is one in which fairness, sharing, and openness within the family is stressed, it conflicts with the actual asymmetry of child-care found in these families. Backet argues that the contradiction had to be resolved by negotiation, a difficult and subtle process involving a range of mechanisms, which was sometimes successful, sometimes not. Husbands' helping, she found, often served as just such a mechanism, designed to create a feeling of fairness: 'occasional proof of willingness or ability to carry out child-care tasks was sufficient for respondents to sustain a belief in the existence of 'active' fathering' (Backet 1982: 228). Showing their interest and involvement in this way was important, but Backet contends that whereas motherhood had several taken-for-granted fundamental characteristics, such as responsibility and constant availability, the 'construction of paternal behaviour was a highly problematic exercise' (Backet 1982: 221). Backet comments: 'Essentially this was because it was more difficult for couples to sustain belief in their much valued precept of the father having a *direct* involvement with the children' (Backet 1982: 221).

Backet not only contends that there is little evidence that the women's movement has had much of an impact on fathers' participation in child-care, indicating that the father's role is basically peripheral, but also suggests that a radical change in social attitudes is necessary if there is to be more equitable parenting, particularly *vis-à-vis* the allocation of responsibility for child-care. In addition she argues that there need to be structural changes, such as more flexible occupational arrangements. This is the type of change stressed by Boulton who regards the basic sexual division of labour and the organization of men's work as the major factors that lead to the strains of motherhood and, consequently, are the avenues of change if shared responsibility for parenting is to be achieved. She comments 'the major restriction on a man's involvement in child care, and therefore to a large extent his understanding of his wife's world, is his obligation to his job' (Boulton 1983: 209). One might add that the contradiction which Backet identifies between ideology and actuality permits some optimism about the potential for attitude change, if some of the recommended structural changes could be effected. Her own study showed that while men tended to legitimize leaving a particular task to their wives on the grounds that they had greater knowledge and experience, those who did attempt to tackle the task in question found that they could accomplish it satisfactorily and were, as a result, more willing to help in future.

The arguments for attention to the needs of women as mothers and the difficulties they encounter do not merely stem from the temporary vulnerability that the responsibilities of motherhood may help to generate in women to other pressures, such as unemployment, poor housing, death of a close relative, and so forth, as Brown and Harris's (1978) study of the *Social Origins of Depression* brought out. They also stem from the impact they may have on the child's experiences and subsequent behaviour, the issues which so concerned earlier researchers. One cross-cultural study cited by Boulton showed that 'mothers who are primarily responsible for the care of their children are variable in their expressions of warmth and do not gear their hostility to the behaviour of their children' (Boulton 1983: 200). Consequently, 'women who have excessive responsibility for their children and who are forced to spend long periods of time caring for them without help and without break are likely to be irritable and emotionally unstable in their dealings with them' (Boulton 1983: 200). This means that even if our primary concern is with the behaviour and values of the next generation we cannot ignore the experiences of the mothers or fathers themselves, since their experiences affect how they act towards their children.

The argument here is an argument about the conditions in which parenting takes place in present-day advanced industrial societies, in particular about the oppressive nature of the circumstances of mothering for many women, including, of course, the fact that for many women paid work in the labour market simply increases the tasks which have to be performed, since women are still expected to do most of the domestic work on top of their paid labour (Berk and Berk 1979). However, the implication of existing studies is as much that parenting needs to be shared as that it must be shared between mother and father. Sharing can be achieved in a number of ways. It can be achieved by intergenerational support with a woman's own mother and female relatives helping to spread the burdens and responsibilities as well as the rewards of child-care, although this still leaves women with the responsibility for child-care (Young and Willmott, 1962). It can be achieved by much better child-care services, such as free day nurseries, which again are arenas within which caring will usually be done by women. Or it can be achieved by real sharing of responsibility and labour between mothers and fathers or other couples. All the evidence suggests that it is isolated, unsupported child-care which is oppressive. And unfortunately the ideological focus on motherhood, with its suggestion of a natural maternal instinct and its emphasis on the child's needs for a mother's love, has blinded us to concern for the social conditions in which child-care occurs. Under what social conditions do parents love their children and treat them well? Under what conditions do individuals find child-care a satisfying and rewarding experience? Under what conditions do men start to take a real share in the responsibility of child-care?

Significantly, however, the political and ideological changes of the first half of the 1980s appear to be producing a shift of attention away from the parent and back on to the child. The Conservative Government's concern to strengthen the family as the basic unit of the social order and to cut back the state's role in the provision of a range of services is associated with a set of ideas which emphasizes the responsibility of parents for the actions of their children and, while paying lip-service to ideas about the increasing equality of men and women, none the less assumes that women's proper place is caring for the family, whether children, husbands, or parents. These ideas and assumptions can be seen whether we look at the official response to moral panics about drug addiction amongst the young, or at the government's commitments to community care programmes for sick, handicapped, and elderly people, or at the cutbacks in public expenditure for nursery provision. Such ways of thinking are counterposed by critical, feminist analyses and politics and the outcome of the ideological and political struggle cannot be predicted with any certainty. It is essential, however, to recognize the ideas, assumptions, and political inclinations which underpin the scientific analyses of parenting and structure the terms of the debates, the questions asked, the avenues explored, the theories proposed, the methods adopted, and the knowledge obtained.

REFERENCES

Adorno, T.W., Frenkel-Brunswik, E., Levinson, D.J., and Nevitt Sanford, R. (1964) *The Authoritarian Personality* (first published 1950). New York: Wiley.

Anderson, M. (1980) *Approaches to the History of the Western Family, 1500–1914*. London: Macmillan.

Antonis, B. (1981) Mothering and Motherhood. In Cambridge Women's Studies Group, *Women in Society*. London: Virago.

Aries, P. (1973) *Centuries of Childhood*. Harmondsworth: Penguin.

Backet, K.C. (1982) *Mothers and Fathers: A Study of the Development and Negotiation of Parental Behaviour*. London: Macmillan.

Berger, P.L. and Luckman, T. (1966) *The Social Construction of Reality*. London: Allen Lane.

Berk, R.A. and Berk, S.F. (1979) *Labour and Leisure at Home: Content and Organisation of the Household Day*. Beverly Hills, Calif.: Sage.

Blurton Jones, N.G. (1974) Ethology and Early Socialisation. In M.P.M. Richards (ed.) *The Integration of a Child into a Social World*. Cambridge: Cambridge University Press.

Boulton, M.G. (1983) *On Being a Mother: A Study of Women with Pre-School Children*. London: Tavistock.

Bowlby, J. (1946) *Forty-four Juvenile Thieves: Their Characters and Home-Life*. London: Ballière, Tindall & Cox.

Bowlby, J. (1952) *Maternal Care and Mental Health*. Geneva: World Health Organisation.

Bowlby, J. (1953) *Child Care and the Growth of Love*. Harmondsworth: Penguin.

Breen, D.L. (1975) *The Birth of a First Child: Towards an Understanding of Femininity*. London: Tavistock.

Brighton Women and Science Group (1980) Technology in the Lying-in Room. In Brighton Women and Science Group *Alice Through the Microscope: The Power of Science over Women's Lives*. London: Virago.

Brim, O.G. and Wheeler, S. (eds) (1966) *Socialization after Childhood*. New York: Wiley.

Bronfenbrenner, U. (1959) Socialisation and Social Class through Time and Space. In E.E. Maccoby, T.M. Newcomb, and E.L. Hartley (eds) *Readings in Social Psychology*. (3rd edn) London: Methuen.

Brown, A. (1982) Fathers in the Labour Ward. In L. McKee and M. O'Brien (eds) *The Father Figure*. London: Tavistock.

Brown, G. and Harris, T. (1978) *Social Origins of Depression*. London: Tavistock.

Burgoyne, J. and Clark, D. (1984) *Making a Go of It: A Study of Stepfamilies in Sheffield*. London: Routledge & Kegan Paul.

Busfield, J. (1974) Ideologies and Reproduction. In M.P.M. Richards (ed.) *The Integration of a Child into a Social World*. Cambridge: Cambridge University Press.

Busfield, J. and Paddon, M. (1977), *Thinking about Children: Sociology and Fertility in Post-War England*. Cambridge: Cambridge University Press.

Cartwright, A. (1979) *The Dignity of Labour? A Study of Childbearing and Induction*. London: Tavistock.

Central Statistical Office (1984) *Social Trends, 1984*. London: HMSO.

Clarke, A.M. and Clarke, A.D.B. (1976) *Early Experience: Myth and Evidence*. London: Open Books.

Clausen, J.A. (ed.) (1968) *Socialisation and Society*. Boston, Mass.: Little, Brown.

Donnison, J. (1977) *Midwives and Medical Men: A History of Inter-professional Rivalries*. London: Heinemann.

Douglas, J.W.B., Ross, J.M., and Simpson, H.R. (1968) *All Our Future*. London: Davies.

Dreitzel, H. (ed.) (1974) *Family, Marriage and the Struggle of the Sexes.* New York: Macmillan.
Erikson, E.H. (1965) *Childhood and Society*. Harmondsworth: Penguin.
Ferri, E. (1976) *Growing Up in a One-Parent Family*. London: NFER–Nelson.
Ferri, E. and Robinson, H. (1976) *Coping Alone*. London: NFER–Nelson.
Firestone, S. (1971) *The Dialectic of Sex*. London: Cape.
Fraser, D. (1984) *The Evolution of the Welfare State*. (2nd edn) London: Macmillan.
Freidson, E. (1970) *The Profession of Medicine*. New York: Little, Brown.
Glass, D.V. (1973) *Numbering the People*. Farnborough: Saxon House.
Hobsbawm, E.J. (1969) *Industry and Empire*. Harmondsworth: Penguin.
Johnson, T.J. (1972) *Professions and Power*. London: Macmillan.
Lewis, C. (1982) The Observation of Father–Infant Relationships: An Attachment to Outmoded Concepts. In L. McKee and M. O'Brien (eds) *The Father Figure*. London: Tavistock.
Lewis, J. (1980) *The Politics of Motherhood*. London: Macmillan.
MacIntyre, S. (1976) Who Wants Babies? The Social Construction of 'Instincts'. In D.L. Barker and S. Allen (eds) *Sexual Divisions and Society*. London: Tavistock.
McKee, L. and O'Brien, M.(eds) (1982) *The Father Figure*. London: Tavistock.
Mackie, L. and Pattullo, P. (1977) *Women at Work*. London: Tavistock.
Marsden, D. (1969) *Mothers Alone*. London: Allen Lane.
Miller, D.R. and Swanson, G.E. (1958) *The Changing American Parent: A Study in the Detroit Area*. New York: Wiley.
Morgan, D.H.J. (1985) *The Family: Politics and Social Theory*. London: Routledge & Kegan Paul.
Newson, J. and Newson, E. (1965) *Patterns of Infant Care in an Urban Community*. Harmondsworth: Penguin.
Newson, J. and Newson, E. (1968) *Four Years Old in an Urban Community*. Harmondsworth: Penguin.
Newson, J. and Newson, E. (1974) Cultural Aspects of Childrearing in the English-Speaking World. In M.P.M. Richards (ed.) *The Integration of a Child into a Social World*. Cambridge: Cambridge University Press.
Newson, J. and Newson, E. (1976) *Seven Years Old in the Home Environment*. London: Allen & Unwin.
Oakley, A. (1976a) *Housewife*. Harmondsworth: Penguin.
Oakley, A. (1976b) Wisewoman and Medicine Man: Changes in the Management of Childbirth. In J. Mitchell and A. Oakley (eds) *The Rights and Wrongs of Women*. Harmondsworth: Penguin.
Oakley, A. (1981) *From Here to Maternity: Becoming a Mother*. Harmondsworth: Penguin.

Oakley, A. (1982) *Subject Women*. London: Fontana.

Parsons, T. and Bales, R.F. (1956) *Family, Socialisation and Interaction Process*. London: Routledge & Kegan Paul.

Phillipson, C. (1982) *Capitalism and the Construction of Old Age*. London: Macmillan.

Pollock, L.A. (1983) *Forgotten Children: Parent–Child Relations from 1500 to 1900*. London: Cambridge University Press.

Popay, J., Rimmer, L., and Rossiter, C. (1983) *One Parent Families: Parents, Children and Public Policy*. London: Study Commission of the Family.

Richards, M. (1975), Non-Accidental Injury in an Ecological Perspective. In Department of Health and Social Security *Non-Accidental Injury to Children*. London: HMSO.

Riley, D. (1983) *War in the Nursery: Theories of the Child and Mother*. London: Virago.

Rutter, M. (1972) *Maternal Deprivation Reassessed*. Harmondsworth: Penguin.

Sears, R.R., Maccoby, E., and Levin, H. (1957) *Patterns of Childrearing*. Evanston, Ill.: Row, Peterson.

Thomas, K. (1974) *Attitudes and Behaviour*. Harmondsworth: Penguin.

Whiting, B.B. (ed.) (1963) *Six Cultures: Studies of Child-Rearing*. New York: Wiley.

Whiting, J.L. and Child, I.L. (1953) *Child Training and Personality: A Cross-Cultural Study*. New Haven, Conn.: Yale University Press.

Wilson, E. (1977) *Women and the Welfare State*. London: Tavistock.

Wright, P. and Treacher, A. (1982) *The Problem of Medical Knowledge*. Edinburgh: Edinburgh University Press.

Young, M. and Willmott, P. (1962) *Family and Kinship in East London*. Harmondsworth: Penguin.

Young, M. and Willmott, P. (1973) *The Symmetrical Family*. London: Routledge & Kegan Paul.

4
From the celebration to the marginalization of youth

Frank Coffield

'one in four of the European Community's 48 million 15 to 25 year olds are unemployed – a rate three times greater than that for adults over 25.'

(*Times Educational Supplement*, 6 December, 1985: 14)

INTRODUCTION

In little more than ten years the economic crisis in western societies has transformed the golden age of youth into a massive social problem. The dominant images until very recently were of free-spending and pleasure-seeking young people, enjoying the best years of their lives; now the pictures are of depressed young adults lying in bed or watching television until their giro cheques arrive. In the 1960s young people were celebrated as the embodiment of sexuality, freedom, health and progress; before the end of the 1970s they had again become economically marginalized and began to be treated in the same way as other stigmatized groups such as black immigrants or disabled people. Witness this extract from an article in *The Times*:

> 'The nub of the problem is that there are almost no jobs at all for the academically unqualified and those best suited for manual work. The lesson seems to be that if Britain does not do something drastic about this very soon, in months rather than years, it will be saddled with an unemployed, unemployable *Lumpenproletariat* capable only of causing social problems. The legion of the lost could easily become a cohort of the damned.'
>
> (*The Times*, 6 October, 1981: 6)

The first argument of this chapter is that the major generator of change in our ideas about and treatment of young adults is not advances in biology or psychology but fluctuations in the economy. This is a development of the ideas marshalled by Tucker (1977: 26) to answer the question, what is a child? He wrote: 'the whole concept of childhood could be said to be a man-made phenomenon. Thus childhood may be lengthened and prolonged at some periods of history, and abbreviated at others, according to adult perceptions, needs and expectations.' Adolescence, similarly, may be extended or curtailed according to the needs of industry and commerce.

It is not, however, being suggested that young adults are somehow being subjected to special social changes which have left other age groups untouched. The claim is rather that the seriousness of the economic crisis is most marked among the young whose hold on the labour market has historically been very tenuous in capitalist countries. Young people have for generations been the most expendable section of the work-force and writers like Tawney (1934) and Jewkes and Winterbottom (1933) make clear the historical continuity of the problem: what is new is *long-term* unemployment for young adults.

The world recession, technological advances, the loss of markets to cheap labour in Third World countries, the run-down in manufacturing jobs, and the increased numbers of young people have all contributed to unprecedented levels of unemployment and major restructuring within the economy. As a result, adults are painfully learning to adjust to much more frequent moves in and out of the labour market and to regular periods of retraining. In the words of Ken Roberts

> 'adulthood has become less certain, more fluid. Adolescence used to be a transitional phase between two known statuses – childhood and adulthood. ... The problems of youth were essentially transitional. School-leavers needed "bridges" which would provide them with the additional skills, and technical and social qualifications that were needed to tackle adult jobs. ... This view of youth as a transitional phase between known and secure statuses is fast becoming obsolete. ... Traditional gender roles are being challenged. Family life is also changing. Life-long monogamy is now just one of several patterns. ... Rather than basing life styles upon stable occupational and domestic statuses, many individuals now appear to spend their entire lives in transition.'
>
> (Roberts 1984: 6–7)

If this analysis is accurate, how is it possible for the Manpower Services Commission (MSC) to believe that it 'is about providing a permanent bridge between school and work' (Manpower Services Commission 1982: 7). The organization which successive governments have entrusted with the industrial retraining of Britain appears to be trapped in the language and the ideas of the past.

This chapter, because of the shortage of space, will concentrate on the following issues: the real suffering of unemployed young people, the impact of their unemployment on families, the particular difficulties of young women, cultural continuities and regional differences in times of rapid change, and a few general conclusions which contain implications for social policy.[1]

THE SUFFERING OF UNEMPLOYED YOUNG PEOPLE

Above, I quoted approvingly from Ken Roberts's book *School Leavers and their Prospects* (1984). It contains, however, a discussion on the ability of young people to cope with unemployment better than middle-aged adults, a view with which I would want to disagree strongly as a result of our fieldwork. Roberts's view is shared by many commentators including Watts (1983), Warr (1983), and Kelvin and Jarrett (1985). Part of his argument is that 'school-leavers have no occupational identities to shatter ... their personalities cannot be assaulted in quite the same way as lifelong steelworkers and dockers' (Roberts 1984: 73). I have no desire to detract from the anguish of middle-aged or skilled workers with mortgages and young families who are suddenly made redundant. Margaret Owen (1986: 159) has drawn particular attention to the problems of professional married women over the age of forty-five who are *inter alia* ineligible for the dole. But concern for these groups should not obscure the plight of young adults who have never had any job nor any opportunity to develop an occupational identity. Such young people cannot even claim to be out-of-work secretaries or painters, they are simply *unemployed*.

Nor can I accept Roberts's (1984: 73) additional claim that 'school-leavers have the better grounds for hope. They can realistically expect their prospects to improve, unlike the redundant middle-aged, many of whom are sentenced to *de facto* early retirement. Irrespective of Britain's economic fortunes, time improves school-leavers' prospects.' There are at least two counter-arguments. First, there are crucial regional differences (of which more will be said later). The economic prospects for the north of England were recently assessed by a team from the Centre for Urban and Regional Development Studies in Newcastle University and their conclusion was that 'some young people may never work' (Robinson 1982: viii). Second, of the north's 125,600 long-term unemployed adults who were eligible for placements on the MSC's community programme in 1983–84, only 10 per cent were provided with places. The young adults we met were all too well aware of the dismissive attitudes of employers to workers who were considered to have been too long on the dole.

The choice in the near future for employers will be between twenty-two- and twenty-four-year-olds who have not held a regular job since their six-month Youth Opportunities Programme (YOP) scheme ended when they were sixteen, and bright-faced eighteen-year-olds from a two-year Youth Training Scheme (YTS). It is possible that a whole generation of young people may remain in the dole queues, namely those who left school from the mid-1970s onwards and who failed to obtain permanent employment. This group are likely to present social policy decision-makers with a particularly severe test as their cynicism continues to deepen and more and more of them retreat into drugs. Moreover, government action to drive down the wages of young workers (for example, the removal of the protection of Wages Councils from under-twenty-one-year-olds) may make it even harder for long-term unemployed adults in their twenties to enter (or re-enter) the labour market.

Without exception, all of those in our sample who became unemployed experienced serious financial problems, and some sank into social isolation, while still others quarrelled bitterly with their parents and left home. The suffering was no less real because it was often disguised and, more frequently, not even admitted to us until the young adult in question had landed a temporary or part-time job. Such reactions are likely to undermine the results of questionnaires or any research methods where there is no long-term relationship of trust and respect between the researcher and the young adults in question.

THE EFFECTS OF YOUTH UNEMPLOYMENT ON FAMILIES

It is not being overly melodramatic to suggest that the new phenomenon of long-term youth unemployment may be creating a crisis for the family, especially in the homes of parents who entered the labour market in the 1950s or 1960s. The parents of our sample, for example, had in the main moved with comparative ease from school to employment, picking and choosing as they went; for these parents short periods of unemployment were a regular and unworrying feature of their search for a job which suited them better. Having become regular wage-earners in a job of their own choice, the parents had then been able to establish adult status and independence with homes and families of their own. Parental expectations for their children's material advancement and occupational mobility grew as their children grew.

The contrast in the external conditions facing these two generations is very marked in that the labour market for young people is now radically different from the one most parents *think* their daughters and sons are experiencing. Parents in the north-east, for instance, are still trying to obtain apprenticeships (particularly for their sons) and do not understand the widespread collapse of that system. The new forest of acronyms (YOP, TOPS, WEEP, WOC, CPVE, TVEI, CP, and so on) only adds to their disorientation.

The problems cannot, however, be left outside the family's front door. The ever-extending period of transition to adulthood means that young people, in the eyes of some parents, are 'moping round the house' for days, weeks, and months on end. Their offspring need not only emotional support but also seemingly unending financial help for clothes, improving training skills (like driving lessons), and money for travel to job centres, 'snake bites' (cider and lager), 'tabs' (cigarettes), discos, concerts, newspapers, and cups of coffee to help pass the time. One can readily understand the pressures and tensions arising from sharing physical space with people who are getting older and older without correspondingly gaining any more control of their surroundings. The physical overcrowding is likely to be all the greater when some of the parents, elder brothers or sisters, uncles or aunts are themselves unemployed. One member of our sample spent each winter at home with his father as both could find only seasonal jobs as gardeners in spring and summer.

We also saw a whole continuum of family reactions from parents who sympathized with and supported their offspring to those families where the tensions led to periodic quarrels and on to those where young people left home because they felt the friction had become intolerable. Most families were not, however, easily categorized and parents veered from recriminations to being over-protective. Leaving home only introduced single young adults to a new set of problems such as the lack of rented accommodation available for them, and the government restrictions on board and lodging regulations, aimed specifically at young people under twenty-six years of age (see Matthews 1985), which came into operation after our fieldwork had ended. The official thinking behind the new regulations, which were successfully challenged in the courts, appeared to be that young people should live at home.

In addition, the financial burdens on families have been increased by changes in social policy. In April 1983 'housing requirement' of £3.10 (now £3.90) was withdrawn from any unemployed person under twenty-one living at home. The resulting poverty can be judged from the fact that, in January 1986, after giving their parents £10 per week for their keep, young unemployed sixteen- to eighteen-year-olds were left with £8.20 a week (and eighteen to twenty-one-year-olds £13.60) to pay for all their needs.

The anger felt by parents at the treatment of their young, whether in terms of unemployment, low wages, or 'slave labour', is well caught by Allatt and Yeandle's study of family structure and youth unemployment in the north-east:

> 'The encouragement parents give their children, the nagging, the threats, the irritability when their off-spring seem to be constantly watching television or spending long hours in bed, the 'job creation' within the household, the amount of joking . . . are not only means of keeping a work ethic buoyant but, from a parent's point of view, an attempt to control the unclean, the danger which threatens the categories by which they have ordered their lives and brought up their children. . . . For the threat posed by unemployment is not so much that the unemployed can survive without working, but that they may be content to do so.'
>
> (Allatt and Yeandle 1985: 9–10)

THE PARTICULAR DIFFICULTIES OF YOUNG WOMEN

Another consequence of the economic crisis has been a hardening of attitudes which exposed more clearly to some young women in our sample the force of patriarchy within the family and of sexism in the work-place. Arguments over money and domestic chores between parents and unemployed daughters who had been drawn back into unpaid work in the home served only to bring out into the open within some families the power relations rooted in gender (and age), and the consequent sexual division of labour within the household.

The majority of young women in our study, however, accepted without question the rather restricted roles envisaged for them by their fathers, partners, and employers, and were unwilling to explore why the choices available to them were even more limited than those open to their brothers. Both the women and the men in our study had views about each other based upon stereotypes. They tended to respond to each other not as individuals but in terms of the biological characteristics generally thought to be typical of women or men. Their beliefs and their behaviour were shot through with patriarchy, which is best thought of as a means of distributing power among people. The values associated with patriarchy have been passed down from generation to generation in the north of England and they are so much part of the structure of relationships and daily life that their significance at first went unremarked by our sample and by ourselves. Patriarchy has meant that working-class women tend to be paid less, are much more likely to be in part-time jobs and to hold down lower-level jobs, and have fewer chances of training or promotion. They tend to be in sole charge of running homes and rearing children, to have their sexuality controlled first by their fathers and then by their boyfriends, and are often discounted in public by their own menfolk as scatter-brained, emotional, or frivolous. At best, they are thought to be a pleasant, ornamental, and at times exciting distraction after the 'real work' of society has been completed by men.

This traditional pattern of expectations is being challenged in certain areas of the north-east, where frequently the bread-winner is no longer the 'macho' male working in dirty and dangerous conditions in mines, steel mills, or shipyards, but is the wife employed as a part-time, low-paid machinist, making shirts for Marks and Spencer. The consequences for relations between the sexes and for the family have still to be worked out.

Paul Willis has reported from the west Midlands

> 'A trend towards early pregnancy and the setting up of single parent homes. This is also one way to "get off the register" at the careers office or Job Centre. It cuts out the embarrassments and failures of trying to find work. More positively, child rearing offers a clear role for young women. You are meeting the needs of someone else, and you are achieving a transition to adult status. Whether or not pregnancy is chosen as a conscious strategy, it is certainly now much more acceptable to become a "welfare mother" in state housing.'
>
> (Willis 1984: 13)

Willis could have been writing about Detroit or Newark where for generations there have been large numbers of black households run by young mothers in what has been called 'the feminisation of poverty' (Hall, 1985: 22).

Only some of the young women in our sample (but, predictably, even fewer of the younger men) were beginning to question and to oppose actively the constraints on the lives of women. Some, for example, struggled against fathers and fiancés to win the sexual freedoms which their brothers have always been accorded, and which most of their middle-class sisters have already won for themselves.

One young woman of eighteen sometimes had to contend with the violent possessiveness of her father who objected to her boyfriend, who refused to allow any of the family to attend her engagement party, and who tried to prevent her meeting her future husband by locking her in her room. She eventually packed her clothes and moved in with her fiancé who in turn wished to distance himself from the sexist behaviour and attitudes of his mates. They referred to his girlfriend as 'the missus' or 'the little lady'. For all the good intentions of both parties, shortly after they began living together (and even more so after their marriage), more traditional patterns asserted themselves, and the wife took over the running of their flat while the husband watched television and was waited on.

Although as Nissel (Chapter 9) shows for women in general there are now far more opportunities for paid employment than existed in previous generations, young women are just as much subject to male expectations in the labour market as they are at home (Griffin 1985). The widescale adoption of new technology is also likely to have a disproportionate effect on the young female worker. The Equal Opportunities Commission has, for example, calculated that the introduction of the word processor will lead to a national loss of 170,000 jobs by 1990. Those most affected will be female copy typists. Programmes of positive discrimination in favour of young women appear necessary and yet those already in existence (like the MSC's projects to attract women into the new technologies) are not overly successful as the very low number of women attending Information Technology Centres testifies. The effects of generations of socialization, which starts from the cradle and continues throughout the life course (Burgoyne, Chapter 2) are not likely to be dissipated quickly by a new initiative from the MSC or anywhere else.

CULTURAL CONTINUITIES AND REGIONAL DIFFERENCES

So far, attention has been centred on the economic crisis in western societies, the collapse of the job market for young people, and the rapidity of technological advances. Our field-work, however, kept reminding us of two issues which were just as powerful in moulding the lives of our sample: deep cultural continuities and regional differences. La Fontaine (1985: 41), while discussing a number of anthropological perspectives on the family and social change, raises the interesting question of how much continuity is found in societies which have experienced considerable economic change and concludes that 'there seems to be more evidence for the resilience of traditional kinship structures in the face of economic change than for their breakdown'.

Let me give an example of such resilience from our fieldwork in the north-east. Neither prolonged personal experience of unemployment, nor the high national level of unemployment, nor controversial calls for the right to useful unemployment (Illich 1978), nor arguments in favour of a move to a 'life ethic' (Clemitson and Rodgers 1981) in any way shook the attachment of young adults to the Protestant work ethic. All of our sample, without exception, wanted a job and saw no other possibility of attaining independence and personal dignity except through a wage.

In the writing of Paul Willis the wage is not simply money but the crucial pivot for such processes as setting up home, forming a couple, preparing for a family, and becoming a consumer with some real power in the market-place:

> 'the wage is still the golden key (mortgage, rent, household bills) to a separate personal household, away from parents and away from the boss. . . . A separate home is a universal working class objective. Its promise of warmth and safety more than offsets the risk and coldness of work. No wage means no key to the future.'
>
> (Willis 1984: 476)

Also, we were still able to discern twenty years later, some of the long-term effects of the depression of the 1930s upon the north-east, which had been noted by Christopherson in 1966:

> 'That experience established the tradition that . . . for the majority – and it was a larger majority here than in many parts of the country – the best, indeed often enough the only possible, course was to leave school as soon as the law allowed, and to take a job, any job, which would contribute to the family income and offer some possibility of security.'
>
> (quoted by Townsend 1985: 106–07)

Similarly, sexism, racism, and the negative aspects of localism, such as the unwillingness to travel even to a local though unfamiliar area for a job, were still virulent in all three of the areas we studied. We also detected an intensification of some established patterns of behaviour. Connections between family networks and local firms, for instance, seemed to tighten as, on the one hand, relatives tried to restrict job openings to other members of their family and, on the other hand, personnel managers learned to use the extended working-class families in the north-east to fuller advantage. Allatt and Yeandle (1985: 21) conclude that 'the shift in the balance of power in the labour market also denotes a shift to a more traditional society. Change in the labour market enhances the familial power of some parents fortunate enough to have access to the job market.' Considerable adaptations might have been expected in response to economic crisis and decline but, in the words of La Fontaine (1985: 55), 'great changes may be absorbed with little obvious effect on norms and ideals of behaviour. The study of stability is as important as the study of change.'

The second issue concerns the deep-seated regional differences which make up the structure of opportunities within which all young people in a particular area have to live out their lives. Just as Connell *et al.* (1982: 180) have argued that 'the situation of a working-class schoolboy is always different from the situation of the working-class schoolgirl', so the job prospects for either the working-class young woman *or* man vary markedly from one part of the country to another. Regional differences need to be added to those of gender and class, and all three sets of differences need to be assessed together if we are to understand what is happening in any one particular area. There is, as Massey and Meegan (1983: 418) have shown in detail, 'a new geography of jobs', which has produced a new form of regional inequality – 'based not simply on differences in levels of unemployment, but also on differences in the type of jobs on offer'. Their argument is that peripheral areas like the north-east are expanding but are able to attract only repetitive, low-paid jobs for women in 'a branch plant economy', while the professional, scientific, and high-level administrative jobs continue to be concentrated in a contracting centre in the south-east.

Regional differences have been well illustrated by Trew and Kilpatrick (1984: 129), who found that the unemployed men they surveyed in Belfast suffered less psychological distress than their counterparts in Brighton. They further suggested that 'unemployment is less of a social stigma in Belfast then elsewhere'. Similarly, to grow up in a region like the north of England with its long tradition of high unemployment and with currently more than one-quarter of a million unemployed adults out of a total population of just over 3 million, and to live on an estate where seven out of ten male adults are unemployed, is obviously to be in a social setting of a different order, irrespective of one's class or sex, from leaving school in a town with 4 per cent unemployment and factories specializing in the latest technologies. And, as Trew and Kilpatrick have proposed, the combined effects of the historical experience of joblessness and the resulting system of local support are likely to lessen the psychological impact of unemployment.

This is not the place for a detailed statistical breakdown of the economy of the north, but one central issue can be addressed: Britain's regional aid policies. The north's industrial base has not collapsed of its own accord: it has been pushed over the cliff by the policies adopted by such nationalized industries as the National Coal Board, British Rail, and the British Steel Corporation. The full argument is well rehearsed by Hudson (1985: 76–7) who concluded that the net result of implementing various state policies 'has been that people in the Northern Region have suffered a serious qualitative and quantitative loss of employment opportunities, often concentrated in particular locations within the Region, resulting in sustained net out-migration and high levels of unemployment'. Not only are these regional policies uncoordinated and chaotic but they are also, according to Hudson, 'to a very considerable extent, the major proximate cause of employment decline'.

The future for the north-east and for other similar areas like Scotland, South Wales and the north-west has been made even gloomier by the present government's plan, announced in November 1984, to cut regional aid by £300 million. The decision was made after the EEC had calculated that Britain already had ten out of the Community's fifteen most disadvantaged regions. The EEC analysis, based on unemployment and productivity, showed that, in the words of the latest report of the North of England County Council Association (NECCA):

> 'Northumberland, Tyne & Wear, Durham and Cleveland are in the bottom 12 out of 131 regions in Europe. They are accompanied by the recognised "poor men of Europe", such as Calabria, Sardinia, Sicily and Northern Ireland.'
>
> (NECCA 1984: 1)

The vulnerability of the region has been increased since the Second World War by attempts to diversify the industrial base by attracting into the region branches of multinational companies without centres of research and development. Control over the local economy has now passed into the hands of either nationalized industries or firms with headquarters in Rotterdam, Detroit, or Tokyo. This historical domination of the job market by a small number of very large firms means that there is no tradition of self-employment in the area and generations of workers expect to be given a job rather than to create one; it also means that the closure of any major works such as at Consett or Shildon has far-reaching effects in the community.

Our sample, then, has inherited a bleak legacy from the north's industrial past. A combination of interlocking disadvantages in employment, health, and education has produced a set of opportunities which are markedly inferior to those of their contemporaries in other more prosperous parts of Britain and Europe. Their immediate prospects are worsened by the fact that in 1987 the twenty to twenty-four age group will peak in numbers, with 20,000 more in the north-east at that time (NECCA 1983: 20). The loss of manual jobs is also expected to accelerate over the same period, and the north's stake in the new technologies is not an impressive one (Thwaites 1983). The outlook, therefore, is that greater numbers of unskilled young people than ever before will be competing throughout the rest of the 1980s for a declining number of dead-end jobs.

Faced with a crisis of this proportion, we felt obliged – in the full account of our fieldwork – to outline a new social contract for young people. Here there is only space for a few of the conclusions of that study.

SOME CONCLUSIONS

For some years to come millions of young adults in western countries are likely to be excluded from responsible participation in society because they are wageless. They will form a poverty-stricken, frustrated, and apathetic under-class who are unlikely to seek redress for their grievances through political action. That particular generation of young working-class adults who became sixteen in successive years from 1975 onwards have borne the brunt of the world economic recession and of the structural changes in British industry. The greatest risk they now run is that, even if there is an economic recovery, whatever new jobs are created are more likely to go to their younger, better-trained, and less embittered sisters, brothers, cousins, and neighbours. Such an outcome would leave them unemployed, state pensioners for a lifetime, marrying and raising children on the dole. If, as seems most probable, there is increased investment in new technologies and jobless growth, their chances of breaking into the job market as untrained and unskilled employees are further reduced. Compared with earlier generations who left school in the 1950s or 1960s, they are 'secular victims' of an economic crisis which has affected their adolescence more deeply and more lastingly than any hormonal changes. Their worst predicament remains the lack of individual, communal, or regional choices which would enable them to break out of their poverty and their dependence.

The international character of the crisis which has destroyed the juvenile labour market in many countries coupled with specific changes in social policy in Britain (to which reference has been made earlier) have combined to place new and heavy burdens on the family. Unless the housing needs (primarily the need for decent rented accommodation) of young adults who are struggling to become independent on state handouts are recognized, there may be an explosion in the number of homeless youngsters seeking emergency shelter.

We also need to break out of what I call 'the training only trap', namely the idea that a two-year YTS scheme is an adequate response to the current range of predicaments of young people. No matter how many hundreds of millions of taxpayers' money are invested in training, and no matter how many employers are persuaded to share some of the financial costs (and a two-year YTS will test their commitment to training), it must be stressed that training *alone* creates no jobs. The experience of the West Germans, with their long-established system of vocational training, should be giving us pause for thought: in 1985 '84,000 young skilled workers have become unemployed immediately after finishing their apprenticeships – almost 15 per cent of the total of those passing the exam' (James 1985). What young Germans as well as young Britons need is an interactive trio of education, training, *and* employment – and the least of these is training.

Nissel (Chapter 9) points to the lower age levels at which young people have reached adulthood. Yet recently the age at which in Britain an adolescent is officially or administratively considered to have become an adult has begun to rise; witness the proposal contained in the Green Paper of June 1985 on *Reform of Social Security* which will pay all single people under twenty-five a reduced weekly benefit rate *on grounds of age alone*. Other initiatives, like the Social Democratic Party's strategy document *Tertiary Education for All* (1985), which would remove all sixteen- and seventeen-year-olds from full-time employment, point in the same direction. As young people's labour is no longer needed by industry and commerce, they are to be placed in 'ageing vats', to use Grubb and Lazerson's phrase (forthcoming). The age of majority, having been lowered from twenty-one to eighteen in 1967, is set to rise again even if all the psychological and biological findings about earlier maturity (Tanner 1978) remain valid and unchallenged.

Within the total population of young adults, the problems of certain groups will tend to intensify: those most at risk are likely to be young blacks and young women. Of all the English regions the north-east has the lowest percentage (less than 1 per cent) of black immigrants and yet our fieldwork clearly showed that ordinary young people in the region could not be budged from their openly racist beliefs. That uncomfortable fact will have to be faced squarely by the community in the area and by its political and educational leaders. Traditional female jobs will also disappear at an increasing rate. More part-time jobs without training or promotion prospects are already being offered, and ideological pressures to ease unemployment by forcing or persuading women to remain at home to look after either employed or unemployed men will grow. Another generation of young women will run the risk of sacrificing their own lives for others, of sinking into social isolation, or of jumping prematurely into sexual relationships in order to escape from home into some form of independence. In the words of Paul Willis (1984: 14): 'Single parenthood may involve a passive dependence on the state and acceptance of an isolated life of poverty.'

A leitmotiv running through this chapter has been the need for a strong regional dimension in all aspects of government policy. As I have argued earlier, the northern region has been transformed from the end of the Second World War into a 'global outpost' (Williamson and Quayle 1983: 29). It has neither the economic resources nor the political clout to solve its own problems. The regions of England require a minister of Cabinet rank like the secretaries of state for Scotland and Wales to protect their interests. The overwhelming majority of the young adults we got to know well were politically ignorant and deeply cynical about the democratic process: government in Whitehall was viewed as distant, unconcerned, and irrelevant to their own personal lives.

Whatever changes in social policy are introduced by whatever government to cope with the catalogue of problems mentioned in this chapter, the greatest injustice would be committed and the greatest blunder would be made if decision-makers thought they were dealing with millions of untalented, dull, and unteachable young people. Irrespective of a general lack of formal qualifications, the young adults we met displayed a whole range of intellectual, emotional, physical, and social qualities which had, in the main, been left untapped and unrecognized by their schools, their MSC schemes, and their employers (if they had any). The challenge to social policy is to take this finding seriously and to involve young adults in the formation of new structures. The official world is full of the rhetoric of participation – it was after all one of the three themes of the United Nations International Youth Year in 1985 and was used in the title of the Thompson Report (1982) on the Youth Service in England – but, as we all know, the voices of young adults are not heard where it matters. How else would 12 million of them in Europe be unemployed?

NOTE

1 A fuller account is available in *Growing Up at the Margins* by Coffield, F., Borrill, C. and Marshall, S., a three-year participant observation of around fifty young adults in the north-east.

REFERENCES

Allatt, P. and Yeandle, S.M. (1985) Family Structure and Youth Unemployment: Economic Recession and the Concept of Fairness. Unpublished paper. University of Durham.

Clemitson, I. and Rodgers, G. (1981) *A Life to Live: Beyond Full Employment*. London: Junction Books.

Coffield, F., Borrill, C., and Marshall, S. (1986) *Growing Up at the Margins: Young Adults in the North East*. Milton Keynes: Open University Press.

Connell, R.W., Ashenden, D.J., Kessler, S., and Dowsett, G.W. (1982) *Making the Difference: Schools, Families and Social Division*. Sydney: Allen & Unwin.

Griffin, C. (1985) *Typical Girls?* London: Routledge & Kegan Paul.

Grubb, W.N. and Lazerson, M. (forthcoming) *Vocationalism in American Education*.

Hall, P. (1985) The Social Crisis. *New Society* 22 November: 20–2.

Hudson, R. (1985) The Paradoxes of State Intervention. In R.A. Chapman (ed.) *Public Policy Studies: The North East of England*. Edinburgh: Edinburgh University Press for the University of Durham.

Illich, I. (1978) *The Right to Useful Unemployment*. London: Marion Boyers.

James, H. (1985) The Disillusioned Apprentices. *The Times* 13 December.

Jewkes, J. and Winterbottom, A. (1933) *Juvenile Unemployment*. London: Allen & Unwin.

Kelvin, P. and Jarrett, J.E. (1985) *Unemployment: Its Social Psychological Effects*. Cambridge: Cambridge University Press.

La Fontaine, J.S. (1985) Anthropological Perspectives on the Family and Social Change. *Quarterly Journal of Social Affairs* 1 (1): 29–59.

Manpower Services Commission (1982) *Youth Task Group Report*. Selkirk House, London: MSC.

Massey, D. and Meegan, R. (1983) The New Geography of Jobs. *New Society* 17 March: 416–18.

Matthews, R. (1985) Out of House and Home? The Board and Lodging Regulations. *Poverty* 62: 20–5.

NECCA (1983) *The State of the Region Report*. North of England County Councils Association.

NECCA (1984) *The State of the Region Report*. North of England County Councils Association.

Owen, M. (1986) On the Scrapheap. *New Society* 24 January: 159–60.

Roberts, K. (1984) *School Leavers and their Prospects*. Milton Keynes: Open University Press.

Robinson, F. (1982) *The Economic Prospects for the North*. Newcastle University: Centre for Urban and Regional Development Studies.

Social Democratic Party (1985) *Tertiary Education for All: A Strategy for Education and Training of the 16–19's*. Green Paper 25. London: Jaguar Press.

Tanner, J.M. (1978) *Education and Physical Growth*. London: Hodder & Stoughton.

Tawney, R.H. (1934) *The School-Leaving Age and Juvenile Unemployment*. London: Workers' Educational Association.

Thompson Report (1982) *Experience and Participation: Report of the Review Group on the Youth Service in England*. London: HMSO.

Thwaites, A. (1983) Technology and the Prospects for Employment in the Northern Region of England. In B. Williamson and B. Quayle (eds) *Technology and Change in the North East*. University of Durham: North East Local Studies.

Townsend, A.R. (1985) A Critique of Past Policies of 'Modernisation' for the North East. In R.A. Chapman (ed.) *Public Policy Studies: The North East of England*. Edinburgh: Edinburgh University Press for the University of Durham.

Trew, K. and Kilpatrick, R. (1984) *The Daily Life of the Unemployed: Social and Psychological Dimensions*. Queen's University of Belfast: Photographic Unit.

Tucker, N. (1977) *What is a Child*? London: Fontana–Open Books.

Warr, P. (1983) Work, Jobs and Unemployment. *Bulletin of the British Psychological Society* 36: 305–11.

Watts, A.G. (1983) *Education, Unemployment and the Future of Work.* Milton Keynes: Open University Press.

Williamson, B. and Quayle, B. (1983) Work, Technology and Culture in the North East of England. In B. Williamson and B. Quayle (eds) *Technology and Change in the North East.* University of Durham: North East Local Studies.

Willis, P. (1984) Youth Unemployment: 1. A New Social State; 2. Ways of Living; 3. The Land of Juventus. *New Society* 29 March, 5 April, 12 April: 475–77, 13–15, 57–9.

5
Changing partners: marriage and divorce across the life course

DAVID CLARK

There have been few attempts to adopt a life course perspective in relation to marriage and divorce in Britain, though some of the groundwork for developing such a perspective has been undertaken, chiefly in the writings of the Rapoports (1975, 1977, 1982) and in the publications of the Study Commission on the Family (1983; Rimmer 1981). Rather too much has been made in some of these works however of the idea of family *pluralism* as an organizing framework, championing *diversity* in family life as a positive manifestation of greater freedom, choice, and healthy variation. Such appeals to voluntarism can often serve to mask the more structural constraints of class, gender, age, and ethnicity which shape and mould family experiences. In this chapter I want to explore some of these variations and constraints in relation to marriage and divorce through the life course. Such processes remain poorly understood and call for the examination of various forms of data; I shall begin by considering some relevant historical and demographic trends, along with their ideological correlates, before narrowing the focus in the consideration of selected case studies, drawn from my own fieldwork.

CHANGING EXPECTATIONS: LONGEVITY, MARRIAGE, AND DIVORCE

In 1851 the average expectation of life in Britain was forty years for men and forty-two years for women. One hundred years later these figures had increased to sixty-six and seventy-one respectively; in the mid-1980s they reached seventy and seventy-six (Dominian 1980: 13; Burgoyne, Chapter 2). By contrast, at the beginning of this century the mean age at marriage was 27.2 years for bachelors and 25.6 for spinsters; by 1983 bachelors were marrying at an average age of 25.7 and spinsters at 23.4 (Rimmer 1981: 17; Office of Population Censuses and Surveys 1984). These two factors, though the first is clearly more important than the second, have important consequences for our thinking about marriage and divorce in relation to the life course. They show that for those who ever marry, and that is perhaps 90 per cent of the population on recent estimates, the expected duration of marriage to death is higher than ever before (Nissel, Chapter 9), at all ages. Of course the significance of this trend is greater for those who enter into marriage as a lifelong monogamous relationship, since such an expectation must be evaluated in the context of current divorce rates. It is worth noting though that the idea of marriage as a lifelong arrangement, enduring 'till death us do part' had very different sociological implications for mid-nineteenth-century newly weds than it does for their late-twentieth-century counterparts, even allowing for the fact that only just over a half of the latter will have entered into marriage via a religious ceremony which makes explicit the notion of lifelong monogamous commitment.

A number of complex effects and questions are raised by relatively straightforward changes in life expectancy and age at marriage. These relate in particular to beliefs about the marital relationship, as well as the institution of marriage. As Morgan (1981) has pointed out, there has been a tendency to place increasing emphasis on the relational aspects of marriage, at the expense of the institutional. This is evident in the inclination to explain the incidence and prevalence of divorce and remarriage as consequences of the higher expectations which couples have of their relationships (Berger and Kellner 1964), so that when disappointed with one marriage, they are prepared to divorce, prior to beginning again with a new spouse. Such 'choices', it is argued, are more likely to emerge when marriage is experienced through a lengthening life course (Study Commission on the Family 1983).

Recent historical work, along with evidence from sociology and anthropology, can cast some light on changes in expectations of marriage, including gender, class, and regional variations. Jane Lewis has shown for example that in the 1870s working-class attitudes to marriage, as reflected in the marriage ceremony, were perfunctory, contingent, and highly pragmatic. This was related in turn to a set of 'financial obligations, services and activities that were gender specific' in marriages which 'did not enjoin romantic love or verbal and sexual intimacy' (Lewis 1984: 9). In the middle class the separation of male and female worlds was even more visible; for whereas their working-class sisters did engage in paid work outside, middle-class women were subjected to total confinement in the private world of home and family. Victorian bourgeois womanhood was idealized as 'the angel in the house': dependent, passive, and sexually innocent (Lewis 1984: 77).

It has been argued (Goldthorpe *et al.* 1969) that some blurring later took place in these class-related expectations and practices and in particular that the marital 'partnership', advocated by Beveridge and envisaging the equality of differing but complementary tasks, gained widespread acceptance in Britain after the Second World War. Ideologies of 'companionate' marriage (Fletcher 1977) and 'symmetrical' families (Young and Willmott 1975) which followed, however, have been variously attacked by feminists as more apparent than real, unattainable, and even undesirable (Barrett and McIntosh 1982). Leonard's well-known study of courtship and marriage in Swansea does suggest, however, a growing congruence in class expectations of marriage, at least on the basis of an analysis of marriage rituals, which show 'how little the form of weddings varies by class: the weddings of the elite ... differ only in detail and scale from the "proper" weddings of the provincial lower middle and working class'

(1980: 256–57). It should be added, however, that the sociological and anthropological record in Britain is almost completely silent on ethnic variations in relation to these issues.

There can be no doubt that even if the subject of marriage expectations has been largely ignored by academics, it has generated considerable popular discussion in the press, radio, and television. In recent years we have seen the development of a climate of opinion which has drawn attention to various issues, including sex and gender roles in the family, the domestic division of labour, and fathers' involvement in child-rearing. Discussions around these have called into question many previously taken-for-granted aspects of domestic life and opened up new ways of thinking about family and gender issues. Our knowledge of the social and geographical distribution of this body of opinion, however, remains impressionistic and subject to considerable speculation.

A further piece in this particular jigsaw can be found in the shape of a series of ideas which draws upon notions of personal growth and self-actualization through the marriage relationship. These are much in evidence for example in *Marriage Matters*, the report of the Working Party on Marriage Guidance (1979), a document which has recently been subjected to a critical sociological scrutiny by David Morgan (1985). Lasch (1980), addressing himself more specifically to the North American setting, has also analysed the 'culture of narcissism' which supports such a view of marriage and in two other works has examined ways in which the 'private world' of marriage and family life has come to be falsely regarded as the ultimate source of personal rewards, gratifications, and meaning (Lasch 1977, 1985). A host of writers from liberals such as Sennett (1977) to feminists like Barrett and McIntosh (1982) have castigated this 'privatization' of values as socially detrimental and damaging to the individual's genuinely public life. The tendency nevertheless feeds on an ideology of marriage based on romantic love, as a relationship which should change, develop, and grow while the 'partners' move through different phases of the life course. The commonplace rationale for explaining the ending of a marriage – 'we just grew apart' – perfectly reflects these assumptions.

Making sense of all this requires a framework which acknowledges individual contributions to both the theory and practice of marriage and family life; within a sociological frame of reference a theoretical position which makes use of the concepts of symbolic interactionism (Rock 1979) would seem to be an appropriate one. From this perspective it is possible to give an account of the micro-processes wherein the social world of marriage and the family are constituted (Askham 1984) while at the same time recognizing the broader structural context which sets the boundaries for such processes, constraining, shaping, and modifying individual motivations and outcomes. In acknowledging the significance of understanding both the micro and the macro we therefore free ourselves to seek a better appraisal of the private and public aspects of marriage and family life, and in particular the ways in which they intermesh over the life course.

This dynamic is made particularly clear in relation to public perceptions of divorce, which was an example used by C. Wright Mills himself when making the distinction between 'private troubles' and 'public issues' (Mills 1967: 9). The breakdown of a marriage which ends in divorce may seem at first sight to represent a uniquely personal trauma in the lives of the individual partners; yet when we consider a society in which one marriage in three now taking place can be expected to result in divorce, there is a sense in which the emphasis has shifted from the private to the public arena. This does not mean of course that divorce can be seen only as a public issue, though the rate of divorce in any society will have implications for its social planning, employment, housing, welfare, and other arrangements. There are also interpersonal, psychological, and individual dimensions to the phenomenon. Too often however particular disciplinary specialisms lose sight of the complex interactions between private and public aspects of divorce. Until recently for example much clinical and therapeutic writing on the subject concentrated on the 'syndrome' of marital breakdown, to an extent which wholly denied the significance of socio-cultural changes in the relationship and institution of marriage (Epstein 1975). Similarly much sociology has concentrated on the implications of divorce for other aspects of the social system, in a way which gives little or no recognition to subjective experience. In exploring marriage and divorce from a life course perspective there is clearly scope for an approach which combines human relations, psychodynamic, and even analytic insights with a broader recognition of social norms and structures.

This drawing together of perspectives is not merely an academic concern; it is one which is certainly in evidence among some of the practitioners who deal with divorce and its consequences: doctors, lawyers, counsellors, and personal social service workers. More significantly, it is probably becoming a factor in shaping popular beliefs, particularly among those who have been or are divorcing. Burgoyne and Clark (1984) found for example that some of the men and women they interviewed in their Sheffield remarriage study saw themselves as part of a modern social trend, in which divorce was becoming more acceptable. This did not prevent others from describing themselves because of their experience as 'the black sheep of the family'. Again there is considerable scope for class, age, and gender variations in attitudes of this kind. A recent survey conducted in Aberdeen and Sheffield (Clark and Samphier 1983, 1984) showed that only one in five of the adult population of those two cities had no one among their personal acquaintances who had been divorced or separated. If the majority of the population have friends or relatives who have been divorced, the possibility of maintaining a 'deviant' view of divorce as the product of individual failure is seriously diminished. But precisely because most people now have a personal knowledge of divorce, through their own or someone else's experience, the divorce 'phenomenon' cannot be viewed simply as something going on 'out there', with little or no individual relevance. Because contemporary divorce implies the *mass* breakdown of *personal* relationships, so it creates special problems for social analysts and commentators.

It is against a normative backdrop of this kind that the more detailed scenes of individual life are played out. Whereas it is indicated by a number of studies (Voysey 1975; Burgoyne and Clark 1984) that background expectations do certainly inform individual experiences in marriage, it is also clear that several specific factors intervene to signpost the unfolding life course in more concrete ways. The most obvious of these are such things as employment, having children, and growing older. Their importance is often highlighted during periods of transition: starting a new job, adjusting to a first baby, coping with an illness. Most marriages are influenced by the ways in which these experiences interrelate, both for the partners and for family and network members. It is therefore important to look at experiences of this kind as they connect with the underlying processes of constitution, conflict, and resolution within marriages, only some of which 'end' in divorce. This is not of course to ignore known correlations between divorce and factors like early, precipitated marriage, or indeed social class and unemployment. The point is rather that such analyses must be combined with an appraisal of complex, processual issues, especially if they are to illuminate the present volume's concerns with 'social' and 'biological' time.

CONTINUITY AND CHANGE IN MARRIAGE AND DIVORCE ACROSS THE LIFE COURSE

Before moving into a description of some of these processes, it is important to make some further reference to recent trends in marriage and divorce. It is a truism to note that sociodemographic data is at one level merely an aggregate of individual life experiences. The relationship is better conceived therefore as a dialectical one. For there is a sense in which the well-known trends in patterns of marriage and divorce, which frequently achieve popular attention in the media, also feed back into the norms and values of the culture, shaping as well as reflecting individual action.

There has been a recent decline in the absolute number of marriages occurring in Britain. In 1971 459,000 marriages took place, compared to 389,000 in 1983 (Central Statistical Office 1985: 36). These figures are of course related to the age and marital status structure of the population at a given time and reflect the numbers who are eligible for marriage. They also imply a real decline, mainly accounted for by falling rates of first marriage (Central Statistical Office 1985: 37); these involve especially a reduction in the levels of teenage marriage. During the 1970s there was a halving in the numbers of teenage women getting married for the first time. In 1972 one in three spinsters marrying was a teenager; ten years later this had declined to a little over one in five. There has also been a reduction in the number of women under the age of twenty who are pregnant at marriage (Central Statistical Office 1985: 42). Such reductions are likely to have long-term implications for particular cohorts, since it has been recognized for some time that youthful, precipitated marriages are likely to carry a disproportionately high risk of divorce.

Burgoyne, Ormrod, and Richards (1986) suggest that there may be some association between the reduction in these sorts of marriages and the levelling out in the divorce rate which has taken place since the late 1970s. The increase in the practice of cohabitation has also been linked to this debate, with discussion centring around whether or not cohabitation should be seen as a 'trial period' leading up to marriage or as a substitute for it. The practice of cohabitation is likely to have contributed to the general increase in age at marriage and we have already seen in Chapter 2 that 7 per cent of British women aged twenty to twenty-four were cohabiting in 1981–82. Likewise about one-quarter of first marriages may be expected to be preceded by the partners living together. Mansfield (1985) has suggested that this should be regarded as a change in courtship patterns, however, rather than a major shift away from marriage. Cohabitation prior to a second or subsequent marriage is much more common and is now found in about two-thirds of all cases (Chapter 2). This is a particularly interesting point when we take into account the fact that one marriage in three is a remarriage for one or other of the partners.

It is well known that a major increase has taken place in United Kingdom divorces since the early 1960s. In 1983 162,000 decrees were made absolute compared to 80,000 in 1971 and 27,000 in 1961. There has been almost a sixfold increase in the rate of divorce in England and Wales over the same period. Nearly 50 per cent of divorces in 1983 occurred before the couple's tenth wedding anniversary and 20 per cent took place before five years of marriage (Central Statistical Office 1985: 39). In addition to the specific contra-indications of youthful, precipitated marriages, there is also a clear relationship between social class and divorce. A number of writers (Gibson 1974; Thornes and Collard 1979; Haskey 1984) have shown the inverse ratio between rates of divorce and social class. Using the husband's occupation as the measure, with the exception of social class III non-manual, divorce rates exhibit a steady decline as the class hierarchy is ascended. Haskey's England and Wales survey for 1979 shows a rate of divorce of seven per thousand in the professional class, rising to thirty per thousand among unskilled manual workers (1984: 12). Such data provide striking confirmation of the ways in which the 'private trouble' of divorce is channelled by major structural constraints. The point is further underlined by Haskey's figures on unemployed men of all classes, for whom a divorce rate of thirty-four per thousand was produced. While seeking at all times to maintain the relevance of interpersonal factors when considering marriage and divorce therefore, we must also accept the significant ways in which the 'private sphere' of marriage, home, and family is publicly scripted.

Marriage, divorce, and the remarriage which so often follows are best seen as a series of events and circumstances concentrated for many within a fairly narrow band of the life course. General Household Survey data combined for 1981–82 have shown that over a half of women who separated in 1970–74 below the age of thirty-five had remarried within six years. It should also be noted that rates of remarriage are three to four times higher for men than women and that the risk of re-divorce is gender specific. Divorced men who remarry are more than one and a half times as likely to divorce as single men of the same age marrying for the first time; for divorced women the chance is twice that of their first-married counterparts (Central Statistical Office 1985: 38). Indeed, remarriages provide interesting examples of what the North American literature refers to as marital heterogamy; as I have shown in an earlier article (Clark 1983), taking into account the principal combinations of age, previous marital and parental status, remarriages exhibit a considerable diversity of forms. Any appraisal of patterns and processes of remarriage and family reconstitution should therefore be alive to considerations of the *life course*. Not only may partners be more widely separated by age than in first marriages, but also in at least half of all 'remarriages', one of the partners is experiencing matrimony for the first time. Likewise the familiar generational distinctions of unbroken nuclear families are less common; there are variations associated with custody and access arrangements, and the age profiles of step- and half-siblings may be longer and less evenly distributed. Although we know very little about the consequences, the reconstituted family may have four sets of grandparents, each in different ways seeking a continuing relationship with the offspring of their divorced children. These problems therefore highlight some of the advantages of a perspective which goes beyond a mechanistic view of the family life cycle to a position from which account may be taken of the nexus of relationships, particularly those concerning gender and generation, which proliferate in a society characterized by high rates of divorce and remarriage.

MARRIAGE AND DIVORCE IN THE LIFE PROCESS

Making a Start

The sociology and anthropology of courtship and marriage in Britain have not been widely documented. Undoubtedly the key work to date is Leonard's Swansea study (Leonard 1980). The Early Years project, which has been carried out at the Marriage Research Centre, will also provide valuable material on a group of couples who married in London in 1979 and who have been followed up after five years of marriage (Mansfield 1982, 1985). The following data come from a study of newly married and newly remarried couples, interviewed in Aberdeen and district in 1981–82 (Clark 1982, 1983). Like the Welsh and London studies, they are drawn from a non-representative group of couples, who were interviewed at some length by the author. The study should be regarded as a modest contribution to the ethnography of marriage and family life in Britain. It is not intended here, however, to try to summarize all of the material, but rather to illustrate some of the particular concerns of this chapter through an examination of selected case studies.

John and Jean Farquhar,[2] aged nineteen and eighteen, are living in a caravan on the outskirts of Aberdeen; their rent has been in arrears for several weeks. They have just married in the local registrar's office, but lived together in the caravan for several months before that. John is an apprentice electrician;

he suffers from fibrosis and is currently in receipt of sickness benefit. Jean is a secretary, but has been unemployed for the last eight weeks. They were first interviewed in March 1981, the month of their marriage. John and Jean had met about a year previously and accounts of their subsequent courtship were heavily laden with details of difficulties with their respective parents. Shortly after they met, John was 'thrown out' by his separated mother and had gone to live with his grandmother. Jean had been receiving psychotherapy through her general practitioner and had a long history of difficult relations with her mother:

> 'Well my mum, she's been in and out of hospital for various operations and, well . . . she got pretty bad with her nerves and she always ends up crying . . . once I had a fight with her . . . I've never really gotten on with my Mum, I don't know why. I don't think I ever will. She does nae want to know me now.'

Jean's parents clearly disapproved of her boyfriend and when she started spending weekends at his house, John recalled, the situation came to a crisis.

> 'Her folks did nae sorta like this and she was having rows with her folks and there was a big sorta row and Jean took an overdose 'cos she'd been rowing with her parents . . . and I took her to hospital and she was put in.'

The outcome was that Jean moved in with John and his grandmother. Relationships within the family network then deteriorated further; as Jean put it:

> 'There was a bit of trouble between my mum and dad and his dad. His dad was supposed to have beat up his own wife – his ex-wife now – and my mum started saying things about his father. I told John not to tell his father but John went running to his dad and said everything that my mum had said. Then when my mum was confronted by it, his dad was going to take my mum to court for slander, but my mum said "Oh, I

never said none of that''. She sort of left me, sort of taking the blame.'

Meanwhile grandmother had become increasingly disaffected with her two young lodgers, who played records loudly and came in drunk at night. John's aunt also came to live at the house after a period in a psychiatric hospital; she was quickly followed by his unemployed father, who came to convalesce after a heart attack. About this time, some six months after they had first met, John and Jean got engaged, and began looking for rented accommodation of their own. Although they bought a ring, the engagement was ignored by their families.

In December 1980, with John now working only intermittently due to illness, they moved into the caravan. Neither of them saw the cohabitation as 'trial marriage' – they had already decided to marry, but Jean would have preferred a longer engagement if arrangements had worked out with grandmother:

> 'But I mean, if we'd got on well with her and all the rest of it, we wouldn't have had to have moved out until we had enough money for a proper wedding. 'Cos really that's really what I wanted to do, get married in a church, but I just knew we couldn't afford it.'

Early in the year, Jean lost her job. Financial problems began to bear in on them and she claimed that he wasted on alcohol what little money they had. Following a disagreement with his doctor over a sick note and accusations of feigned illness, John began seeing a social worker. Then at the suggestion of a friend of the family, they decided to get married in the belief that it would enable them to be housed by the local authority. None of Jean's family attended the wedding, though John's mother and father were there and, along with friends, a party was held afterwards. The entire day cost about £100, including the marriage fee.

The following months were exceedingly difficult. The couple's rent arrears increased; they began to argue with one another and he would go out with his friends leaving her alone in the caravan; John's health did not improve and they both became irritable and depressed. On one occasion he struck Jean and kicked her in the stomach as she lay on the floor. Her mother's advice echoed in her own comments:

> 'I don't like to start arguing with him 'cos he really does turn fierce – well that's what my mum says to me about his father. She says "oh, he's just going to turn out to be like his father" and his father's lazy, and as far as I know his father did sort of hit his wife. And I just hope John doesn't turn out like that.'

Six months after their marriage John and Jean had been evicted from the caravan and had gone to live once again with John's grandmother. About the same time she became pregnant. They were then rehoused by the local authority into a tenement flat. They were both now unemployed.

This picture of early marriage illustrates some of the interconnections between social class, economic, and health status; it also reveals the way in which these factors intermesh with attitudes and values relating to marriage. At the psychological level it demonstrates how parental influences and family dynamics have a direct bearing upon the experience of courtship and marriage. In the case of John and Jean, marriage appears to have been as much motivated by a desire to escape parental influence as to achieve any intrinsic rewards within the marriage relationship. Neither he nor she had a close friend as a teenager; they both described their attraction to one another in terms of a relatively platonic friendship. It would appear that their objective circumstances would make that friendship difficult to sustain.

A set of circumstances for comparison is provided in the case of another Aberdeen couple who were married in the same month. Jim and Jennifer Fairburn are aged twenty-three and twenty-six years; he is an electrician and she (like Jean Farquhar) is a secretary. They are both in full-time paid employment and live in a tenement flat which was modernized just before they purchased it on a building society mortgage.

Jim and Jennifer met in August 1979 in a night club. Both members of a wide circle of friends, their courtship centred initially around clubs, dancing, and general social activities. They got on well together from the beginning, though they were conscious of the age difference between them ('but my mother was two years older than my father . . . so it didn't bother me at all' – Jim). Within three months of meeting they began to talk about marriage and in February 1980 they were formally engaged to one another. She wore an engagement ring, a notice was placed in the local newspaper, they had a meal with Jennifer's parents and Jim's mother (his parents are divorced). They received in subsequent weeks a large number of gifts and she had also been accumulating a 'bottom drawer', even prior to meeting Jim.

Following the engagement, their gregarious life style changed. They began to see each other almost every day, as Jennifer put it:

> 'I stayed in about two nights of the week, just to have a bath and wash my hair . . . but all the rest of the time I just saw Jim. I gave up all my friends really.'

About the same time Jim's best friends also got engaged and although they continued to have a regular night 'out' together (the equivalent of her night 'in') their contact diminished. For both Jennifer and Jim engagement meant personal economy, saving, and a regime of material preparation for the world of marriage. Like many of the young women described by Leonard (1980) Jennifer was greatly assisted in this process by her mother, who cut down her 'board' money by a third and saved the difference in order to purchase her wedding dress. Jim's mother, he acknowledged, also declined a realistic rent from him. Jim and Jennifer both took part-time jobs working in a bar in the evening to raise extra money. In October 1980 they had amassed enough savings for the deposit on a flat, which they went on to redecorate throughout.

Such thoughtful and conscious planning was mirrored in the sexual side of their relationship. Just prior to their engagement they 'took a risk' on two occasions, but then Jennifer began taking the pill after, as Jim put it 'she was absolutely certain in her mind that there was some kind of a bond between us'. The question of living together before marriage was weighed up equally carefully, though neither of them had any friends who had cohabited. For Jim such an arrangement has 'no follow up'; living together leads inevitably to marriage so as an end in itself is 'just a waste of time'. Jennifer was a little more definite in her views:

> 'We did think about it when we first got the flat, but no . . . I wouldn't like it. No, I thought we'd be better getting married and then moving into the flat, doing it the right way.'

In March 1982 they were married in church. Jennifer explained her reasons:

> 'Well I believe in the church and I've always wanted to get married in a church. I think it's nice, I've never wanted to get married in a registrar, I just like the church and all our family's been married in the church. I was baptized in that church. We used to live down that way and I was always at Sunday School.'

The wedding was a 'quiet' one in the eyes of Jim and Jennifer, who had 'only' twenty guests at the reception. Nevertheless, all of the formal aspects of a 'white wedding' were in evidence: limousine, flowers, bridesmaids, morning suits, photographers, and a reception at a country hotel, followed by the honeymoon. The total cost was over £600, a proportion of which was met by the bride's father. In addition the parents provided substantial wedding gifts including carpets, a bed, washing machine, and items of furniture.

Jim and Jennifer's ability to sustain the material comforts of domestic life was further enhanced in the period around the marriage. Jim changed his job to work for a firm situated within easy walking distance of the flat; in six months he had two pay rises and could do as much paid overtime as he wished. Jennifer also had a rise, though interestingly this was described as being offset by an increase in the mortgage rate. These early months were much taken up with the establishment of a domestic regime in which cooking, cleaning, and budgeting were seen as essential activities in the pursuit of an ordinary married life together. The question of the domestic division of labour between husband and wife, both of whom were in full-time paid employment, was treated with an embarrassed amusement, also found among other couples in the study.

> '*Jim:* It's all one sided there (laughs).
>
> *Jennifer:* I do all the shopping, just shop as I go along. Saturday I really hate going into town; as far as cleaning . . . I just do it when I come home from work. Washing, well I've got an automatic so I'm not over a hot sink scrubbing. There's not much to clean really. Jim does clean as well, he cleaned the windows on Saturday (laughs).
>
> *Jim:* Boost me up a bit (laughs).
>
> *DC:* How do you feel about it Jim?
>
> *Jim:* I think of chores that both of you can help in. If there's only one vacuum cleaner there's only one person can clean obviously. As for doing dishes . . . I help out, give a hand in the kitchen.'

There are echoes here of Mansfield's comments that in modern 'companionate' marriages 'men have entered the kitchen but as visitors rather than co-workers' (1985: 14).

Generational and kinship factors also played an important part in the early phase of marriage for Jim and Jennifer. Their wedding was to a large extent overshadowed by the sudden death of Jim's brother-in-law, whose funeral took place just one day earlier. A considerable amount of their time and energy was subsequently spent in giving support to the bereaved sister and her children. Relationships with parents proved problematic. Jennifer uncharacteristically had a number of arguments with her mother, who claimed that her daughter was not visiting her often enough. At the same time visits to Jim's mother increased; she had recently begun to suffer with arthritis and he was clearly concerned about the implications of this in relation to longer-term caring obligations.

> 'I had thought that with me going away from my mum she would be on her own. I wouldn't have liked to have thought that she was going to be, just going to have a lonely life from

the moment I left. You know, with the ups and downs, the barneys that we did have I wouldn't have in no way liked to have seen her left a sad and lonely person . . . she was fit and healthy person really . . . she had to give up her work. She was retiring in November anyway. She finished work when the arthritis attacked. I didn't realise I was going to have to cope with anything like that.'

Although both of them denied it at first in the interview, such relationships with other members of the family did have an effect on their marriage. The situation continued for a period of a few months, and several weekends seemed to 'end in a row'. This was described as jealousy in relation to parents' demands, but also as 'expecting too much out of each other . . . not giving each other a wee bit of freedom' (Jim) and being 'more tired than I used to be . . . I suppose I've got more work . . . I can't seem to sit down when I come home, always finding jobs to do' (Jennifer).

Quotations from interviews with this couple carry certain of the hallmarks of 'marriage as a project': something consciously planned and executed, having its own personal and structural milestones within which a sense of meaning and purpose can be created. Whereas some writers have argued that this style of marriage is in the ascendant and is increasingly common to all social groups (Young and Willmott 1975) there is also evidence to suggest that its distribution is at best patchy (Edgell 1980) or indeed more illusion than fact (Finch 1983). Jim and Jennifer Fairburn's accounts of early marriage are not distinguished by a high level of reflection or interpretation; they are above all descriptions of practical experience and action. There is a sense in which these actions of getting engaged, saving money, buying a flat, and so on are highly meaningful, even though the meanings may be only weakly articulated. The ability to perform such actions, and in so doing to demonstrate a degree of control over their circumstances, should be seen as a dimension of Jim and Jennifer's position in the labour market. However, that alone is not the sole determinant; the couple clearly had access to certain family resources which provided some of the wherewithal and the springboard to embark upon marriage within a particular set of material circumstances, along with a set of attitudes and expectations which were more or less syntonic.

Making the break . . . and starting again

In an earlier study of remarriage carried out with Jacqueline Burgoyne (Burgoyne and Clark 1984) I became particularly interested in exploring how accounts of courtship and marriage might have specific hallmarks when they related to the second and subsequent marriage of one or both of the partners. For just as the descriptions of the Farquhars and the Fairburns in their different ways convey many of the qualities of first marriage and are instantly recognizable as such, so too we find that in *remarriage* other and somewhat different themes commonly recur. In Sheffield we found that many accounts of second courtship began with first marriage and its breakdown; for it was only in the context of understanding an earlier marriage that the full implications of a second one could be explained. There were again good reasons here for adopting a life course perspective, for although our study had begun as an examination of relationships in step-families, it was apparent that these families could not be separated as a distinctive phase in the life cycle. To understand step-families we would also have to understand the circumstances out of which they emerged and came into being.

This was clearly not just an important procedure for sociological enquiry. It was quite apparent that many of the couples we interviewed had also engaged in similar interpretations. Indeed courtship itself was often much taken up with mutual disclosure and sharing of previous experiences; this applied in the main to the adult partners, but at times also included children of former marriages, to the extent that one father described it as a process of 'all courting one another'. Courtship therefore provided opportunities for reworking the past, for going over earlier experiences, placing them in context, and attaching some meaning to them. 'Courtship as confessional' (Burgoyne and Clark 1984: Chapter 3) was not merely catharsis, however, the dumping of feelings and emotions carried out of earlier experiences: the process was also one of actively *building* a new perspective and dimension to the interpersonal world (Berger and Luckmann 1971). In the following case study, taken from the Aberdeen project, I shall explore some of the ways in which these tendencies were worked out in the experience of a couple who came together in the wake of a marriage breakdown.

Ronald Rankin (age forty-six) and Pamela Rankin (age thirty-nine) were married in Aberdeen in October 1981, after living together for three years. Ronald left school at fifteen and had a variety of sales jobs over a thirty-year period; he is now a general manager with a national company. He was first married in 1961 and divorced twenty years later; he has a son and daughter from the marriage, aged eighteen and fifteen, who both live with their mother in Aberdeen. Pamela Rankin also left school at fifteen and was married three years later; she has two daughters (twenty and fifteen) and two sons (nineteen and sixteen) from the marriage which ended in 1972 after twelve years. One of the sons now lives with his father, but the other three are with Pamela. In recent years she has run her own small video business in the centre of the city. Both Ronald and Pamela, interviewed separately on the first occasion shortly after their marriage, spoke at length about how they had met and the circumstances in which their relationship had developed.

Ronald began the interview by saying that he and Pamela had first become acquainted when he was still married to his first wife. The marriage had, however, been unhappy for some considerable time. From an early stage his wife had been a 'problem' drinker, and he explained the repercussions of this at some length. He had misgivings about the marriage from the outset; indeed he had tried unsuccessfully to call it off at one stage, but gave in to family pressure. Their early years had been taken up with moving around the country as he progressed in his job. His wife found it difficult to make friends and was lonely and isolated in the home with small children. She began to drink heavily during the day and became aggressive and violent at times. On several occasions she started 'accidental' fires in the home, and caused consternation among their neighbours.

A number of times he changed jobs and they moved in order to escape the 'embarrassing' consequences of her drinking, as well as to bail themselves out of financial difficulties. There was clearly a fear on his part that his wife's drinking problem constituted a social liability. As an escape from problems in the relationship he buried himself in voluntary work of various kinds, but he was constantly concerned that their standing in the community might be diminished, if his wife's behaviour became more public and in particular if she got in trouble with the police.

As his anxiety increased, so his health deteriorated; he was unable to sleep, and indeed feared at times for his own physical safety. His wife refused to acknowledge her difficulties and declined any offers of outside professional help.

Like many men and women who experience separation and divorce, he was able to identify a particular turning-point in the marriage, when a decision was made that the relationship must end. The decision was his:

> 'It was nearly a spur of the moment decision although it had been well thought out long before that. I went to a dance, the annual dance of the golf club and I . . . y'know, I had to make a bit of a speech. Now it was a kind of important night for me, and I said: "Now the thing is . . . tonight of all nights you've got to keep the head". And quite honestly she duly did . . . there was no scenes, no collapsing – this had happened at other social functions. And . . . we went home from the function, but of course she got steamed into the whisky bottle and I went off to bed. Got up next morning, went to the football match in the afternoon, went home at teatime and she was lying absolutely paralytic on the couch. She lay there and I just didn't want any further contact . . . I saw her there and that was the final straw. I went out that night and just never went back.'

In common with Ronald, Pamela's account also identified early difficulties in her first marriage; she was married at the age of seventeen, her husband was four years older. Initially they shared accommodation with her mother, staying there until just before the birth of their third child, when they were allocated a council house. By this time, she explained, her husband, a mechanic, had developed 'an allergy to work', having previously been a fastidious employee, who took regular overtime. She remained bewildered by this apparent change in his personality, though it had important consequences. Her husband spent increasing amounts of time outside the home, drinking with his friends. When he was at home, he was inclined to violent outbursts. The first began 'when he was under the influence of alcohol. But then, as the years passed, he didn't even need that excuse'.

These were years of great difficulty. Her second child developed a severe illness in infancy and 'was on steroids and many other drugs until the age of nine or ten and was a semi-invalid all these years'. Two more babies followed in rapid succession and she found it increasingly difficult to make ends meet. In common with many other women in such circumstances she not only took a job to eke out the household budget, but also carried a burden of guilt, blaming herself for the multiple difficulties of the whole family.

> 'I couldn't talk about it, I felt ashamed, felt a failure really. I often used to ask myself the question, why . . . y'know, was I doing something wrong, was there something wrong with me as a person that this was happening . . . of course I was told so often by my first husband that I was an idiot, a fool . . . and, eh . . . if you're told these things often enough, you begin to believe them after a while.'

In Pamela's case it was a violent beating from her husband which finally precipitated her decision to leave him after ten years of marriage. He returned one night after a heavy drinking session and beat her unconscious; when she came to, she went to her neighbours for help. It was the first time she had done this; she needed hospitalization for her injuries and afterwards went with the children to stay with her mother. 'And that was it . . . I just didn't ever go back.'

Neither the separation nor the divorce which followed it were the conclusion of her difficulties however. She was continually harassed by her former husband, who threatened her with obscene calls at her mother's home and followed her around outside. Eventually she was rehoused by the local authority and moved with the children to a flat ('I specified that I would like somewhere upstairs, where it wasn't so readily accessible for him'). A niece moved in with her as a companion, and gradually her life began to improve. She recalled a particular occasion:

> 'Through in the sitting-room the children were laughing and I can remember, I was at the cooker, and I felt . . . "Oh, this is fantastic". Y'know, my front door was locked, I knew he couldn't come in and disturb us . . . I think it was the first time that I actually felt peace of mind . . . well maybe not peace

> of mind, I hadn't quite managed to acquire that, but I was beginning to.'

The descriptions of Ronald and Pamela, albeit presented here in somewhat truncated form, reveal contrasting experiences and different concerns. A strong sense of a particular kind of family morality pervaded his account. There was not only concern for and eventual disgust with his partner, but also an underlying unease about the social implications of the problem, both for him and the family as a whole. In common with men in the Sheffield study (Burgoyne and Clark 1984) he was inclined to connect the development of 'private' troubles within the marriage to his own 'public' biography in the work-place, linking both the causes and the consequences of his wife's drinking problem to changes in his employment.

Pamela's description of her first marriage revealed a different set of concerns, of a kind documented in detail in an earlier Aberdeen study (Askham 1975) and which show the close relationship between deprivation and fertility. Early marriage and sharing accommodation with mother, followed by the births of four children within a six-year period, one of whom had a serious illness, combined with her husband's apparent psychological problems and violent behaviour, all took a significant toll. They served not least to shape subsequent expectations of a satisfactory family life, which as we can see from her last quotation, were couched initially in straightforward material terms. The beginnings of 'peace of mind' came with physical safety and an uninterrupted domestic routine.

Nevertheless, for Pamela the next few years brought further difficulties; she received no alimony from her ex-husband and had few prospects in the labour market. She therefore made the decision to take a secretarial course at technical college, and on completion was able to find a job. The pay was poor, but she managed for a while on secondhand furniture and clothes and with the help of friends and her mother. Gradually, though, her finances became more tightly stretched.

> 'The children were getting older, bigger, wanting more fashionable clothes, needed shoes more often, and things like . . . were eating more and my wages just weren't keeping up with this . . . the standard of living became poorer and poorer,

which I found very upsetting, because during the years of marriage I hadn't had very much, but I accepted that ... didn't enjoy it, I accepted it because I felt that the blame was really at my door.'

She therefore took another job, working in a video shop; the basic wage was better and she also received a quarterly bonus. There was a steady improvement in their living standards; she was able to pay her bills on time, saving a little each week, 'the food was more plentiful and everything just got better'.

Later she took part-time work in a pub and it was there she met Ronald. Previously she had one other relationship with a divorced man, which had led to a proposal of marriage which she declined. Whereas that relationship had been more physical than emotional, her friendship with Ronald developed in the opposite way. Over a period of several months they became increasingly attracted to one another, though they did not meet for long periods and did not begin a sexual relationship for some time. He was still living with his wife, and was determined to stay there until his daughters had finished their education. In that sense, Pamela felt, the relationship promised her little. On the other hand:

'Ron was the very first person I really and truly opened up to ... I'd spent quite a few years hiding all the facts of my private life, and that became a habit ... Ron always described me as a person behind a wall, he said I have a wall there, a defence mechanism.'

Their increasing ability to share such private concerns placed a growing strain on Ronald's resolution to remain with his wife. Pamela was careful not to put pressure on him, but when he asked if he could come to live with her she said yes, though for him it was 'dreadfully difficult to walk out on his wife and children'.

Their subsequent life together bears many of the hallmarks of remarriage as a conscious attempt to rebuild a normal family life out of the legacy of the past (Burgoyne and Clark 1984). For remarriage is a two-edged sword, representing both a new opportunity to 'begin again', while at the same time making evident the constraints imposed by a variety of circumstances surrounding first marriage. These include emotional, material, and financial factors, which combine in various ways to set the limits on aspects of life in the 'reconstituted' family.

Pamela and Ronald's eagerness to establish a domestic regime fell foul of a number of difficulties. He related some of these:

> 'Pam had been a very good mother I think. Under the conditions that she had, the financial conditions, I think she did a marvellous job. But ... of course there were tensions in the home. A father figure appeared and, eh ... life had to be ... started living differently and a degree of regimentation had to come into the home, because ... if that was to be my home I was going to ... start improving it.'

There were problems in particular with Geoff, Pamela's twelve-year-old son, who was having difficulties at school, which led to his expulsion and later a police prosecution.

Pamela too found difficulties in adjusting to a new way of life, 'after having had years of being the boss'. For both of them this period of living together was seen as a necessary prelude to marriage imposed by Ronald's circumstances. Obtaining a divorce however created certain complications. Ronald's wife did not wish to dissolve the marriage at first; there were misunderstandings with the solicitor and a great deal of concern on Ronald's part that 'there should be no mud-slinging', either in terms of past events or financial settlements. As a result they had to postpone wedding plans at one stage and were not married until three years after beginning to live together, by which time they had moved to another house and started up a joint business venture.

Both Pamela and Ronald wanted to marry in church, but failed to obtain the permission of their bishop. As a result they married in a register office, followed by a formal blessing in church. In most other respects they had a 'conventional' Aberdeen wedding – over one hundred guests, a reception in the evening, and a total outlay in excess of £2,000.

Six months later, when interviewed jointly, they talked about establishing a 'new' married life together, including reference to the various complications. These had centred in particular around Geoff, Pamela's son, who had gone to live with his father. For Ronald these difficulties with Geoff were a source of considerable regret:

> 'If you were to really press me, it is *the* disappointment that we couldn't have been here as a team, as a complete team . . . I mean we've come through with the other three and all showed our difficulties, make no mistake about it, and out of it comes a stronger relationship and I wish he'd have been here, enjoying all this.'

Pamela however was more prepared to look at their 'successes', and in so doing summarized a variety of hopes and aspirations for their family life together:

> 'My children have the advantage really over Ronald's . . . they're actually living with us and they see our happiness day to day and I think it is rubbing off on my children. Whereas they were fairly mixed up kids four or five years ago . . . I think that that is fading into the background day by day and I think our happiness is rubbing off on them and I hope that our relationship and our happiness can be a goal.'

CONCLUSIONS

The case studies which have been examined here share two conflicting characteristics. At one level they are culturally available as 'typical' accounts of the process of getting married, divorcing, and marrying again. Accordingly they contain a familiar repertoire of motives, actions, and outcomes, so that even if we have no first-hand experience of couples like the Farquhars, the Fairburns, or the Rankins, we nevertheless respond to the social categories they portray. They too draw on a range of background assumptions in their interviews, referring to implicit definitions of 'satisfactory' and 'unsatisfactory' circumstances and relationships. These background expectations have an over-arching quality and reveal some of the shared understandings of marital and family morality within the culture.

Yet at the same time the case studies reflect an enormous range of experiences within the 'familiar' world of domestic life. We see here intimacy and estrangement; growing together and growing apart; affection and violence; affluence and poverty; employment and unemployment; experience and inexperience. When we consider that these case studies were themselves selected from within a fairly circumscribed set of categories, then the full enormity of marriage, divorce, and remarriage across the life course begins to reveal itself.

To date social science has been largely concerned with either objective structures or subjective processes. There have been few attempts to meet C. Wright Mills's (1967) call for the integration of history and biography. Such an integration is essential for a full understanding of marriage through the life course. It is long overdue.

NOTES

1 Two groups took part in the project: twenty couples who had recently married for the first time and twenty where one or other of the partners was remarrying. Letters inviting the couples to take part in the study were included by the local registrar with their marriage licence. The couples were interviewed separately and together, immediately after the marriage and six months later. The project was carried out at the MRC Medical Sociology Unit, Aberdeen.

2 All names are pseudonymous.

REFERENCES

Askham, J. (1975) *Fertility and Deprivation*. London: Cambridge University Press.

Askham, J. (1984) *Identity and Stability in Marriage*. London: Cambridge University Press.

Barrett, M. and McIntosh, M. (1982) *The Anti-Social Family*. London: Verso.

Berger, P. and Kellner, H. (1964) Marriage and the Construction of Reality. *Diogenes*: 1–23.

Berger, P. and Luckmann, T. (1971) *The Social Construction of Reality*. Harmondsworth: Penguin.

Burgoyne, J. and Clark, D. (1984) *Making a Go of it: A Study of Stepfamilies in Sheffield*. London: Routledge & Kegan Paul.

Burgoyne, J., Ormrod, R., and Richards, M. (1986) *Divorce Matters*. Harmondsworth: Penguin.

Central Statistical Office (1985) *Social Trends*. London: HMSO.

Clark, D. (1982) Marriage and Remarriage: New Wine in Old Bottles. In *Change in Marriage*. Rugby: National Marriage Guidance Council.

Clark, D. (1983) Restarting a Family: Having Children in Second Marriages. *International Journal of Sociology and Social Policy* 2(3).

Clark, D. and Samphier, M. (1983) Public Attitudes to Marital Problems. *Marriage Guidance* Autumn.

Clark, D. and Samphier, M. (1984) Attitudes to Custody, Access and Maintenance. *Adoption and Fostering* 8(1).

Dominian, J. (1980) *Marriage in Britain 1945–80*. London: Study Commission on the Family.

Edgell, S. (1980) *Middle-Class Couples*. London: Allen & Unwin.

Epstein, J.E. (1975) *Divorce: The American Experience*. London: Cape.

Finch, J. (1983) *Married to the Job: Wives' Incorporation in Men's Work*. London: Allen & Unwin.

Fletcher, R. (1977) *The Family and Marriage in Britain*. (revised edn) Harmondsworth: Penguin.

Gibson, C. (1974) The Association between Divorce and Social Class in England and Wales. *British Journal of Sociology* 25(1): 79–93.

Goldthorpe, J.H., Lockwood, D., Bechhofer, F., and Platt, J. (1969) *The Affluent Worker in the Class Structure*. London: Cambridge University Press.

Haskey, J. (1984) Social Class and Socio-Economic Differentials in Divorce in England and Wales. *Population Studies* 38.

Lasch, C. (1977) *Haven in a Heartless World*. New York: Basic Books.

Lasch, C. (1980) *The Culture of Narcissism*. London: Abacus.

Lasch, C. (1985) *The Minimal Self*. London: Pan.

Leonard, D. (1980) *Sex and Generation*. London: Tavistock.

Lewis, J. (1984) *Women in England 1870–1950*. Brighton: Wheatsheaf.

Mansfield, P. (1982) A Portrait of Contemporary Marriage: Equal Partners or Just Good Companions? In *Changes in Marriage*. Rugby: National Marriage Guidance Council.

Mansfield, P. (1985) *Young People and Marriage*. Occasional Paper 1. Edinburgh: Scottish Marriage Guidance Council.

Mills, C.W. (1967) *The Sociological Imagination*. London: Oxford University Press.

Morgan, D.H.J. (1981) *Berger and Kellner's Construction of Marriage*. Occasional Paper 7. University of Manchester: Department of Sociology.

Morgan, D.H.J. (1985) *The Family, Politics and Social Theory*. London: Routledge & Kegan Paul.

Office of Population Censuses and Surveys, (1984) *Marriage and Divorce*. OPCS Monitor FM2 84/2. London: OPCS.

Rapoport, R., Rapoport, R.N., with Strelitz, Z. (1975) *Leisure and the Family Life Cycle*. London: Routledge & Kegan Paul.

Rapoport, R., Rapoport, R.N., and Strelitz, Z. (1977) *Fathers, Mothers and Others*. London: Routledge & Kegan Paul.

Rapoport, R.N., Fogarty, M.P., and Rapoport, R. (eds) (1982) *Families in Britain*. London: Routledge & Kegan Paul.

Rimmer, L. (1981) *Families in Focus*. London: Study Commission on the Family.

Rock, P. (1979) *The Making of Symbolic Interaction*. London: Macmillan.

Sennett, R. (1977) *The Fall of Public Man*. London: Cambridge University Press.

Study Commission on the Family (1983) *Families in the Future*. London: Study Commission on the Family.

Thornes, B. and Collard, J. (1979) *Who Divorces?* London: Routledge & Kegan Paul.

Voysey, M. (1975) *A Constant Burden*. London: Routledge & Kegan Paul.

Working Party on Marriage Guidance (1979) *Marriage Matters*. London: HMSO.

Young, M. and Willmott, P.L. (1975) *The Symmetrical Family*. Harmondsworth: Penguin.

6
The mid life phase

Mike Hepworth

'*Middle Age*: When you begin to exchange your emotions for symptoms.'

(I. S. Cobb)

INTRODUCTION

In this chapter I wish to describe key changes in western beliefs about mid life and their implication for certain aspects of family life in contemporary society. In particular I wish to focus on the notion that mid life is a relatively new phase in what is increasingly referred to as 'the life course'. I shall describe this phase as 'the new middle age' in contrast to a more traditional view of the middle years characteristic of the centuries preceding the Second World War (Hepworth and Featherstone 1982). I should warn, however, that my use of the term 'new middle age' does not imply that the emergence of what are essentially 'modern' ideas concerning the nature of the mid life phase has involved any sudden or complete break with the past or that all members of a particular generation, cohort, or age group are equally influenced by the culture of ageing I shall detail below. Indeed, in the pages which follow I shall be largely concerned with the *ideals* symbolically expressed in the culture of the new middle age; the light the expression of these ideals can shed on changing expectations of family life; and ultimately, the great diversity of ways in which men and women from various walks of life transform these ideals into 'reality'.

For good sociological reasons, the evidence I shall give is derived from an extensive range of sources, including the mass media; prescriptive literature; personal correspondence and communications; and, where available, academic research. Because there is a comparative dearth of systematic empirical research into the 'reality' of the mid life phase in the United Kingdom (as experienced by members of any section of society), I shall use material from the USA to draw attention to parallels in expression at the cultural level, and their implications at the level of everyday experience for that ever-changing network of human relationships we call 'the British family'.

THE MID LIFE PHASE

It is not within my remit to present a detailed history of western attitudes to middle age (Featherstone and Hepworth 1985) but it is important to remember that the middle years of both men and women have always occupied a special place in the individual life history. In his brilliant analysis of changing attitudes to death in eighteenth-century France, John McManners (1985: 78) shows how middle age was widely considered to be 'the end of youth'. Although advances in medicine and hygiene were beginning to alter attitudes to illness and death, and the onset of physical decrepitude was to some extent delayed amongst the advantaged classes, there was general agreement that 'the best of life was over at fifty'. McManners points out that those commentators who

> 'put the peak of "vitality" in the forties did not deny that physical decline was setting in. We grow in stature, Buffon had said, to the age of eighteen, and thereafter thicken out

> and strengthen to the age of thirty; from thirty-five onwards (rather later for women), the cartilages harden, the skin wrinkles. . . . Whatever "youth" was, everyone agreed it was lost by thirty-five.'

The assumption, then, that the price of 'maturity' is the loss or 'end of youth' has a long and respectable history. The outwardly visible physical changes associated with middle age have for centuries been a poignant reminder that the life course is at least half over and the run-down to death has begun. Writing from a woman's perspective, the novelist Margaret Drabble vividly captured the sense of unease an awareness of middle age can bring:

> 'Slowly, Allison Murray rose to her feet, and shut the curtains, and crossed to the wardrobe mirror. Slowly, she inclined her face towards the mirror. The harsh light fell without mercy. Yes, there were wrinkles. There would be more. There was strain round the eye, the mouth, the nose. The neck was slightly ringed. Rings, dark and grave, lay also beneath the eyes: dark red, weary. She bared her teeth at herself: yes, her gums were receding, slightly, they were creeping back in distaste from her too-large, too old, nicotine-stained teeth. Her face felt stiff; it woke stiff, took all day to soften, then stiffened again each evening. Her hair was touched with grey: she had always admired young women with grey hair, with white streaks in the black, had not minded her genetic inheritance: but a young woman with grey hair was one thing, an old woman with grey hair another. Meditatively, she untied her wrap, and stared at her body. There it was, source of so much pleasure, so much self-congratulation. And still lovely: hardly a mark upon it, hardly a sign of wear, a body of a young woman. But for how long, she said to herself, panic beating noisily in her ears: for how much longer? When will it collapse? Will it collapse overnight, like Dorian Gray? It is unnaturally preserved already, as it was unnaturally endowed in the first place. When will I cease to be able to look at myself naked in the mirror? And God, O God, what then, what then will I do?
>
> (Drabble, 1978: 94–5)

Facial and bodily changes associated with middle age are unwelcome reminders not simply of the passage of time but also that life chances are gradually becoming more restricted and the future is unlikely to be as sweet as the past. In the eighteenth century this negative perception was rooted in the knowledge that life itself *was* short and that to reach middle age was a considerable achievement: most people could not realistically expect a very long future. But in the late-twentieth-century version of middle age, the 'bodily betrayals' which are its primary identifiers derive their significance from the fact that for the majority of men and women, there *is* a lot of life left to live. The central preoccupation of the new middle age is, therefore, with the implications of various physical signs of passage into middle age for the *quality* of life in the decades of existence which (barring accidents) lie ahead.

Many of the contemporary students of the new middle age have described the perception and utilization of time as twin hallmarks of the mid life phase. Irene Friese, for example, has argued that the feeling that time is running out leads to an urgent desire to maximize experience and live life to the full (Friese 1978). While, as I shall show below, the concept of the 'mid life transition' is now the centre of controversial debate, there are few investigators and commentators who would disagree over the time factor (Collin 1984). Bernice Neugarten, a leading researcher of social aspects of ageing in the USA, observed in the late 1960s that the central psychological task for middle age relates to the use of time, and the essential polarity is between the mastery of time and capitulation (Neugarten 1968).

The physical changes which ageing produces, and which first become visible during the middle years, derive their subjective significance primarily from the particular meanings western culture attaches to time and the nature of the individual human life or life course. Gerontologists and other professionals with an interest in the ageing process agree that ageing is 'multifaceted'. There are no immutable laws of ageing except 'men and women are born, grow up, and die, and that now in industrialised societies, most people grow old before they die' (Neugarten 1985: 294–300). The process of growing old involves a complex interaction of physical, psychological, and social variables which are themselves subject to the not entirely predictable effects of culture and history. Central to this process is the subjective experience of self-assessment neatly illustrated in the following passage from Nina Bawden's novel, *A Woman of My Age*:

> 'When I look in the mirror . . . not to see if the grey roots are beginning to show before the next tinting, but in the same way I used to look at myself when I was seventeen, at *what, whom* and *why* . . . I remain, as I did then, cloudy, fading, sadly out of focus. The important thing is that I am in the middle of my life and feel as I did when I was adolescent, that I do not know where to go from here.'
>
> (Bawden 1976: 8–9)

It is not therefore the passing of time itself, or the physical effects of that passage on the face and body, which in the final analysis endow middle age with a particular personal and social significance, but the particular interpretations we make of the impact of these changes on our lives. There are three arenas of life where social inducements to self-awareness and self-re-evaluation have become especially noticeable during recent years:

1 Relations between the generations.
2 Gender relations and sexuality.
3 Work and leisure.

Although it is axiomatic in sociology and in life that these three arenas are closely linked together, I shall for the purposes of the discussion which follows artificially disentangle the first two and concentrate on what I take to be the central issues in any analysis of the implications for the family of the new middle age. The key to any understanding of the interaction between these configurations and the subjective experience of the new middle age is, of course, social change.

THE FAMILY

Relations between the generations, gender relations, and sexuality are all clearly 'family matters' in western society. The reason I have chosen to discuss the mid life phase in relation to these two arenas rather than in terms of 'the family' as such is that the latter is so notoriously difficult to define.

Sociologist Donald W. Ball argued some years ago that the most useful basic definition of the family is as a group of people who live together in domestic and sexual relations. As a network of human relationships the family is characterized by 'two dimensions of differentiation which are fundamental to social structural arrangements in all societies: age and sex' (Ball 1974: 36). Although Ball's definition has been criticized on the grounds that sexuality and the family are by no means synonymous (one predominant image of the new middle age is of the prospect of a sex life *outside* conventional marriage), it does have the advantage of being open-ended and can be used as a point of departure for the interpretation of the *quality* of the various types of family life it is possible to experience. The view, for example, that marriage and the family pass through a typical 'life cycle' (Dominian 1980) can be tempered with the knowledge that there is not yet sufficient information available about family life to establish indisputable criteria of a 'normal' cycle. Certainly there are 'common stages' through which many families pass, and which are the subject of statistical analyses and reports, but it is also well known that members of diverse social groups do not conform to these patterns. Hogan, for example, has noted how neglect of the familial transitions of males in the USA (and, it may be added, elsewhere) has 'resulted in an inaccurate picture of the changing probabilities of marriage, divorce, and remarriage among Americans since age-specific rates of these behaviors differ substantially by gender for both whites and blacks' (Hogan 1985: 71). The most realistic response to this awareness of considerable social variation is to accept the 'multidimensional' nature of life course, life course transitions, and thus the process of human ageing.

In her sensitive analysis of interaction between a sample of husbands and wives in Aberdeen, Janet Askham has drawn attention to two important issues. First, that marriage as an institution is invested with such a degree of privacy that it will only 'explode into public view' when some sort of catastrophe occurs (a theme further developed by Clark in Chapter 5). Second, that one of the major changes taking place in expectations of marriage, especially at the younger end of the age spectrum, is 'a growing emphasis upon self-fulfilment and identity pursuit' (Askham 1984: 194). Askham detects two conflicting activities in contemporary marriage: the desire to establish and maintain a sense of individual personal identity, an identity which is not completely submerged in the life of the partner; and a desire to preserve the stability of the marriage. Since the latter will necessarily involve compromise and an adjustment to the expectations and needs of the partner, marriage becomes something of an exercise in walking the tightrope. Conflict between the two goals of independent self-realization and the maintenance of the stability of the marital relationship may be minimized, she suggests, by identification with the cultural concept of the 'married couple', a concept reinforced by the immediate social network within which the marriage has its being.

At the same time, there is no shortage of evidence of the existence of dreams of personal change and self-realization and of their sometimes traumatic consequences. Not every marriage partner is prepared to endure a life of closed options and unspoken desires. And it is, as Janet Askham has indicated, from the various kinds of domestic 'catastrophes' that hit the headlines from time to time, that traces can be found of the workings of the strong subterranean current in family life to which she alludes.

During the early part of 1985 Roger Marshall's 'Missing From Home' was serialized by BBC–1. The story followed in fictional terms the efforts of a middle-aged, middle-class housewife to trace her middle-aged, middle-class husband who had suddenly and inexplicably gone missing. By episode six the errant husband had been tracked down and returned to his family to explain his absence. His motive was described as a kind of identity voyage in mid life – a quest for more personally satisfying experiences than those offered by his marriage. This information came as a revelation to his wife who, until his disappearance, had assumed that all was well. In effect the serial was about disillusionment: as a result of her search for her husband the wife not only discovered *his* unshared desires – his inner sense of unfulfilled identity – but also was brought to an awareness of the gulf between the outwardly ideal image of happy family life and the inner world of self-assessment and reappraisal often said to lie at the heart of the mid life crisis.

'True life' stories which bear some resemblance to Roger

Marshall's serial appear quite regularly in the popular press. I give below two not untypical examples:

> *Boss and his secretary vanish*: featuring a managing director, aged 54, and his secretary, aged 30.[1]

> *Mystery of the missing head and the sixth form blond*: featuring a headmaster of 45 years of age and one of his teenage pupils.[2]

Events such as these are, of course, deeply embedded in the popular culture of the younger-woman–older-man, and I shall refer again to this element of self-awareness, ageing, and gender relations below. In the meantime the connections between the motives for this kind of physical disappearance and the more legitimate variations of 'falling in love', which itself has been described as an identity voyage, are obvious.

A recent report from a study by Lawson of adultery involving a sample of 600 married or long-term cohabiting couples, most of whom were adulterers, suggests that by the age of forty, 40 per cent of women and 60 per cent of men will have committed adultery. The lack of fit between these figures reflects the finding that more married men have affairs with younger women. But more than this, it is the general conclusion that an affair tends to make both men and women feel 'alive' and that their lives are more 'worthwhile'.[3] Two or three years before this report, Lake and Hills, writing from a psychological perspective, confirmed the benefits an affair could bring to both middle-aged men and women provided, of course, they knew what they were doing:

> 'For those in their fifties, sixties and seventies who stayed married to one person while children were born and grew up, middle age is often a period of awakening. An affair at this stage may well bring even more stability to a stable marriage, enabling one partner to feel alive in new ways without in the least threatening the other.'
>
> (Lake and Hills 1979: 149)

If the optimistic (and, some would say, exhilarating) vision of Lake and Hills is to be realized, both partners in the original marriage must be in on the act. Whether or not this is the case, affairs in mid life do provide suggestive glimpses of the inner world of family life and thus clues to the ways in which certain individuals and social groups (especially members of the middle class and higher reaches of society) are responding to the impact of social change.

RELATIONS BETWEEN THE GENERATIONS

As in the cases of 'family' and 'middle age' the concept of generation is surprisingly difficult to define. It is another of those concepts which exert a profound influence over beliefs, values, and ideals yet which is hard to pin down in the empirically observable world. At the heart of the generational idea is a belief in the discontinuity of age groups: the implication that society is divided into categories which can be defined primarily in terms of their age (Wohl 1980). The dichotomy between 'youth' and 'age' is, of course, crucial here and derives from the processes associated with modernization; youth being seen as essentially bound up with 'progress' and forward movement, in sharp contrast to age which is stigmatized as traditional and hidebound, concerned only with a futile celebration of the past. For many, it has been argued, the great watershed in generational awareness was the First World War (1914–18) and its aftermath. Historians of the 'roaring twenties' have long recognized that western culture was remade during that decade. This period has been described as a time when

> 'youth appeared suddenly, dramatically, even menacingly on the social scene. Contemporaries quite rightly understood that their presence signaled a social transformation of major proportions and that they were a key to the many changes which had remade the society. Contemporary perceptions of youth were, as a result, heavy with the excitement and anxiety of that perception.'
>
> (Fass 1977:6)

The key words in this passage are 'contemporary perceptions of youth', 'excitement', and 'anxiety'. For, as Wohl's painstaking study of the 'generation of 1914' shows, strong expressions of faith in the regenerating power of youth over an ageing establishment received scant fulfilment in the political and economic realities of life following the peace (Wohl 1980). Nor, as Fass's careful investigation of American youth in the 1920s also shows, did the symbolic fervour of the 'jazz age' produce that dramatic break with traditional values and practices which the older generation feared. The youth of the 1920s 'did not reject the authority of their nurture, nor were they symptoms of the irrelevance of the society's norms. On the contrary, they were an indication of the success of both. The young translated the changes in nurture into new behavioural norms which continue to organise our lives' (Fass 1977: 7).

In effect the changes which distinguish the generations are changes of 'translation': old values and norms are translated into new, or refurbished to accommodate the transformed realities of social life in the 1980s. As I observed in my introductory remarks on the new middle age, the use of the term does not imply a complete break with the past on the part of a new generation of 'mid-lifers' but is rather a loosely defined collection of ideals which intersect (sometimes by chance) around the concept of youth*fulness* and its capacity for personal and social change. It is not by chance that frequent comparisons are made in the present-day prescriptive literature of the new middle age between youth and middle age: both are now seen in western culture as periods of crisis and change; of increased anxiety and self-doubt and yet also of enhanced self-confidence and hope. The reference point of the ideal imagery of the new middle age is the conception of a 'generation gap' which finds expression in two ways, one general and one specific. On the general level can be found a sense of breaking with convention or what has been described in certain pre-retirement literature as loosening the 'chronological bonds' of traditional attitudes to ageing (Featherstone and Hepworth 1984). On the specific level can be found an appeal to the shared experiences of a particular generation of men and women who are urged to discover a common identity and a common cause; it is towards this expression of a sense of distinct 'social destiny' that I now wish to direct attention.

The first point I wish to make refers to comparisons between youth or adolescence, and middle age ('middlescence' as it has sometimes been called), which occur not infrequently in the prescriptive literature. The purpose of such comparisons, as I have hinted above, is to highlight subjective experiences of stress and turmoil which have been identified by most commentators as one of the hallmarks of middle age: 'the sandwich generation' (sandwiched, that is, between the younger and the older generation and thus likely to experience specific pressures and needs).

One of the least ambiguous and certainly most personal of these expressions of the generational factor can be found in Eda Le Shan's book, *The Wonderful Crisis of Middle Age* (1974). Here the author firmly locates her own awareness of the new middle age in the context of family relations with the younger generation of the 1960s. She sees the middle years in explicitly generational terms and in particular in terms of the limitations of the traditional boundaries of family life. The explicit appeal of her book is to the shared experience of bringing up the 1960s generation of young people:

> 'We were the Freudian Generation, the first parents armed with knowledge of unconscious causes of behaviour; we were the Mental Health Age parents, the first to study parenthood, the first to see cause-and-effect relationship between the experiences of childhood and adult adjustment.'
>
> (Le Shan 1974: 106)

For Le Shan, and by implication her audience, interaction with teenage children involves exposure to new values and fashions and stimulated self-awareness and identification in mid life with youth rather than age. Membership of the 'sandwich generation' – caught between youthful idealism and feelings of despair and failure – should not be a source of regret for a wasted life but a stimulus to self-realization. Middle age becomes a time of 'wonderful opportunity' to discover 'that until we learn to please ourselves ... we can give little genuine pleasure to anyone else' (Le Shan 1974: 18).

Similar expressions of the 1960s generational factor can be discovered in Gail Sheehy's *Passages*, subtitled *Predictable Crises of Adult Life* (Sheehy 1977), in which Sheehy distinguishes 'mid life', defined as a transitional phase or *status passage*, from middle age which is described as the *goal* of a successful passage. The essential prelude to the mid life passage is an 'authenticity crisis' or what Le Shan described as 'the wonderful crisis of middle age'. Such a crisis must therefore not be avoided but actively sought out and lovingly embraced. It is the living permeable membrane which separates the older version of middle age from the new: 'most people who have allowed themselves the authenticity crisis are ready to accept entry to middle age and to enjoy its many prerogatives' (Sheehy 1977: 375). They become members in effect of a new generation of mid lifers with an entirely new array of perceptions, values, dreams, and goals which transform them into 'pathfinders' (Sheehy 1982). As in Le Shan's book and the works of other popular prescriptive writers, the qualities required for the realization of a successful middle age are those which come to be associated with the younger generation: energy; flexibility; and a self-conscious rejection of outworn attitudes and beliefs.

In a more recent book, *Taking Stock* (1983), Handy has reaffirmed the theme of shared experience amongst the specific generation of those aged between fifty and sixty. The underlying premise of this book, which accompanied a BBC–1 television series, is that men and women now entering their fifties are breaking into new territory. The nature of social change is such that those entering their fifth decade in the 1980s will not as a rule find the traditional models of middle age relevant to the challenges they are about to face. What is required is a new process of 'taking stock' which will help individuals to relate their own experiences to those of others; develop a clearer understanding of their difficulties; and pave the way for practical solutions by relating personal difficulties to the broader social changes taking place in the wider world.

It should now be clear that the appeal to specific generations' experiences, which is one of the marked characteristics of the new middle age, is but one facet of a broader challenge to the traditional imagery of ageing, which is now a central feature of changing attitudes towards retirement in the western world. Since its first appearance in Britain in October 1972, the retirement and leisure magazine *Choice* (originally entitled *Retirement Choice*) has mounted an attack on the 'chronological bonds' of traditional images of retirement and their association with a socially inactive or disengaged old age (Featherstone and Hepworth 1984). In the second issue of the magazine (November 1972: 2) readers were sternly advised that 'in the interests of the community there must be a quite dramatic change in attitudes to the whole question of retirement'. For too long retirement had been associated with passive old age and it was the responsibility of society to transform it into a positive and active phase of life. In the section on women's clothing the assault on the traditional image of retirement was even more vigorous. Women readers were informed they need no longer dress themselves in the 'dull uniform' of retirement: 'Time was when once you were forty or so you could climb into a "uniform" of a long black skirt, severe blouse and sensible shoes, sit back and officially enter old age for ever'. The days were gone when they could skimp on make-up and wear something old and comfortable around the house: 'Now, when your husband is going to be home most of the time, is the moment to make him sit up and take notice of your elegant new image' (*Retirement Choice*, November 1972: 18–19). Perhaps as an added inducement the photographic models demonstrating fashionable aids to this new image for women were much younger than the prospective readership.

But times, as the mid life literature is so fond of reminding us, are changing and the models employed in recent issues of the much glossier successor, *Choice*, are now more likely to be elegant older women. Male models drawn from a similar age group to that of the target readership (fifty-plus) are now regularly featured, and they too carry their years well. In addition, comparisons are often made between generations to highlight the particular combination of youth*ful* appearance (not youth itself), and vibrantly mature years which is the ideal state of the new middle age. For changes in the circumstances surrounding retirement *are* helping to produce the new generation of pathfinding mid lifers which both the authors of the rather breathless prescriptive literature I have sampled, and authors of comparatively sober excursions into speculative social policy, expect to encounter.

GENDER RELATIONS AND SEXUALITY

Thus far in my discussion of the mid life phase, and its relation to specific features of family and marital life, I have tended to underplay the subject of gender differences in favour of an examination of trends which seem to me to apply to both women and men. But there remain, of course, a number of thorny issues pertaining to relations between the genders and to sexuality in general which cannot be ignored. And the first of these I wish to consider is the relationship between the younger woman and the older man.

As I observed earlier, the theme of the passionate and rejuvenating pursuit of a younger woman by a middle-aged man is so deeply entrenched in the popular imagination that in some circles it has come to be dignified with the status of a 'law of nature'. It reflects the belief that as men move into middle age, and their wives become menopausal, such husbands are likely to develop a strong pyscho-sexual interest in the attractions of the younger woman. And there are, as the feminists have shown, plenty of well-publicized examples of middle-aged male tributes to the life-enhancing properties of a relationship with a younger woman. At the same time 'May and December' relationships do not always result in lasting satisfaction and it must not be forgotten that the pursuit of the younger woman is not at all times the subject of unqualified approval – even by men. Indeed, like many of the issues related to middle age, the cultural imagery of the older man–younger woman syndrome is deeply ambivalent. The following quotation taken from Ernest Raymond's masterly novel about an English domestic murder in the 1930s is an interesting example of what I mean. In this story the accused has murdered his shrewish and overbearing wife, is arrested, and stigmatized in court by the prosecuting counsel as

> 'a middle aged man, poor, earning but little money at a private school in the neighbourhood, worried about his future and deeply entangled in an intrigue with a young woman he desired with all that lamentable – they might think rather despicable – infatuation to which middle aged men of a weak, flaccid and romantic type so frequently succumbed.'
>
> (Raymond 1973: 408)

What is of concern to feminists, of course, is evidence that the negative effects of ageing are unequally distributed between the genders and bear down more heavily on women. According to this analysis it is more permissible for a husband to seek youthful relief from the 'flatness' of a middle-aged marriage and other compensations are also unfortunately available for men as they grow older. Our society, Susan Sontag has observed,

> 'offers even fewer rewards for ageing to women than it does to men. Being physically attractive counts much more in a woman's life than in a man's, but beauty, identified, as it is for women, with youthfulness, does not stand up well to age. Exceptional mental powers can increase with age, but women are rarely encouraged to develop their minds above dilettante standards.'
>
> (Sontag 1978: 73)

Middle age for women is not only bedevilled by the 'double standard of sex' but also by the 'double standard of ageing', and these unequal standards inevitably have a significant influence on relations between the genders. While there is much truth in these arguments, I also wish to suggest that there are good grounds for adding yet another layer to the imagery in order to do justice to the complexity of the subject. Certain of these complexities become apparent if we consider contemporary interpretations of the menopause and 'male menopause', the second of the issues pertaining to gender relations and sexuality that I wish to take into account.

Physiologists, endocrinologists, psychologists, and sociologists who have studied the menopause tend to agree that the symptoms of which women complain during the years when their reproductive powers are gradually in decline are the product of a process of interaction between the physical (hormonal change), the psychological, and the social (Hepworth 1982). Because historical analyses (Wilbush 1980; Featherstone and Hepworth 1985) and cross-cultural studies (Hepworth 1982) reveal considerable variations in the meanings attached by different societies to the menopause (Davis 1983), it may be concluded that in the context of the contemporary western culture this phenomenon has become a convenient metaphor for the expression of consciousness of the new middle age. A brief overview of the interdependency of the menopause and 'male menopause' in present-day popular thinking will perhaps explain what I mean.

Over the last two decades or so the public definition of the menopause has been dramatically transformed at least on the symbolic level. It is no longer part of the 'silent crisis' of female middle age but is indeed proudly identified as the prelude to the personal and sexual liberation of what in some quarters has been defined as 'the bolder, older woman'. Sheila Kitzinger, for example, asserts that 'For each woman the menopause has its own meaning . . . and even if it is often a time for self assessment, it can be seen as a fresh beginning' (Kitzinger 1985: 232). In order for this particular type of successful status passage to occur, women must, she argues, abandon the male language of the menopause (created by a male-dominated medical profession) and find one of their own: they must discover a new metaphor for change which reflects their own experience of ageing and the life course. In other words, they must confront the double standards of ageing and transform themselves into 'pathfinders':

> 'the emphasis can be on how you are going to use the rest of your life. Some women see it as a fresh beginning, opening the door on a new phase of existence. Many say that they are forced to ask themselves who they are and what they want to be and do and that though the process can be painful it results in exciting change and possible development.'
>
> (Kitzinger, 1985: 239–40)

Inevitably this challenging approach to middle age will necessarily influence relations between the genders and, of course, the generations. For the central irony of the idealized imagery of the new menopause (for both women and men) is the simultaneous vindication of age and the celebration of youth. In certain prominent texts, for example, the tables are neatly turned on the older men–younger women syndrome in favour of the older women–younger men. The younger generation of men not only have the advantage of familiarity with and acceptance of the values of the new mature woman, but also are aware, as followers of the Masters and Johnson sexual revolution (Masters and Johnson 1970), that the menopause is far from being the end of active sexuality for a woman and the odds are that she is likely to have a stronger sexual appetite than her contemporary males.

I am not suggesting for one moment that efforts to create a new language of the new menopause which more faithfully expresses the experience of women necessarily leads to a pre-occupation with sex with younger men although this is clearly a notable feature of the image. What I am suggesting is that the identification of youth with sexuality, flexibility, progress, and change is now so deeply embedded in western culture that it is increasingly difficult to avoid its lure. Just as the new metaphor of the menopause as personal and sexual enhancement has legitimized the image of the older woman and the younger man – the exact cultural counterpart of the younger woman and the older man – so it has had significant repercussions on the concept of male middle age; namely in the shape of the so-called 'male menopause'.

Of particular interest in the expanding literature of the 'male menopause' is the way in which descriptions of the symptoms and treatment of this phenomenon parallel those of the female menopause. In an article entitled 'Is Your Man Going Through the Change?' published in *Woman*, 14 May, 1977, Helen Franks asserted that middle age could be as depressing for a man as for a woman. The principal cause was the male menopause. The self-questioning which seemed to be one of the central characteristics of the male mid life transition, might well be influenced by the emerging independence of women: 'nothing could be harder for a man than to be challenged by his wife's new-found confidence when he is casting doubts upon his own. Male sexuality, for instance, ever fragile and often dependent on boasts and conquests, is never more vulnerable than in mid-life' (Franks 1981:58).

The existence of a variety of disturbing symptoms, loosely described as 'the male menopause' has received wide confirmation in both professional and lay literature over the last few years. While there is no conclusive evidence that the majority of men undergo a hormonal 'change of life' equivalent to that found in women, it has become clear that a significant number *do* experience psychological and social difficulties at some point in middle age and that these difficulties may well have a sexual component. Since the 1960s (although some commentators such as Marjorie Fiske would trace the movement in the USA back to the publication of Arthur Miller's play *Death of a Salesman* in 1949: Fiske 1979), interest in the problem of men in mid life has notably expanded and made its contribution to the vocabulary of the new middle age. Terms such as 'male climacteric', 'prime time', and that catch-all category, 'the mid life crisis', which can apply equally to women and men, have become part of everyday speech. The most recent example of prescriptive writing to be published in the United Kingdom contains the unequivocal assertion that 'Therapists today estimate that only twenty per cent of the Western male population' avoid the distressing effects of the male menopause which is responsible for 'injecting a considerable amount of havoc and unrest in their lives' (Aquilina Ross 1984: 3). Eight years previously Bowskill and Linacre described the 'male menopause' as a 'disastrous watershed for Twentieth Century Man' (Bowskill and Linacre 1976: 9). In their eyes the male menopause was 'the malaise of our time', increasingly reported by 'Friends, wives, doctors and agony columnists', as well as many others who 'tell of hundreds of men who define their problems as the "male" menopause' (Bowskill and Linacre 1976: 33).

Two aspects of this popular concern are of interest here. First, the suggestion made by Helen Franks and others that the symptoms to which the label 'male menopause' is attached arise at least partly in response to changing relations between the genders, and often in family situations. Second, that these symptoms, as in the case of those associated in modern western thought with the menopause, are not trivial manifestations of a fleeting reaction to passing events (the traditional 'silent crisis'), or merely the preoccupation of an identifiable generation, but have a collective significance symbolically connecting these interpersonal events with broader historical and yet less tangible changes in western culture. Changes which can themselves be traced back at least to the early nineteenth century (Featherstone and Hepworth 1985). In 1981, for example, the Marriage and Marriage Guidance Commission of the International Union of Family Organizations considered the issue significantly urgent to organize a conference in Toronto around the 'Male Crisis'. The crisis in question was defined not as 'one single phenomenon' but as several distinct and interrelated aspects of 'contemporary man's adaptation to changing social conditions', particularly as they seemed to be affecting his roles of husband, father, and worker. At the close of the conference the Commission concluded that evidence to warrant the belief in the existence of a male crisis *was* gradually emerging in western society, and that although often a source of 'fear and anxiety', it could also be interpreted as a prelude to positive 'personal growth' and 'creative change' (Tyndall 1982). In other words, not merely as a 'malaise'.

PERSONAL CHANGE IN ADULT LIFE

The historian Edward Shorter has described the movement towards what he calls the 'postmodern family' as the gradual emergence of an 'emotional unit' which is dependent for its stability not on traditional communal constraints but upon the bonds of sentiment and sexuality. The family has thus evolved into an essentially private unit held together by the capacity of the couple to maintain a mutually rewarding romantic and erotic relationship. For Shorter romance is 'a vehicle of self-exploration and self-development' (Shorter 1977: 24) in a society where 'individual self-realisation takes precedence over community stability. The careers and happiness of individual members of the family triumph over the continuation of the lineage as a whole' (Shorter 1977: 27). While reservations may be expressed about the universal applicability of Shorter's thesis, the language is undoubtedly that of the apologists of the new middle age with whom my previous discussion was largely concerned. The overriding preoccupation of the new mid lifers with personal growth and change is closely linked to increasing dependence on 'rewarding' interpersonal relationships rather than reliance upon enduring or stable external social structures that Shorter has described as characteristic of pre-modern family life. Indeed, the central tension in much of the literature of the new middle age – between the negative terminology of the symptoms (depression, anxiety, a sense of life closing down, personal unworthiness, failure) and the positively optimistic tones of the prescriptive literature – is eloquent testimony of this view.

But what I have tried to show in the preceding pages is that although a case can be made for a significant cultural trend in the changing imagery of middle age, such images are in the last analysis as deeply ambivalent as any practical everyday realization of the dreams they embody. As I stated in my introduction, the break with the past is by no means as clean as some would have us imagine and there are in any case untold numbers of middle-aged men and women whose day-to-day lives are relatively untouched by the new middle age and whose life courses are shielded from its challenge. Thus when it is accepted that the world needs new models of middle age which correspond with increasing pressures for personal change in adult life, what we are really being told is that *certain groups* of individuals have discovered or are discovering a 'need' for new models of personal fulfilment in mid life. Those, for instance, who have been labelled the 'pacesetters' and who represent the specific experience of a segment of an identifiable generation in the sense that Wohl (1980) uses the term.

As with 'the family', and 'generation', and indeed all concepts of which I have made use in this discussion, there is more than enough room for further empirical research. Not so long ago, sociologists Nancy Datan and Dean Rodeheaver noted that the 'incidence of rebirth in middle age is considerably less than Sheehy would have us believe; but the hunger for rebirth, to judge from the extraordinary impact of her book is immense' (Datan and Rodeheaver 1983: 283). What I have tried to argue is that when all the sociological reservations it is possible to muster have been taken into account, there is no doubt that the options for both men and women in mid life are more open and flexible than they have ever been in the past.

NOTES

1 *News of The World*, 14 March, 1971.
2 *News of The World*, 6 February, 1977.
3 Reprinted in the *Guardian*, 22 November, 1982.

REFERENCES

Aquilina Ross, G. (1984) *How to Survive the Male Menopause*. London: Elm Tree Books.

Askham, J. (1984) *Identity and Stability in Marriage*. Cambridge: Cambridge University Press.

Ball, D.W. (1974) The 'Family' as a Sociological Problem: Conceptualisation of the Taken-For-Granted as Prologue to Social Problems Analysis. In A. and J. Skolnick (eds) *Intimacy, Family and Society*. Boston, Mass.: Little, Brown.

Bawden, N. (1976) *A Woman of My Age*. Harmondsworth: Penguin.

Bowskill, D. and Linacre, A. (1976) *The 'Male' Menopause*. London: Frederick Muller.

Braine, J. (1978) *Stay With Me Till Morning*. (first published 1970) London: Magnum Books.

Collin, A. (1984) *Mid-Career Change: An Exploratory Study of the Process of 'Career' and of the Experience of Change in 'Mid-Life'*. Unpublished Ph.D. thesis. Loughborough University of Technology.

Conran, S. (1981) *Futurewoman: How to Survive Life*. (first published 1979) Harmondsworth: Penguin.

Datan, N. and Rodeheaver, D. (1983) Beyond Generativity: Toward a Sensuality of Later Life. In R.B. Weg (ed.) *Sexuality in the Later Years*. New York and London: Academic Press.

Davis, D.L. (1983) *Blood and Nerves: An Ethnographic Focus on Menopause*. St John's, Nfld: Memorial University of Newfoundland, Institute of Social and Economic Research.

Dominian, J. (1980) *Marriage in Britian 1945–80*. London: Study Commission on the Family.

Drabble, M. (1978) *The Ice Age*. Harmondsworth; Penguin.

Fass, P.S. (1977) *The Damned and the Beautiful*. New York: Oxford University Press.

Featherstone, M. and Hepworth, M. (1984) Changing Images of Retirement – An Analysis of Representations of Ageing in the Popular Magazine *Retirement Choice*. In D. Bromley (ed.) *Gerontology: Social and Behavioural Perspectives*. London: Croom Helm.

Featherstone, M. and Hepworth, M. (1985) The History of the Male Menopause, 1848–1936. *Maturitas* 7.

Fiske, M. (1979) *Middle Age: The Prime of Life*. London: Harper & Row.

Fogarty, M. (1975) *Forty to Sixty: How We Waste The Middle Aged*. London: Centre for Studies in Social Policy.

Franks, H. (1981) *Prime Time: The Mid-Life Woman in Focus*. London: Pan.

Friese, I. (1978) *Women and Sex Roles: A Social Psychological Perspective*, New York: Norton.

Green, M. (1984) *Marriage*. London: Fontana.

Handy, C. (1983) *Taking Stock: Being Fifty in the Eighties*. London: BBC Publications.

Hepworth, M. (1982) Sociological Aspects of Mid Life. In P.A. van Keep, W. H. Utian, and A. Vermeulen (eds) *The Controversial Climacteric*, Lancaster: MTP Press.

Hepworth, M. and Featherstone, M. (1982) *Surviving Middle Age*. Oxford: Blackwell.

Hogan, D.P. (1985) The Demography of Life-Span Transitions: Temporal and Gender Comparisons. In A.S. Rossi (ed.) *Gender and the Life Course*. New York: Aldine.

Kitzinger, S. (1985) *Women's Experience of Sex* (first published 1983) Harmondsworth: Penguin.

Klapp, O. (1969) *Collective Search for Identity*. New York: Holt, Rinehart & Winston.

Lake, T. and Hills, A. (1979) *Affairs: The Anatomy of Extra Marital Relationships*. London: Open Books.

Le Shan, E. (1974) *The Wonderful Crisis of Middle Age*. New York: Warner Books.

McManners, J. (1985) *Death and the Enlightenment: Changing Attitudes to Death among Christians and Unbelievers in Eighteenth-Century France*. Oxford: Oxford University Press.

Masters, W.H. and Johnson, V. (1970) *Human Sexual Inadequacy*. Boston, Mass.: Little, Brown.

National Action Forum for Midlife and Older Women Inc, Summer (1985) *Hot Flash: Newsletter for Midlife and Older Women*. New York: State University of New York at Stony Brook.

Neugarten, B.L. (1968) The Awareness of Middle Age. In B.L. Neugarten (ed.) *Middle Age and Ageing: A Reader in Social Psychology*. Chicago, Ill.: University of Chicago Press.

Neugarten, B.L. (1985) 'Interpretive Social Science Research on Ageing'. In A.S. Rossi (ed.) *Gender and the Life Course*. New York: Aldine.

Raymond, E. (1973) *We The Accused* (first published 1935) London: Corgi.

Retirement Choice. November 1972.

Rimmer, L. (1981) *Families in Focus: Marriage, Divorce and Family Patterns*. London: Study Commission on the Family.

Sheehy, G. (1977) *Passages: Predictable Crises of Adult Life*. New York: Bantam Books.

Sheehy, G. (1982) *Pathfinders: How to Achieve Happiness by Conquering Life's Crises*. London: Sidgwick & Jackson.

Shorter, E. (1977) *The Making of the Modern Family*. London: Fontana.

Sontag, S. (1978) The Double Standard of Ageing. In V. Carver and P. Liddiard (eds) *An Ageing Population: A Reader and Sourcebook*. London: Open University Press.

Tyndall, C. (1982) Male Crisis. *Marriage Guidance Journal*, March.

Wilbush, J. (1980) The Female Climacteric. Unpublished DPhil thesis. University of Oxford.

Wohl, R. (1980) *The Generation of 1914*. London: Weidenfeld & Nicolson.

7
The transition to retirement

Chris Phillipson

INTRODUCTION

The emergence of retirement has been one of the most significant social trends of the past fifty years. This new social institution has raised important policy issues in terms of social relations, economic resources, health planning and management, family life, and leisure. The *expectation* of retirement at a fixed age (or earlier) now affects the thoughts and plans of millions of men and women. Few are likely to have paid employment after leaving their full-time occupation. For those who either want to, or who, because of poverty, are forced to work, the range of available jobs will be limited, and will invariably mean some element of occupational downgrading (Phillipson 1982).

The exclusion of older people from employment has been hastened both through the economic recession and by policy measures aimed at weakening the position of older people in the labour market (Walker 1984; Guillemard 1986). Labour statistics reveal a major transformation in work experiences: in 1931 one-half of men aged sixty-five and over were in the labour force, in 1951 the figure was 31 per cent, and by 1983 it had fallen to just 9 per cent (OPCS 1984). The position of women is more complex, with the location of older (and younger) married women in part-time work in the service industries, giving them a limited measure of protection during the recession (Dex and Phillipson 1986).

In reality, the separation of people from work may be experienced as a relatively sudden event: through the announcement of factory closures; through the implementation of a 'voluntary' early retirement scheme; or through the operation of the retirement condition which governs the receipt of the state retirement pension. Alternatively, and for a minority of individuals, retirement may be part of a 'planned' experience, supported through access to an occupational pension and with the cushion of savings from regular employment.

These examples illustrate the point that we need to be aware of a range of conditions and influences bearing upon the retirement transition. We must also acknowledge at least three distinct periods surrounding retirement, although these may be telescoped depending on the environment faced by the individual. These periods comprise a pre-retirement phase; the retirement event itself; and the post-retirement phase. Each of these will have its own particular dynamic, with the individual being presented with new tasks and developmental changes. In addition we must also recognize variations produced by the life histories of people entering retirement. As George Maddox has argued:

> 'Interpretations of retirement are [often] seriously marred by the inadequate attention to variations both in the social context within which retirement takes place and in the personal biographies of elderly individuals. Too often retirement is treated implicitly as a fact with a given social meaning, rather than as a sociological variable to be understood within the social life-space of an individual.'
>
> (Maddox 1966: 163)

It might also be said that retirement has often been artificially separated from other events taking place in the life course. Retirement may, for example, occur alongside an increase in responsibilities within the family network (for example caring for an elderly relative);[1] it may occur within the context of a gradual or sudden change in the retiree's health status; it may be preceded or followed by widowhood. Retirement, in short, is rarely a singular event or experience. It may have many layers: biographical, sociological, social-psychological, medical, and familial. Because of this multiplicity of events, processes, and relationships, we must, in a single chapter, be selective in the description and analysis provided. Given the focus of this book, our review will consider first, the theoretical models which have been used to explain the transition; second, empirical accounts of its impact; third, its effect on family life, in particular the relationship between wife and husband in the early post-retirement years. Finally, we shall consider some policy issues relating to the retirement transition.

THEORETICAL PERSPECTIVES

Two different types of theoretical models have been used to explain attitudes and behaviour in the transition to retirement. On the one side are functionalist accounts such as role theory and disengagement theory, emphasizing the divisions between pre- and post-retirement lives; on the other, perspectives which stress elements of biographical and sociological continuity. In the case of role theory, divisions are attributed to a range of sociological factors like the predominance of the nuclear family, urbanization, high rates of geographical mobility, the importance of work as a central life interest (Tibbitts 1954; Burgess 1960). As a result of the interplay of these forces, retirement, it is argued, is experienced as a 'roleless role', one which separates the individual from valued relationships and resources. The apparent ambiguity in the social position of the retiree was summarized by Talcott Parsons:

> 'In view of the very great significance of occupational status and its psychological correlates, retirement leaves the older man in a peculiarly functionless situation, cut off from participation in the most important interests and activities of the society. . . . Retirement not only cuts the ties to the job itself but also greatly loosens those to the community of residence.

> It may be surmised that this structural isolation from kinship, occupational and community ties is the fundamental basis of the recent political agitation for help to the old. It is suggested that it is far less the financial hardship of the position of elderly people than their "social isolation" which makes old age a "problem".'
>
> (Parsons 1942: 616)

In the case of disengagement theory, the older person's withdrawal from social life is seen as part of a mutual agreement between the individual and society. As with role theory, the central task for men is considered to be their work. Retirement – or the giving up of work – means that a man's central life-task is finished, and it is from this point that disengagement begins. The process is made easier for the individual by the setting of fixed retirement ages and pension schemes – developments which undercut individual dilemmas about when to disengage. Retirement is seen, in fact, as a form of permission for men to disengage from demanding social roles; for women, widowhood is considered to be the formal marker of disengagement. In addition it is also argued that disengagement or withdrawal from social relationships will lead to the individual maintaining a higher morale in old age – higher, that is, than if he or she attempted to keep involved in a range of social affairs and activities. Thus disengagement is seen as both natural and desirable, producing, in the individual, a stronger sense of psychological well-being. Finally, this feature of ageing is suggested as a universal phenomenon, associated with ageing in all cultures (Cumming and Henry 1961; Cumming 1963).

In contrast to these theories, a number of researchers have identified continuities between pre- and post-retirement life styles. Robert Atchley's (1971) identity continuity perspective suggests an underlying stability in life styles and attitudes through the retirement transition. For example, individuals might still see themselves as teachers or coal-miners even though they are no longer actively performing such roles. At the same time, people will draw upon their existing interests, or develop new ones, to form a bridge between work and retirement.

The political economy approach provides a critical edge to the idea of continuity. First, there is the notion of continuity as a product of social class. Poverty, for example, is seen as the result of both low economic and social status *prior* to retirement, as well as depressed social status *after* leaving work (Walker 1981). Secondly, there are the positive and negative continuities derived from the type of social and occupational rewards accumulated through life. Taking the experience of social isolation, for example, Guillemard (1982) explores these continuities as follows:

> 'In the classical analyses of old age, isolation was often described as one of the attributes of the process of aging, as an inherent characteristic of a particular stage of life that was defined by retirement from professional life and by the decline of the parental functions. In the new perspective, isolation appears as the product of certain class positions and of the repeated, cumulative processes of requalification in these positions, which the individuals holding them have constantly undergone through their life course. Isolation, then, emerges as the effect of certain positions within social relations that have prevented the establishment and continuation of a framework of sociability to accompany the individual's advance in age.'
>
> (Guillemard 1982: 226)

In the analysis of the retirement transition, I shall examine the available research data in the context of the above theories. Having established which is the most useful and relevant, I shall consider its implications for understanding domestic life in the retirement transition.

THE RETIREMENT TRANSITION

The pre-retirement period

In the years or months leading to retirement important changes and developments may be experienced. The loss of a job in middle age can cause considerable hardship and distress, with an extended period of unemployment and consequent loss of income (Parnes and King 1977). For those remaining at work, there may be social pressures arising from early retirement programmes, technological changes in the work-place, and adjustments due to the impact of health problems. A minority may feel and express concern about their future retirement. Parker's (1980) British survey found 35 per cent of women workers under pension age expecting that they would find it difficult to settle down when they retired; the figure for men was 27 per cent. Both groups anticipated similar types of problems, financial difficulties being uppermost. Overall in Parker's survey, two-fifths of older workers were looking forward to retirement, one in eight were definitely unhappy about the prospect, and the rest had mixed feelings.

Research indicates that the availability and size of (occupational) pensions influence decisions about retirement.[2] The availability of an occupational pension is related to whether a job is full- or part-time. Since many women are in part-time jobs or have spent some proportion of their working life in part-time work, their eligibility for occupational pensions will be limited. Statistics on occupational pensions confirm that this is the case, and that women are distinguishable from men in this respect. The lack of an occupational pension is likely to act as a disincentive for women to retire, and certainly to retire early (Jowell and Airey 1984; Dex and Phillipson 1986).

Surveys in Britain, France, and the USA highlight the importance of health problems as a factor in early retirement. Parker's (1980) survey found 76 per cent of men who had retired under state pension age reporting that they had an illness or disability which affected their activities in some way; 50 per cent of men retiring early gave ill-health as the main reason. Cribier's (1981) survey of Parisian retirees confirms sickness and disability as the major cause of premature retirement. Commenting on this, Cribier makes some important points relating to the difficult transition faced by such workers:

> 'First, many of those who stopped working before the normal age did not realize that they would never work again. Either their illness lasted for years, they were declared disabled by doctors, or they could not, in spite of all their efforts, find another job. Therefore, for many people there exists a period of uncertainty between the end of working life and the beginning of retired life. Some of them were discontented, even anguished, all of them were unable to make any plans and

found it difficult to adjust. Second, retirement from work before the normal age was mainly involuntary (whether it was welcome or not is another matter). Among those who stopped working involuntarily, 58 per cent would rather have retired later. Even some of the women who maintain they retired of their own free will had, in fact, obeyed family obligations (such as caring for a husband or sick relative, or looking after a grandchild to enable the mother to work).'

(Cribier 1981: 55–6)

The above review suggests that the pre-retirement phase may have considerable implications for domestic and family life. For women, as Cribier's analysis indicates, there may be an intensification of caring activities. For men (as well as for their wives) there may be anxieties about the future, particularly as regards financial issues. We know only a limited amount about decision-making within the domestic unit regarding impending retirement. American longitudinal data, following a representative sample of middle-aged working women, found that a majority did not plan to retire at the same time as their husbands (Shaw 1984). Comparable information is not available for the United Kingdom, but the American research suggests that where both partners are in paid work we must be careful of assuming that their retirements will coincide. In general, the American study showed that the husbands' plans did have a strong impact on those of wives, and that having a husband who would be retired made it more likely that a woman would plan to retire. This seemed particularly likely where husband and wife were approaching the same age (Shaw 1984).

It would be valuable to know more about the process of domestic decision-making in the pre-retirement phase. To what extent do we see joint decision-making over financial or housing issues? Are there serious discussions about the division of labour of household tasks? What sort of feelings do partners have about their respective – if both are in paid work – retirements? Amongst British studies, Crawford's (1971, 1972, 1973) research is one of the few to have tackled such questions. The couples in her study, who were five months from retirement when first interviewed, differed in their perceptions of the benefits of leaving work. Amongst the men 'more freedom' was the most popular description; for women it was 'seeing more of spouse'. According to Crawford:

> 'over twice as many wives as husbands saw their spouses' company as an advantage of retirement. In contrast to their husbands, very few mentioned the contribution that their husbands could make round the house. Instead, the most frequent comments concerned their pleasure in their husbands' company and indirectly indicated that they were looking forward to re-engaging in the marital relationship. They reflected the loneliness of the women's lives: "I shall be glad of the company. I wish it was tomorrow and so does he". Their loneliness derived from the fact that [their children had left home] some years earlier and left them without an active maternal role.'
>
> (Crawford 1971: 265)

Many aspects of retirement are, of course, very difficult for individuals to control. The timing of retirement will be set by relatively fixed and impersonal procedures and few people – at least in Britain – are able to construct a retirement of their own choosing. Moreover, few employers help their employees prepare for retirement (for example, by running pre-retirement courses).[3] Many workers thus enter retirement in a state of some uncertainty about their future.

There are, however, positive experiences in the pre-retirement years which should be recorded. There may, for example, be a reintegration within the domestic sphere as children leave home. Leisure activities may be extended, and may replace, in some cases, the benefits derived from work (Kaplan 1979). Accepting gender, race, and class inequalities (to be indicated below), many people enter a new and positive phase of discovery in areas such as education and sport (Bernard 1985; Glendenning 1985).[4] But for all groups in this period, the impending reality of retirement assumes major importance from the early fifties onwards. The next section reviews existing research material on its immediate impact and effect.

Leaving work and the post-retirement phase

Sociological research in the 1950s focused upon the 'crisis' and 'shock' induced by retirement (Phillipson 1982). Leaving work was seen as a disruptive event, separating the individual from a 'central life interest', disrupting family life, and disturbing the balance between work and social relationships. Retirement was in short seen to bring an unwelcome discontinuity into the lives of people, one which invariably caused painful readjustments.

For those writing from a critical perspective, retirement was also seen as a debilitating event – a form of 'social death' (Guillemard 1972). Here, however, the emphasis is placed on structural factors which predispose certain groups to experience alienation in later life (for example unskilled and semi-skilled workers, women, and disabled people).

What have three decades of research told us about the continuities and discontinuities experienced in retirement? First, perhaps on a positive note, we should recognize the gradual shift, in terms of *general social attitudes*, towards acceptance of retirement. This is the overwhelming conclusion from American longitudinal data, which has started to question a number of stereotypes and myths about the retirement transition. Summarizing the findings from various longitudinal studies, Palmore and colleagues write:

> 'Retirement at the normal age has little or no adverse effects on health for the average retiree. Some have health declines, but these are balanced by those who enjoy health improvement. ... Retirement at the normal age has few substantial effects on activities, except for the obvious reduction in work and some compensating increase in solitary activities.'
>
> (Palmore *et al*. 1985: 167)

French research has also confirmed both a 'marked increase in the proportion of people who view retirement as a desirable goal, and early retirement as particularly desirable' (Cribier 1981: 66). The retirees in Parker's British study (1980), while more cautious in their views, had still, in the majority of cases, 'settled down' to retirement at least twelve months after the event.

Despite the above evidence, the language spoken about retirement remains contradictory, and this says much about the wider landscape of class and social relations. Cribier (1981), for example, notes how the proportion of people 'genuinely' satisfied with retirement (40 per cent overall), varied from 34 per cent of male employees and blue-collar workers to 59 per cent of middle- and upper-level executives. Similarly Guillemard (1982) has shown how different types of retirement life styles are related to class position. Thus for working-class retirees, social withdrawal may be a typical mode of response, because their exploited position presents them with few resources to consume and convert into meaningful leisure during retirement. Middle-class retirees, on the other hand, are seen to have the economic and cultural capital to assist the conversion of free time into leisure.

Such findings have also been indicated in the American longitudinal research. Parnes and Less (1983), for example, found that amongst white men, both family income and occupational level had independent effects on the amount of time spent on leisure activity in retirement. They concluded from this that

> 'the kind of work that men do influences leisure activities not only through the income that it generates, but also by conditioning or reflecting their interests. If participation in leisure activities contributes to satisfaction, one might therefore expect men who had retired from high level jobs to manifest above average satisfaction with retirement even when such factors as income and health are held constant.'
>
> (Parnes and Less 1983: 90–1)

Sex differences in adjustment to retirement have been reported by some researchers (Jacobson 1974; Streib and Schneider 1971; Fox 1976). Findings are, however, inconsistent, and there is an urgent need for data which relate women's experiences in the transition to feminist and other sociological perspectives.

Poor health is another factor which may affect the retirement transition, and lead to difficulties in adjustment. Those with a low income and a disability may be most vulnerable to feelings of having 'time on one's hands', with resulting frustration at being unable to convert free time into meaningful leisure.

The findings from empirical research demonstrate continuities (both negative and positive) between pre- and post-retirement life styles. Such research suggests that we need to see the retirement transition as an area where the social ties an individual has developed with society and the type of skills he or she has been allowed to accumulate assume a new importance. In short, it is in the retirement transition that the individual calls upon the resources he or she has developed during the early and middle phases of the life course. In this sense the transition is not a movement from an old to a completely new life (as the disengagement and role theories would suggest); rather it is the final resolution of the advantages and disadvantages attached to given social and class positions. A resolution in the sense that once the advantages accruing from a particular position are consolidated they are likely to be sustained even into very old age. Similarly, where there are disadvantages, retirement and old age may simply add to the individual's sense of powerlessness and loss of control.

But this perspective needs to be extended into the domestic area itself. How do these social and class dynamics affect the relationship between partners in the early stages of retirement? I shall now review some case studies to provide information on this area.

DOMESTIC LIFE IN RETIREMENT

The arguments presented in favour of continuity between work and retirement will now be explored in relation to domestic life. Material will be drawn from research on retirement, carried out by the author, in the late 1970s. The research included tape-recorded interviews with twenty-five retired architects, twenty-five retired car workers, and twenty-five retired miners. All had been retired for approximately four years.[5] The purpose of the research was to place the retirement transition in the context of the individual's work and family biography. In the words of George Maddox, the concern was to understand the 'reaction to retirement as a variable (rather than as a social event with a single meaning) related to the particular configuration of experiences which constitute an individual's biography' (Maddox 1966: 131).

In terms of the ties between work and retirement, the research generated similar continuities to those identified by Guillemard (1982). For the architects, their occupational environment had allowed the development of, and may itself have stimulated, a variety of skills (engineering, painting, carpentry, modelling, writing) all of which could be transferred and developed in the retirement period. In some respects, they straddled both sides of the mental and manual division of labour and the more rounded development of skills and abilities to which this led undoubtedly made retirement both easier to adjust to, and ultimately more fulfilling for the individuals concerned.

Thus the architects were not in the position of having to shed a restrictive work identity and then to assume one which was appropriate for retirement. On the contrary, they carried through both a secure self-image, and a set of skills and resources which could be usefully exploited in the post-work period. Further, they saw (and felt) the advantages which retirement had for them in terms of enjoying these interests and resources within a period free of work responsibilities.

For the car workers, on the other hand, the 'barriers' between 'work' and 'life' made it more likely that retirement would appear as a 'break' and a 'rupture' from past experiences and relationships. In effect, discontinuity was built into the work context. Thus work experiences had done little to develop skills and resources with relevance beyond the factory, and work relationships were usually terminated at the factory gate. If work did have an influence on the 'non-work' areas of life it was usually on the negative side. People working different shifts from week to week would find it difficult to participate actively within the community; people doing assembly work might often be too tired to go out.

Given conditions such as these one should not be surprised that people would often ask: 'What have I got now that I have finished work?' 'What is there left for me?' By this, some meant not that work had an intrinsic value, but that once the obligation to work had been removed there was little else of importance left for them.

So while for one group retirement reaffirmed the value and validity of their past occupational choice, for another it more often provoked a crisis of identity. While for one group the transition to retirement deepened and extended the layers making up the individual's identity, for another there were only 'subtractions' and, on occasions, insults to the integrity of the self.

In the case of the miners, retirement was experienced in a different way again. It was less of an individual burden, and much more a collective experience. Retirement did not involve disengagement from an existing social network; indeed, if anything there was an intensification in activities and relationships in the social and domestic arena. For this group there was consolidation of an existing level of activity, rather than expansion and diversification (as with the architects) or contraction (as with many of the car workers).

I shall now consider how these class and occupational experiences affected domestic life in the early post-retirement years.

Retirement in a mining village

The miners comprised twenty-five men living in a former mining village in County Durham. The majority of those interviewed had been born in the north-east, many coming from the community itself or villages close by. Most had had fathers and brothers who were also miners. Eighteen out of the twenty-five had started in the pits at the age of fourteen, usually working straight through until the closure of the village pit in 1968.

The findings on the domestic life of miners came as some surprise, given that findings from earlier research had suggested that relationships inside the home might be a source of tension in the retirement period (Dennis, Slaughter, and Henriques 1956: 228).This research presented a picture of a home life where a strict sexual division of labour (combined with, and following on from, the nature and organization of the miners' work) fostered an emotional shallowness in the relationship between husband and wife. Indeed, apart from a brief development of intimacy in the early years of marriage, thereafter it was a down-hill run, with an increasing separation of interests and activities between the sexes:

> 'Because of the divisions in activity and ideas between men and women, husband and wife tend to have little to talk about or to do together. It is, therefore, a common feature for no development or deepening of the husband and wife relationship to take place after the initial intensive sex life of early marriage. Indeed those couples which seemed happiest were in the first year or two of marriage when most problems were solved by going to bed. . . . So long as the man works and gives his wife and family sufficient, and the woman uses the

> family's wage wisely and gives her husband the few things he demands the marriage will carry on.'
>
> (Dennis, Slaughter, and Henriques 1956: 228)

None of those interviewed for my study had had any worries about spending more time in the home, and there were no reported instances of domestic conflict because the husband was 'in the way' or 'intruding'. Ten husbands reported that they now helped their wives more with the housework. Six husbands felt they had definitely become closer to their wives since they retired; the rest felt that their relationship was basically unchanged (certainly none expressed any views that their relationship had actually deteriorated).

None of this is to say that the sexual division of labour described by Dennis, Slaughter, and Henriques was non-existent. On the contrary, most wives retained their control over domestic affairs and many husbands would still go out to the workingmen's club alone or with a male friend. But retirement (interacting with an undoubted improvement in the social position of women inside mining communities) did lead to a 'softening' in the more extreme examples of conjugal role segregation: the organization of domestic life becoming more flexible, and the division of labour within the household undergoing some modification. The domestic situation of the miners was thus very different from that found, for example, by Peter Townsend in Bethnal Green, where an existing sexual division of labour was reinforced in retirement; and, further, where the relationships between husband and wife became increasingly strained:

> 'Retirement produced frustrations in men, because they could not fill their time and because they felt they were useless, and it also produced frustrations in women, because they had been used to a larger income and to a daily routine without interference from the husband.'
>
> (Townsend 1963: 89–90)

In contrast to this here are some comments made by both miners and their wives on how they have found retirement:[6]

> 'I'll tell you something about retirement . . . retirement draws you closer together . . . yes . . . we've been close all our lives

> . . . but since I retired we couldn't be any better than we are now.' (miner)

> 'I think we've come closer definitely. I think it's because we are more together and that. I mean I never used to bother with the garden but I'm interested with the garden now. He never used to paper or anything like that . . . but since he finished work he helped me do the staircase and all that.' (miner's wife)

> 'You're more together aren't you? I go down now and help her with the shopping which I never used to do .' (miner)

> 'Since he's been retired he's took more interest . . . the way of living in the home . . . he knows when this has got to be paid and one thing and another and he sees to things like that whereas before he never used to do anything like that.' (miner's wife)

> 'It makes you closer . . . you seem as though you need each other more I think.' (miner)

This reorientation towards domestic life is illustrated further by four men who all had wives who were very ill when they retired; for these men being able to help their wives more gave a decided advantage – as they saw it – to being retired as opposed to working. One man, for example, whose wife died five years after he retired, and who had been an invalid throughout this period, commented: 'I thought twelve months with me helping her might pull her together.' And another, whose wife died three years after he retired, suggested that

> 'probably the main reason why I decided not to keep on working . . . my wife had pains see . . . they were really severe . . . she was going to hospital twice a week for injections . . . I saw the advantage of me being able to help her a certain extent if I finished work . . . which I wouldn't have been able to do if I'd kept on working. That was a decided point in retirement. It made things a bit easier for her the last few years she lived.'

Given that miners' wives have a higher mortality rate than those of other workers, it was unsurprising that their health problems were influential in the retirement experience of many of the miners interviewed, representing, as well, an important component in the reorientation towards domestic life. Two other factors which would seem likely to assist such a reorientation were the migration of children and the death or illness of close friends. Thus the social network which the miner could draw upon – though larger perhaps than for other groups – was a contracting one and one which was shrinking fast because of migration and high mortality rates. In this situation a highly segregated conjugal relationship was changed in retirement. As the separate networks enjoyed by each couple contracted, so they tended to share more activities with each other. The important aspect here is that the structure of the conjugal relationship was sufficiently flexible for this change to take place.

Car workers

The car workers consisted of twenty-five men who had worked at the Longbridge car factory in Birmingham and who lived in the large suburb surrounding the car plant. This community had grown substantially in the inter-war and post-war period. Much of the population was drawn from people moving out of areas closer to the centre of Birmingham: usually couples with young children. As a consequence, the area had a low percentage of people over pensionable age (10.6 per cent) and a population which was primarily concentrated on the inter-war property, around which the post-war additions had been built.

As a result of these demographic changes, the question arose as to whether the social relations of the retiree would be affected not only by his withdrawal from factory-based ties, but also by his return to a community undergoing rapid expansion; the position of older people being that of a minority within a youthful and family-oriented area. To balance against this there was the point that the area (particularly its physical environment) had definite attractions for retired people. Despite the age of some of the properties the level of amenities in them was high, and the surrounding physical environment offered many advantages for the retiree.

However, what emerged from the interviews was the ambiguous social position for retired people in a community dominated by young families and wage-earners. In this environment dependence on the state pension (none of those interviewed received an occupational pension) generated feelings of financial insolvency and, on occasions, social inadequacy. People would speak of the difficulty of forming relationships without a corresponding financial exchange. One wife of a man in this group said they now avoided many of their younger friends who were still working: 'We don't want them to see our poverty', she said. Another man commented:

> 'I've gone to the Woodman [a local pub] and bought myself a drink . . . and just as I was finishing one off someone might say: "What are you going to have?" "Oh, no, can't stop, I've only come to have a quick one." Which I know I've told a lie see, otherwise, if I'd have had it and turned around and said "I can't afford to buy you one" . . . I couldn't have done that . . . it's only that excuse . . . "Oh, no, I've only come in to have this one." And if I'd said: "Have one on me" . . . and he'd taken me up on it, I would have come unstuck on that wouldn't I? . . . these are the things.'

In one important sense, these material constraints were felt more keenly by the car workers than by our other groups. This was a group of men who had worked a greater part of their lives in what had been one of the city's most prosperous industries. This was a group used to certain 'luxuries' – the meal out on Saturday night, expeditions in the car and caravan, the occasional holiday abroad. In other words, it was a life of 'progress' and 'change' from the more 'traditional' life styles in the north-east. But just how much progress can perhaps be best gauged in the terms most relevant to these men, that is had their differing occupational and financial experience given them any more security or freedom to order their lives in a period such as retirement? The answer appeared to be that it had added or given very little. As the following comments suggest, an old tradition of poverty and insecurity had returned:

> 'You've got to face it we knew this would come up sooner or later as far as me and the wife is concerned . . . there's a lot of things as regards that we used to have . . . for instance . . . it might sound child talk to you . . . I used to think of nothing,

you know, of going out and buying two pounds of chocolates and enjoy meself, eating things like that . . . fruit and stuff . . . and then I would think nothing about going into town and bringing a crab back . . . which is all gone for a burton . . . these are some of the things. It's just like . . . it's just the ordinary day to day things to live on you know and . . . er . . . the luxury parts are out of it.'

'It's all right [retirement] for people who have got money . . . who can get about and meet people and who can go here and go there . . . but it doesn't apply to working-class people . . . that doesn't at all.'

An extreme illustration of the financial austerity many had been forced into can be seen in the following example. This man discussed his situation in retirement warily, commenting at first: 'It's not something I like to talk about . . . I keep it to myself'. A not altogether surprising reaction, given the siege economy he and his wife had imposed on themselves. They were still paying for their house when they retired and part of the £500 insurance money received on retirement was used to clear the mortgage. The car and caravan were both sold because they were now becoming too expensive to run. Then social life had itself been pared down to the minimum to keep pace with necessities such as food, fuel, and clothing. The interview concluded with the comment: 'I only keep going for the wife really . . . well without the children's help we wouldn't be able to keep going at all.'

For some of the above, then, it had been anything but a happy retirement. People would find themselves driven back inside the home as external contacts and supports fell away. One immediate effect of this was an increase in conflict within the domestic sphere:

'get on each other's nerves let's be fair . . . well it's a well known thing that is . . . wife's gone to her sister's today . . . thank God for that . . . she's off today. We was all right at first, but as it got on, well, she doesn't do anything . . . I don't do anything. . . . Well at least I read or something like that . . . she just goes and does more housework . . . nothing what you might call cultural.'

> 'Yes ... Yes ... she's never said anything about it, but you know ... I suppose being a housewife, as my wife has been, she's always been a good housewife and so forth and I suppose she's got a daily routine; well with me sitting here as though I couldn't care less ... well, it's obvious to me, you're inclined to feel you're a little bit in the road ... that's how I look at it. I know she's said sometimes: "What time are you going to get up?" I said: "Why?" She said: "I think I'd like to do the house round" ... these are some of the things.'

> 'I think she likes to get me out of the way ... she wouldn't like me sitting here all day.'

Yet, as some of the interviews suggested, the relationship between husband and wife could be used as a way of tackling at least some problems in retirement. The following exchange between a couple talking about their experience brings this point out:

> 'It was a bit strange at first you know ... you got up in the morning ... I used to get up the same time ... turn round and round ... it kind of takes a little bit before it actually hits you that you are finished work. I felt rather strange but she helped me quite a lot and ... er ... eventually you get down to it and settle down. As I say I've got a marvellous wife and I know whatever happened she'd be with me to talk things over ... I think she straightened me up more than I realised.'

> 'Well, of course, you get talking to people that have retired years before your own husband and I mean they tell you things, how he does this or how he don't do that and how he ought to do the other ... he's sitting about doing nothing ... it prepared you sort of thing for when your own retires.'

In this example, the mutual working out of retirement undoubtedly led to a greater closeness and togetherness in the relationship as a whole:

> 'It's kind of brought us more together ... because we're in each other's company more that's probably made the difference ... I mean we've always got on well but since I've retired we've kind of got closer.'

> 'I think you're more dependent on one another really . . . and of course he helps me now.'

The general pattern was for the car workers to report either an unchanged domestic relationship or an increase in conflicts inside the home. These conflicts would most often appear as the individual made the transition from engagement in social activities outside, to increased concentration on activities inside the home; the ease with which he could do this being partly dependent on his own need for a male peer group or for activities outside the home.

Architects in retirement

The third group consisted of twenty-five retired architects living in the west Midlands. In the choice of this sample it was necessary to find a group who would maximize the sort of resources which were thought to be most useful in the retirement period. A number of possibilities were considered, but the architects were eventually selected as being the group most likely to show the outlines of an alternative retirement life style – a life style which would be less affected by the sort of problems that have been documented with the car workers. In particular, it was reasoned that the architects might be able to take into their retirement elements of their occupational lives and support these within a more flexible social and financial framework. The Midlands was regarded as an appropriate area from which to select a group of architects; the post-war industrial boom and extensive housing developments in the 1950s and early 1960s providing a favourable environment for the growth of the profession. Finally, it was thought that in the transfer from work to retirement a more gradual scaling down of activities might be possible (particularly for principals in private practices) and that this might be an important factor in removing the 'anxieties' sometimes associated with retirement.

Most of the architects had a different social background from the other groups we have discussed. Only three out of the twenty-five came from working-class backgrounds; most had been brought up in a home environment where a life in one of the professions was an accepted and 'natural' thing. Fathers had sometimes themselves been architects or builders (in seven cases), and other occupations mentioned included engineer, factory manager, bank manager, and local government official. Virtually all the architects were married and most reported that retirement had had only a limited impact on their domestic life. There were a number of reasons for this. First, many people still employed domestic help in the home. This reduced the pressure to change domestic habits and the household routine. Second, the large size of many of the houses visited was itself an influential factor in allowing an existing pattern of domestic relations to be maintained – as well as helping to reduce the tensions usually attributed to such relations in the retirement period. Third, the above aspects were underpinned by the architects' control over a wide range of resources, making them less vulnerable to the experience of retirement as one of reduced contact with friends and reduced participation in social activities. The architects' wives were also themselves involved in an extensive social and voluntary network.

Notwithstanding these influences, the unchanged nature of domestic relationships remained a striking feature of the architects' retirement. For most, the pre-retirement balance of joint and independent activities had usually been maintained, and few reported any tension in the marital relationship arriving with the onset of retirement:

> 'I think we've got just about enough space to avoid that being a trouble. My wife has a fairly active life too . . . she does voluntary work . . . and this sometimes takes her to London for a day. So I think we are not on top of each other all the time.'

> 'it's understood between us that I go somewhere I want to go . . . that's all right . . . she does the same . . . she has her own little clubs and things and she goes to them . . . I go to mine . . . we meet quite happily for a meal in the evening.'

> 'I had thought we might get out a bit more but it was always difficult . . . she had some meeting on . . . or the hairdressers . . . or a neighbour next door would come around wanting to take her out . . . so on the whole very little changed except that I was more available here. . . . We've lived our own lives and enjoyed them together when it was convenient.'

But the combination of both external activities and internal space was an important one. Most of the houses where the interviews were conducted were large enough to have particular rooms to cater for individual interests and activities. Thus many of the men had their own study or work-room where they often spent a large part of the day writing, painting, doing model engineering, or just reading. The area was their own space and their own territory; an area, however, which the individual could control and manipulate for himself, retaining in the process an important degree of personal autonomy. Mr Oliver reported having a 'hobbies room' where he could go and 'make as much mess as he liked'; Mr Peach showed me two rooms in his house, one (containing accessories such as a kiln) for his wife who was a potter, the other for himself and his tracks of railway line. Here then were rooms where ideas and fantasies could be developed and sometimes put into a material form; more prosaically, here also were areas where people could be alone and be perhaps their 'old' or 'true' selves:

> 'This little house is designed for four bedrooms . . . well there are only two of us . . . we have one bedroom and one guest-room . . . one of the bedrooms is my wife's pottery . . . the other is my own study . . . and we're happy as sand-boys . . . each in our territory . . . we can be as untidy as we like . . . with no complaints.'

> 'We've got a nice working arrangement . . . I come and do what little bit of business that I've got . . . I do my own income tax things . . . and investments . . . I come in here after breakfast and do them on my own . . . left alone . . . and madam gets on with her work . . . goes off shopping . . . then I go into town and she has her bridge. It works very well . . . very satisfactory . . . that side of it has worked quite well . . . I think cash is a terribly important thing in retirement for those things . . . people can afford to carry on their individual pursuits.'

> 'My wife has said she was in the habit of feeling that the middle part of the day was exclusively hers, and the idea of cooking a meal in the middle of the day and indeed having one on the premises, was something to adjust to. But I've got my own . . . I've got a small study where I work . . . and I'm out quite a bit . . . that part worked fairly well.'

Often, of course, the house had been designed by the architect himself (sometimes with retirement in mind), so there was a direct way here in which individuals could secure the space they felt they needed (as opposed to other groups who have more public and bureaucratic definitions of space imposed upon them). Those who did not design their own houses at least had the resources to control and select the type of house they lived in:

> 'I drew up a specification of what I wanted before we bought it . . . and we spent a lot of time finding the one we wanted and this was it. I said you've got to have a double garage . . . a golf course at the back – which it has – a room for me, which I hadn't managed to get before, this is exclusively mine . . . oh . . . various things like that.'

So here were environments designed and selected with the individual's own personality and interests in mind – environments, that is, for living, flexible enough to accommodate the individual both in work and retirement.

CONCLUSION

The transition to retirement: some policy issues

The transition from paid work is showing a number of divergent trends and possibilities. The decreased labour force participation of men is one overriding characteristic; older women may, however, move in the opposite direction, as some of the 300,000 who have traditionally retired every year at the age of sixty now go on working until sixty-five. Surrounding these developments are policy discussions concerned with promoting the idea of greater flexibility in retirement. The government Green Paper, *Reform of Social Security*, lent support to this, with the notion of a retirement decade between the ages of sixty and seventy. This would allow

> 'people to pick the point in the decade at which to retire, knowing what they would expect by way of state pension at each point. There would be no set pension age as such: people would get permanently lower or higher pensions according to whether they retired early or late in the decade.'
>
> (Cmnd. 9518 1985: para. 1.77)

Yet ideas of 'choice' and 'flexibility' sit uneasily with how people may actually experience the transition. Retirement may, as for the car workers we described, mark a re-entry into poverty. In Britain the risk of experiencing poverty is three times greater for those over retirement age than it is for those below retirement age. Around two-thirds of older people (5.9 million) live in or on the margins of poverty (that is with incomes up to 140 per cent of the appropriate supplementary benefit rates) compared with one-fifth of the non-elderly. The retirement transition may also raise issues relating to domestic and leisure relations: What is retirement for? What is its potential? How does it relate to previous life styles and expectations? These are difficult questions to answer, and they may provoke uncertainty and vexation – at least in the early phase after leaving work.

It is even more difficult if such questions have to be explored in a context of financial insecurity. In this context, older people are owed more than just subsistence living. Much of the research that has been done on poverty has shown that, as a result of financial restrictions, there is a 'participation standard' below which it is not possible to take part in the ordinary life of society.[7] Because of this we need to provide financial support which encourages participation in normal life, and maintains continuity between pre- and post-retirement levels of involvement. As a starting-point the flat-rate pension should be steadily increased as a proportion of gross average earnings until it reaches two-thirds of average earnings. In addition, the contribution or employment test which discriminates against substantial numbers of pensioners, especially women, should be abandoned. All pensioners have a need for income *regardless* of whether their previous employment was waged or unwaged.

Underpinning improvements in the basic pension there must be changes in the social relations of work itself. There is the continuing problem of a labour process which leads to the production of ill-health and insecurity (through, for example, redundancy, mass unemployment, and low pay) and an ideology of retirement emphasizing freedom of choice. The contradictions between work and retirement suggest the need for more direct interventions to help some people through the transition. Research suggests that people have achieved a great deal on their own, or as couples, in terms of constructing a viable retirement. However, this has often been achieved despite rather than with the help of, external forms of support. As noted earlier, pre-retirement education (PRE) is almost entirely absent in Britain, particularly for groups such as part-time workers (mainly women), employees of small firms, and unskilled and semi-skilled workers. Moreover, where it is provided, courses are invariably organized almost at the point of retirement, when ideas and plans have already been formulated. However, we need to recognize that the retirement transition may start many years ahead of the event itself, particularly in terms of planning in areas such as finance, health, and leisure.

Probably the best foreseeable alternative is a multi-staged approach to PRE.[8] This would involve major interventions in the life cycle on three occasions: at around the ages of forty, fifty, and sixty years. The goals on each of these occasions would be quite different. At the age of forty we would be concerned with questions of a collective nature: what are the factors in the individual's present environment, whether at work or in the community, which are inimical to long life? We would be concerned with examining how long people had been in jobs which, on the available evidence, were deleterious to health. We would also be concerned with aspects of their social and work roles which influenced behaviour likely to cause ill-health. At the age of fifty it would be important to establish changes at both a collective and individual level. The treatment of middle-aged workers is still highly unsatisfactory. Manual workers face a declining income in their later years, and this inevitably creates difficulties in planning for retirement. They are also vulnerable to long-term unemployment, an experience which drastically reduces any savings they have made. At age fifty, therefore, a pre-retirement policy would attempt to investigate ways of maintaining (if not increasing) the individual's income up to the point of retirement. It would also need to review the implications of long-term unemployment: if it happened, how would the individual cope? What sort of resources are available to provide support?

Some of these questions could be explored in the context of a 'mid-life course' organized at the worker's factory or office. The emphasis would not be on retirement as such (the area of financial planning would be the exception), but on various changes at work and in the family which although preceding retirement influenced the type of adaptation made to this period. Finally, at the age of sixty a retirement course could be organized around the core elements of finance and self-help and political organization. The emphasis in both items would be on how older people – both individually and collectively – can improve the quantity and quality of resources they receive in later life.

In conclusion, the above model suggests the need for radical interventions to assist the transition from work. With retirement likely to grow in importance and popularity over the next decade, policies are urgently required to help individuals achieve their potential in later life. The priority must be for economic and social policies which can provide a secure framework for life in the retirement transition, as well as into old age itself.

NOTES

1 There is a substantial literature showing that it is often middle-aged people who assume a key role in caring for elderly relatives. See, for example, the discussion of this area in Finch and Groves (1983).
2 This research is summarized by Dex and Phillipson (1986).
3 For a history of pre-retirement education in Britain, see Phillipson (1981). Phillipson and Strang (1983) provide an evaluation of this type of work.
4 Mike Hepworth, in Chapter 6 of this book, outlines the changes surrounding the mid life phase and the way it is increasingly portrayed as a period for self-development.
5 See Phillipson (1978) for a full description of the methodology behind this study.
6 The following quotations, along with those relating to car workers and architects, are taken from Phillipson (1978). The names of the retirees are fictitious.
7 For a discussion on this point see Bornat, Phillipson, and Ward (1985).
8 This model is developed further in Phillipson and Strang (1983).

REFERENCES

Atchley, R. (1971) Retirement and Leisure Participation: Continuity or Crisis. *Gerontologist* 11: 13–17.

Bernard, M. (1985) *Health Education and Activities for Older People: A Review of Current Practice*. Working Papers on the Health of Older People 2. Stoke-on-Trent: Health Education Council in association with the Department of Adult and Continuing Education, University of Keele.

Bornat, J., Phillipson, C., and Ward, S. (1985) *A Manifesto for Old Age*. London: Pluto Press.

Burgess, E.W. (ed.) (1960) *Aging in Western Societies*. Chicago, Ill.: University of Chicago Press.

Cmnd. 9518 (1985) *Reform of Social Security: Programme for Change*. (Vol. 2) London: HMSO.

Crawford, M. (1971) Retirement and Disengagement. *Human Relations* 24: 255–78.

Crawford, M. (1972) Retirement and Role Playing. *Sociology* 6: 217–36.

Crawford, M. (1973) Retirement: A Rite de Passage. *Sociological Review* 21: 476–81.

Cribier, F. (1981) Changing Retirement Patterns of the Seventies: The Example of a Generation of Parisian Salaried Workers. *Ageing and Society* 1 (1): 51–73.

Cumming, E. (1963) Further Thoughts on the Theory of Disengagement. *International Social Science Journal* 15: 377–93.

Cumming, E. and Henry, W. (1961) *Growing Old*. New York: Basic Books.

Dennis, N., Slaughter, C., and Henriques, F. (1956) *Coal is our Life*. London: Eyre & Spottiswoode.

Dex, S. and Phillipson, C. (1986) Social Policy and the Older Worker. In C. Phillipson and A. Walker (eds) *Ageing and Social Policy: Critical Perspectives*. Aldershot: Gower Press.

Finch, J. and Groves, D. (eds) (1983) *A Labour of Love*. London: Routledge & Kegan Paul.

Fox, J. (1976) *Women, Work and Retirement*. Ph.D. thesis, Duke University.

Glendenning, F. (ed.) (1985) *Educational Gerontology: International Perspectives*. London: Croom Helm.

Guillemard, A.M. (1972) *La retraite: Une mort sociale*. Paris: Mouton.

Guillemard, A.M. (1982) Old Age, Retirement and the Social Class Structure: Towards an Analysis of the Structural Dynamics of the Latter Stage of Life. In T. Hareven and K.J. Adams (eds) *Ageing and Life Course Transitions*. London: Tavistock.

Guillemard, A.M. (1986) The Social Dynamics of Early Withdrawal from the Labour Force in France. *Ageing and Society* 5 (4): 381–412.

Jacobson, D. (1974) Rejection of the Retiree Role: A Study of Female Industrial Workers in their 50s. *Human Relations* 27: 477–91.

Johnston, S. and Phillipson, C. (1983) *Older Learners: The Challenge to Adult Education*. London: Bedford Square Press.

Jowell, R. and Airey, C. (1984) *British Social Attitudes: The 1984 Report*. Aldershot: Gower Press.

Kaplan, M. (1979) *Leisure: Lifestyle and Lifespan*. London: W.B. Saunders.

Maddox, G. (1966) Retirement as a Social Event. In J.C. McKinney and F.T. de Vyver (eds) *Aging and Social Policy*. New York: Appleton-Century-Crofts.

Office of Population Censuses and Surveys (1984) *General Household Survey: Preliminary Results for 1983*. OPCS Monitor July. London: OPCS.

Palmore, E., Burchett, B., Fillenbaum, G., George, L., and Wallman, L.M. (1985) *Retirement: Causes and Consequences*. New York: Springer.

Parker, S. (1980) *Older Workers and Retirement*. London: OPCS.

Parnes, H. and King, R. (1977) Middle-Aged Job Losers. *Industrial Gerontology* 4: 77–95.

Parnes, H. and Less, L. (1983) *From Work to Retirement: The Experience of a National Sample of Men*. (mimeo) Ohio State University: Center for Human Resource Research.

Parsons, T. (1942) Age and Sex in the Social Structure of the United States. *American Sociological Review* 7: 604–16.

Phillipson, C. (1978) *The Experience of Retirement: A Sociological Analysis*. Ph.D. thesis, University of Durham.

Phillipson, C. (1981) Pre-Retirement Education: The British and American Experience. *Ageing and Society* 1 (3): 393–413.

Phillipson, C. (1982) *Capitalism and the Construction of Old Age*. London: Macmillan.

Phillipson, C. and Strang, P. (1983) *Pre-Retirement Education: A Longitudinal Evaluation*. Stoke-on-Trent: University of Keele, Department of Adult Education.

Shaw, L. (1984) Retirement Plans of Middle-Aged Married Women. *The Gerontologist* 24 (2): 154–59.

Streib, G.F. and Schneider, S.J. (1971) *Retirement in American Society: Impact and Process*. Cornell: Cornell University Press.

Tibbitts, C. (1954) Retirement Problems in American Society. *American Journal of Sociology* 59: 301–08.

Townsend, P. (1963) *The Family Life of Old People*. London: Pelican.

Walker, A. (1981) Towards a Political Economy of Old Age. *Ageing and Society* 1: 73–94.

Walker, A. (1984) Conscription on the Cheap: Old Workers and the State. *Critical Social Policy* 4 (2): 103–10.

8
The life course and informal caring: towards a typology

Clare Ungerson

INTRODUCTION

Recent commentary on social policy has been much concerned with the impact of demographic change on the economy as a whole. The particular statistic which commentators find concentrates their minds wonderfully is the expected very rapid growth in the proportion of elderly and very elderly in the British population. By the year 2001 the number of people over seventy-five years old is expected to increase by 1 million to 4.2 million, of whom 1.1 million will be over eighty-five (Central Statistical Office 1984: 18). As a result of the considerable concern expressed about the ensuing dependency ratio and its generalized economic and fiscal impact, the State Earnings Related Pension Scheme (SERPS) was recently put under very severe threat following the Social Security Reviews (Cmnds 9517–19), although SERPS itself has now been rescued.

It is interesting to note the contrast between the concern

expressed about the dependency ratio in the aggregated context of the British economy and the relative lack of concern about the impact of the very same dependency ratio in the disaggregated context of the 'family'. For example, policies for 'community care' which, if set up on a proper and financially viable footing, would probably constitute a humane and popular way of delivering caring services to the dependent elderly population, are increasingly vulnerable to reductions in public expenditure, in the belief and expectation as expressed by the Prime Minister that caring services at much less cost can be adequately provided within the family (Thatcher 1981).

This chapter is concerned with the effect of that dependency ratio within the intimate context of the household. A study of nineteen families (living in Canterbury in 1984), each containing a person who had been identified by the local social services department as an informal 'carer' of an elderly dependent person, provided the subject matter. In all cases, the person being cared for was a relative, either through kinship or marriage, of the carer; in almost all cases the person being cared for was living in the same household as the carer. In-depth interviews with the carers and, on occasion, other members of their family and/or the person they were caring for, were carried out in the early summer of 1984. (A description of the methodology involved can be found in Ungerson 1985, and Ungerson forthcoming. The sample was in no way a random or representative one.)

It is not my aim in this chapter to demonstrate either how relatively robust the family is when it comes to caring for the elderly, or how such caring can impose considerable stresses and strains on the carers. There is now a very large literature that does exactly that (for example Nissel and Bonnerjea 1982; Briggs and Oliver 1985). Instead my purpose is to posit a connection between life course position and the initiation and continuation of long-term informal care. In particular, I shall do three things: first, I shall describe the life course position of the men and women carers in the sample, and speculate as to why there were considerable differences between the life course positions of, on the one hand, the male carers and on the other, the women carers interviewed. Second, I shall demonstrate that, in contrast to the men in the sample, the women had been in a wide variety of life course positions at the moment when they took up caring. In trying to explain why this variety of life course position seems to exist among women carers, I shall develop a life course typology of care which contains within it reference to women's position as mothers and their position as workers. Finally, as a continuous theme within the discussion, I shall attempt to use the life course typology as a way of teasing out how far the women in this sample had 'volunteered' to care, and how far their life course and their perception of it had 'forced' them to take care of an elderly person.

THE SAMPLE: AGE, SEX, AND MARITAL STATUS

Of the nineteen carers interviewed, fifteen were women and four were men. All of the men were caring for their wives, whereas eleven of the women were caring for someone other than their husband, usually a relative from the older generation. All the men carers were aged over sixty-five, and one of them, at eighty-four, was the oldest carer in the group. In contrast, as one would expect given that it was only the women who were caring for someone of a different generation from themselves, the women's ages spread over a much wider age range with the youngest under forty and the oldest in her late seventies. *Table 1* summarizes the age and sex of the carers and cared for.

Table 1 *Ages of carers and cared for*

ages	carers		cared for	
	men	women	men	women
under 50	–	4	–	–
50–60	–	6	1	–
60–65	–	2	–	–
65–70	1	2	1	–
70–75	–	–	–	3
75–80	2	1	2	5
80–85	1	–	1	3
85 plus	–	–	1	3
total	4	15	6	14[1]

Note: [1]Includes one woman being cared for by a carer of two persons.

The considerable ages of the men carers and, more particularly, the fact that all four of them were caring for their wives as shown in *Table* 2 distinguished them from the women carers, the majority of whom were caring for someone other than their own spouse.

Table 2 *Kin relationship of the carers to the cared for*

child of cared for		child-in-law of cared for		spouse of cared for		other	
men	women	men	women	men	women	men	women
–	7	–	4	4	4	–	1*

*(Mrs Cook for her aunt)

It may well be that these age and marital status differences between the men and women carers have wider reference beyond this small sample, for they neatly illustrate a finding common to many other studies of caring (for example Nissel and Bonnerjea 1982). The point is that the men had taken on caring at a very different point in their life course from that of the women. All the men had been more or less retired when their wives had become incapable of looking after themselves or their husbands. It is highly unlikely, however, that had their wives become ill at an earlier stage in the life course when these men were still in full-time paid work, that they would have taken on full-time caring; almost certainly they would have found someone else (social services, a daughter, a paid employee, or some combination of all three) to take it on, while they continued to earn enough to keep their wives and themselves in their accustomed environment. This suggestion is confirmed by the fact that three of these men held very traditional views about the position of women in society. Far from being unusually radical in their opinions, they had very strong ideas about the nature of the marriage relationship and the appropriate roles of men and women within it. For example, none of the wives of these three men had worked throughout their marriages, and their husbands described them as the kind of women who would never have wanted it otherwise. (The one man whose wife had worked had had a low-paid job all his working life, and his wife had done 'field work' – the Kentish term for seasonal work picking fruit.) However, in the emergency circumstances they were now experiencing, these men were prepared to abandon completely the traditional domestic division of labour within marriage in order to maintain what they perceived to be the more important tradition of marriage itself.

Confirmation that men generally would be very reluctant if not non-existent carers at an earlier pre-retirement stage in their life courses can be garnered from the experiences of four women in the sample who were caring for one of their husband's parents. All four women were married to husbands who were in full-time work. While one of the husbands, an academic, had taken to working at home rather more in order to keep his wife company while she cared for his mother, none of the other husbands had given up full-time work. Their wives had stepped into the breach. It would, as I have suggested above, be very unusual if they had given up work even to care for their wives (unless, as Phillipson indicates in Chapter 7, they were already approaching retirement age). Many men (most?) would be likely to seek the aid of someone else to take over the caring task. This need not be simply a crude reflection of the prevailing sexual division of labour. For many men, particularly those in relatively well-paid and congenial work, a decision to remain in work, even if it means paying someone else to care for their wives, could be justified, not in terms of the traditional sexual division of labour, but in terms of the maximization of household income at a time when household expenses, due to the illness of one of its members, are likely to be high.

Thus, as far as caring is concerned, I am, in keeping with other contributors to this volume, suggesting that the male life course contains definite 'start-up' and 'cut-off' points oriented around paid work. Full-time paid work almost always acts as a buffer between the social and family circumstances of a man and his availability for caring. Once the period in the cycle of full-time paid work is over, a man suddenly becomes available for full-time caring. Indeed, the male life course is typically so full of these sudden changes in life style and lifelong commitment that the prospect of taking up caring as a full-time retirement occupation probably appeals to some men, since their caring role can fill the time that may now hang rather heavily on their hands. Moreover, for a retired man caring for his wife, such caring can be interpreted by him as reciprocity for the servicing she provided for him while she was well, and a way of maintaining and justifying a lengthy marriage. Three of the male carers in my sample did explain their motivation in these terms (Ungerson forthcoming).

THE LIFE COURSE OF WOMEN CARERS

In contrast to the men carers in the sample, the women carers were at a variety of positions in the life course both at the time of the interview and, as we shall see later, at the point in their lives when they took up caring.

Figure 1 Number of women carers, at time of interview, by age of youngest child living at home, by whether or not woman carer in paid work

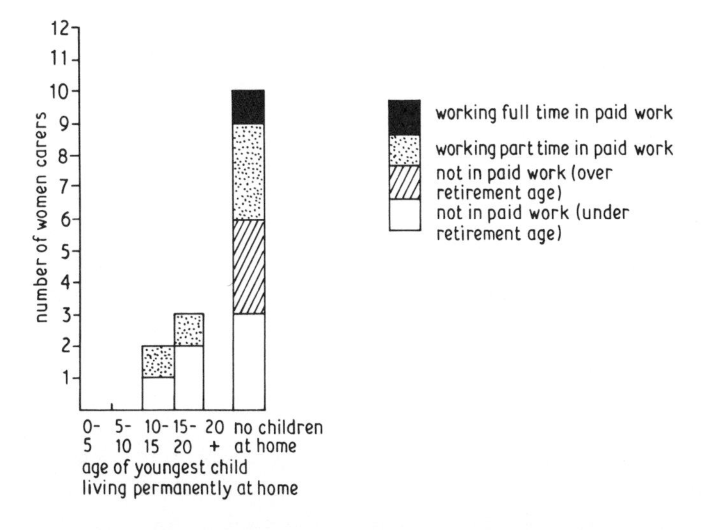

As *Figure 1* in conjunction with *Table 1* shows, at the time of the interview the great majority of women carers (ten out of fifteen) were past the child-rearing, let alone child-bearing, stage. Of those who had had children (thirteen out of the fifteen) only five still had a child or children living permanently at home. It will be seen that only two women were still mothering children under fifteen years of age, and the remaining three women fully expected their children to leave home to enter further and higher education very shortly. None of these five women expected their children to stay at home beyond the age of eighteen to nineteen. They could all put a time limit to the period they would have to provide a steadily decreasing amount of care for their children; their problem was that none of them could put a time limit to the period over which they would have to care for an increasingly dependent elderly person. Thus, just as they were reaching the point in the life course where most women would expect to be able to make somewhat self-indulgent plans for their own futures these women were facing an indefinite period of caring.

Figure 2 Number of married women carers with children, by age of youngest child at 'start' of caring

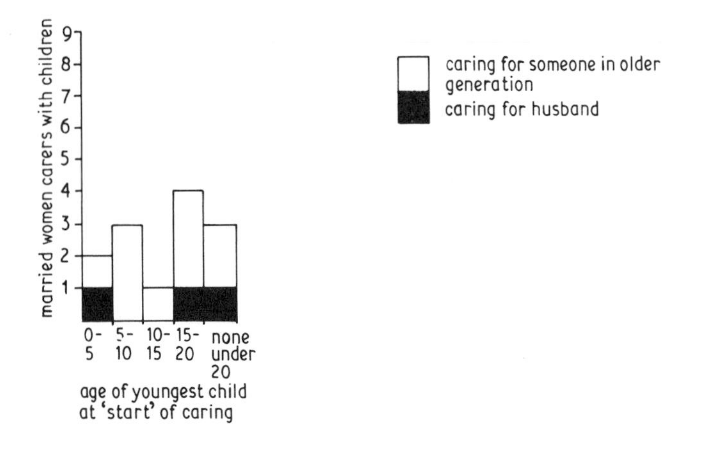

However, it is important to remember that *Figure 1* represents a 'snap-shot' taken at the time of interview. In *Figure 2* I have crudely calculated the ages of the youngest children at the moment when the married women carers with children actually started caring. Such a diagrammatic representation necessarily simplifies the complicated process of becoming a carer by giving the start of caring a definite date; nevertheless, the figure does show that the life course position was rather different and that, at the time they began the tasks of caring, rather more of these married women were responsible for school-age children (and, in two cases, babies) than they were by the time of interview. The most important point made by *Figure 2* is that for many of these women, the initiation of caring for an elderly dependent person *coincided* with child-care. Thus, far from indicating, as *Figure 1* does, an idea of entrapment and frustrated ambitions, *Figure 2* seems to indicate a willingness, indeed a positive choice to care, at a point in the life course when many of these women were already engaged in caring for their healthy, but quite young, children.

In the following paragraphs I shall attempt to set up a typology of women's motivation to care, using life course position and employment prospects as the crucial variables. In the analysis I shall exclude the four women carers who were caring for their husbands and concentrate only on those eleven women carers who were caring across generations. This is on the grounds that, given that I am positing a choice to care, the marriage relationship contains so many coercive elements as to largely exclude options, at least in the short run.

Women who take on caring while their children are still at home

As *Figure 2* shows, five out of the eleven married women carers under consideration started caring when their children were under the age of fifteen and still at school. One woman (Mrs Knowles) started caring for her mother – in the sense that her mother moved into a granny annexe in their house – when she was pregnant with her youngest child. Why did these women take on these additional caring tasks in such a way that they coincided with child-care?

Reciprocal exchange of services

It is frequently argued by commentators (Bulmer 1986) that caring relationships can be satisfactorily founded on some notion of the reciprocal exchange of services. If that is the case, then there seem to me to be two problems about reciprocity across generations. First, the exchange of services can have very long time lags. Elderly people may be able to make some contribution to the care of infants and very small children, but as they grow more frail they will be less and less able to provide such assistance and they themselves will increasingly be in need of care.

Second, the provision of caring services for children has a time limit to it. Children eventually become less dependent, and at certain crucial ages they start to leave home to go, first to school, and then (it is to be hoped) to work. The provision of caring services for old people has no such time limit, nor such obvious landmarks of reductions in dependency. Thus services rendered to old people may stretch over a very much longer period than reciprocated services to children.

Nevertheless, despite these problems, there seems little doubt that some carers do at least start off with some idea of potential reciprocity between carer and cared for. This seems to have been the case with Mrs Knowles. When Mrs Knowles's mother came to live with them in a 'granny annexe' despite the fact that both Mr and Mrs Knowles had regarded the arrival of this sixty-six-year-old lady with some trepidation, they had nevertheless hoped that she would be able to help out with the care of the young family. This she did in fact do. That was thirteen years ago. Since then the reciprocal services between mother and daughter had grown more and more unequal, partly because the need for help with child-care was no longer quite so pressing, but also because Mrs Knowles's mother was increasingly disabled. Mrs Knowles (who was forty-seven years old) was one of the few women in this sample who was clearly now straining at the leash to get out into the labour market: something, she said somewhat wistfully, she hoped to be able to do 'before I reach retirement age!' Thus this case seems to illustrate the general notion that the *idea* of reciprocity may initiate a caring relationship particularly when a carer's children are infants and hence relatively easy to handle. But the *practice* of reciprocity becomes very diluted and increasingly one-sided as the caring relationship continues, such that other feelings like resentment and frustration come to obscure it and even eclipse it altogether.

Construction of elderly person as another infant

It seems clear to me that it is possible that some women will volunteer to care for an elderly dependent person when they have very *young* children at home on the grounds that the old person can be relatively easily absorbed into the already existing daily round of domestic and caring services. In other words, the elderly person can be 'reconstructed' as an infant – at least in terms of the kind of time and services that have to be expended in his or her care, if not in terms of personality. Within this sample, there was no woman who fitted this description exactly, although one woman showed that the reconstruction of an adult dependant into another infant may be one way of handling what would otherwise be a catastrophe. This was Mrs Fisher – one of the four married women whom I have excluded from this general discussion. But it is worth mentioning her to point out that the onset of her husband's dependency as a result of a brain haemorrhage when her son was only one year old meant that, in effect, she became the mother of two 'infants' and the head of a single-parent family. Her disappointment at this terrible turn of events must have been very nearly overwhelming, but the fact that she was already at home caring for one infant may have made it easier for her to take on the care of an additional person.

As children reach school age – caring as a legitimate alternative to paid work

Increasingly in Britain, as women reach the stage in their lives when they are no longer needed at home to care for pre-school age children, they take up part-time work. In 1981 57 per cent of women whose youngest child was over five but under sixteen were economically active and of those women, the large majority were in part-time work (OPCS, 1984: Tables 4–6). As Nissel shows (Chapter 9) the contribution of the wife's earnings to the household resources are crucial and women with school-age children who do not have paid work of any kind are an increasingly small minority. Some of these women may be unable, rather than unwilling, to find work due to the present recession; others, however, may for whatever reason prefer not to work, particularly those women living in households where the resources are already more than adequate for the kind of standard of living to which they and their families aspire. Many women who married in the 1950s and the early 1960s gave up work, not on the birth of the first child, but on *marriage*. Both they and their husbands are likely still to be strongly committed to the idea that women should not work even when their children are old enough to look after themselves, at least for part of the day.

For such women, with children at school and an adequate standard of living, time may well hang heavy on their hands. A number of factors prevent them from taking up paid work: the attitudes of their own husbands, and the fact that they may not have the skills necessary for work that would be congruent with the social standing they have acquired through their husbands' employment and place in the community. A 'career' as a carer does not disturb their own, their husband's, or their community's image of who and what they are.

In this sample there was one woman who demonstrated some of these characteristics. Mrs Barnes had given up work as a fully qualified SRN when she had married Mr Barnes (a prominent local businessman) in 1964. She had not worked since, despite the fact that her own children were now in the sixth form and at school-leaving age. Mrs Barnes thought of the unpaid caring work she did as very like the paid work she used to do; her use of language made this very clear:

> 'I left work when I married. But since then it's been quite incredible how one's "on call" so often for people. I've had lots of 'patients' since! . . . It's definitely true that I'm more willing to care for gran because I'm a nurse. And because I'm a nurse I can look at it as just another job.'

As a result of her mother-in-law's increasing dependency, Mrs Barnes had given up a number of voluntary and community-oriented activities (such as active participation in the Nurses' League and what she called 'my rugby teams for the school') and replaced these activities with other outside activities largely oriented around caring, including being a founder member of the Carers' Support Group and serving on its committee. At no point in the interview did Mrs Barnes indicate that she missed paid work or that she had any intention of returning to it. At the end of the interview she turned to me as I was leaving and said 'I just don't know *what* I'll do when gran goes.'

Thus the case of Mrs Barnes indicates that, particularly at certain points in the class structure, custom and resources simultaneously operate to keep certain women out of the labour market even when they have reached the point in their personal life course when they have the time and the interest to take on some kind of paid work. They are 'career' carers. Such women constitute a no-doubt diminishing pool of domestic labour to whom the opportunity to care for someone might actually come as something of a relief, as a way of avoiding what might otherwise take on the dimensions of a domestic crisis.

I suggest that this is a diminishing pool of unpaid labour for two reasons: first, the number of women who do not expect to combine paid work with marriage at some point in their life course must, by now, be very small (Martin and Roberts 1984: Chapter 12). Second, the number of married couples with dependent children who can, nevertheless, afford to remain a single-earner household must also be diminishing.

As children reach school age – caring in addition to paid work

If women in paid employment take on caring they will be subject to three sets of demands on their time: their husbands and children, their paid work, and the care of the elderly relative. One might expect such women to illustrate a number of themes. First, the demands on their time are such that one might expect many women to avoid the tasks of caring if they possibly can, and for those who do agree to it to be exceptional along some identifiable dimension. Second, one might expect the contribution that such women make to the household finances to be fairly considerable – not necessarily in terms of absolute amounts but in proportionate terms to the total amount of household income. If that is the case then two things would follow: first, they would be reluctant to give up work or reduce their hours in spite of the enormous stresses on their time; but second, they may be willing to give up work altogether or reduce their hours as their children grow into financial independence. Third, it would be surprising if such women were in paid employment that in any sense constituted a 'career'. Given the other demands on their time, their part-time work would have to be of the kind that makes few emotional and motivational demands. It may also be the case that their husbands are either in employment that is not particularly well paid or even that is somewhat insecure, thus making it all the more important that their wives remain in work despite other considerable calls on their time.

In this sample two women (Mrs Cook and Mrs Lee) were continuing to work part time while caring for an elderly relative and had also been – at least when they began caring – responsible for the care of school age children. Similarly Mrs Evans, who had been caring for her mother for twenty-six years, had been in part-time work and looking after a six-year-old when her mother first came to live with her and her family. All three women demonstrated some of the characteristics that I suggest above might distinguish such women who willingly take on caring despite existing calls on their time. First, all of them made it quite clear to me that they thought there were special reasons why, when they first realized that their mothers needed special care, they were the only people in their immediate kin network who could possibly take on that responsibility. Mrs Lee was an only child. Mrs Cook was not an only child but was an only daughter – a social fact to which she herself accorded some significance. She told me that just before her death her mother had said: 'You will take care of father won't you?' At this Mrs Cook commented: 'And being an *only* daughter one just automatically does'. Mrs Evans had been in a somewhat similar position although, in her case, she had two siblings – a brother and a sister. Mrs Evans's brother's wife had always made it clear that she had no intention of having Mrs Evans's mother – not even to give Mr and Mrs Evans a holiday. Mrs Evans's sister had emigrated after the war.

Thus these three women shared one important special characteristic. It so happened that the people they were caring for when they began caring became highly dependent just at the point in the life course when these women had been relieved of the care of a pre-school aged child and had also taken on part-time work. In all three cases there seems to have been a genuine crisis of dependency: Mrs Lee's mother had a severe heart attack, Mrs Cook's mother was diagnosed as having leukaemia, and Mrs Evans's mother was recently bereaved and her sight was failing fast. Moreover, at the time when these crises occurred there seemed (at least to them) to be no one else in their immediate kin network who could do the work. Certain elements of *chance* (mediated by sex role ideology) combined to ensure that these particular women felt under considerable pressure to take on caring even though their time was already heavily committed elsewhere.

None of the three women had, at the time they started caring, been on a 'career' ladder of employment. Mrs Lee had so far found that caring for her mother fitted in with her morning working hours since she could visit her parents in the afternoons before her children came home from school. However, Mrs Cook and Mrs Evans had had to make changes to their working hours and Mrs Evans eventually and much to her regret had given up work altogether.

Unfortunately, it is impossible to state with any clear or certain detail whether these three women made proportionately large contributions to their household's resources as a result of their paid work, and hence whether pressures of financial need largely motivated their willingness to spread their time in three different directions. Certainly none of these three women had husbands in particularly well-paid employment. Among this tiny and unrepresentative sample their household income was probably lower than average.

I have argued, then, that some women will take on caring even though their time is already heavily committed in both paid and unpaid work when basically three conditions hold. First, a fortuitous set of circumstances whereby an elderly person becomes ill combines with another set of circumstances whereby the carer feels that she and only she is available to care for the elderly person. (I emphasize the word 'she' because it is important to bear in mind that no man already active in the labour market is likely to regard himself – or be regarded – as the carer of the last resort in the same way as a woman would.) Second, the carer is not engaged in a 'career' to which she wants to devote herself body and soul and is highly likely to be in part-time rather than full-time work. However, third, the proportionate contribution that the carer makes to the household income is likely to be relatively high, such that the household would be in financial difficulty if she gave up paid work. Finally it is important to bear in mind that some women carers will simply refuse to give up paid work even if it causes enormous strains on their time because it is only at work that they derive some stature other than that of a domestic and unpaid worker in the home. Of the three women who were discussed in this section, Mrs Evans made it clear that she regretted giving up work to care for her mother because she had been lonely ever since. For every Mrs Evans who gives up work there are probably many other women carers who continue to work part-time because they regard their work as crucial to their sense of self.

Women who take on caring as their children are leaving home or long after their children have left home

To prevent the 'empty nest' syndrome

By the time the children are about to or have left home, one can expect that in the 1980s most of their mothers will be in their late forties to early fifties (see Nissel, Chapter 9). Before their marriage most of these women will have worked although very few of them will have left the parental home to do so. After marriage, although most of them will have continued to work until the birth of their first child, between a quarter and a third of them will have given up work on marriage (Martin and Roberts 1984).

The older these women are the less likely are they to have returned to work after the birth of their first child and the longer the time taken to return to work after the last birth (Martin and Roberts 1984: Chapter 9). Nevertheless, paid work is important to women of all ages and, indeed, Martin and Roberts suggest that by the time women at present aged fifty to fifty-nine are sixty, they will have spent 59 per cent of their possible working time at work (Martin and Roberts 1984: Table 9.5). It is nevertheless also true to say that women at present over the age of fifty have, over their recent past, been rather more child-care oriented than work oriented relative to younger cohorts of women.

Mrs Jackson, the wife of an academic, had had four children and was now caring for her mother-in-law. At the time her mother-in-law came to live with the Jacksons they had two children aged fifteen and seventeen still living at home; the older two had already left home. A few years earlier, seeing that her children were well on the way to independence, Mrs Jackson had decided to retrain as a teacher and subsequently got a part-time job as a school-teacher. However, Mrs Jackson discovered she was not altogether happy with her job and when, after a few years she also found that she would need some time off from the school in order to recover from an operation she decided to resign. It was at this juncture, with her children rapidly growing up and away that her mother-in-law became seriously ill at the age of eighty-seven and had to spend some time in hospital. On the discharge of the old lady, Mrs Jackson volunteered to care for her even though others were available to take on the task. Mrs Jackson therefore was both voluntarily prolonging her caring responsibilities and thereby postponing what might otherwise have been a rather painful period in her life. It seems that the moment when the old lady became in need of care coincided with a patch in Mrs Jackson's life when she was looking around for someone to care for, at least in the short run, while Mrs Jackson once again rethought her future. With the end of motherhood staring her in the face, her mother-in-law must have appeared as something of a *deus ex machina*.

There are certain parallels between Mrs Jackson and Mrs Barnes, whom I have previously described as a 'career' carer, and, as we shall see in the next section, with Mrs Green. Both Mrs Jackson and Mrs Barnes had husbands in well-paid work such that their own potential contribution from any paid work they might do was not essential for the financial survival of the household. If paid income was not necessary for the income it generated then, for different reasons, neither did it hold out many other attractions. Both women had taken on unpaid caring in order to avoid or postpone paid work, and prolong domesticity.

Such women cannot be that unusual: as I have already suggested, there is something of a cohort of women who married in the 1950s and early 1960s for whom prolonged domesticity may still conform with their more youthful intentions. There are, however, almost certainly class dimensions that determine who, within this cohort, will now be available for caring, since the decision to care necessarily entails taking on the extra expense of caring for someone at the same time as rejecting the possibility of becoming a two-earner household. Such class dimensions may also coincide with tenure and age dimensions, since, if the household is in owner-occupation *and* the mortgage is paid off, then such households will not only have lost the expense of caring for children but also have, by the time the couple have reached their middle fifties, very considerably reduced housing costs. In contrast, council tenants, whose housing costs tend to rise with inflation and only come down when household income is drastically reduced through retirement, would not be as freely available; almost certainly they would have to combine caring with some form of employment for the female carer.

To talk in terms of the special characteristic of a particular age cohort rather indicates that, in future, women will be less willing to postpone or avoid paid work when their children grow up and away. That may indeed be the case, although there are also countervailing tendencies, one predictable, the other less so. In the first place, given the expansion of owner-occupation in recent years, it will increasingly be the case that many households will find that their children have left home just at the point when their housing costs are also drastically reduced (see Nissel, Chapter 9). Thus, in financial terms, there will be fewer households who find themselves in the position of having to have two earners in order to maintain the standard of living that they have come to expect in their middle age. If that is the case, then it may also follow that women in younger age cohorts will be willing to make themselves available for caring at this point in the life course. Second, the prospects for employment of both men and women are unpredictable; it may be the case that by the time the cohorts of women at present bearing and rearing very small children reach their own middle age, the availability of paid work for them will be somewhat reduced, and they would in principle be available for caring. On the other hand, it is possible that men's unemployment will be higher than women's, particularly in some parts of the country, in which case more women will have to go to work in order for the household simply to survive. Whether unemployed men will take on the tasks of caring is a moot point; the research on domestic labour and paid work rather indicates that they will not (Pahl 1984).

Caring as a legitimate alternative to paid work: the importance of health

As the case of Mrs Jackson above makes clear, there are some women who take up caring because they think they will prefer it to paid work. But there was at least one other woman in the sample who had taken up caring in order to be able to legitimately give up paid work. Mrs Green was married to a local government officer and had, until recently, worked as a cashier/

book-keeper in a multiple store. She told me that she gave up work because 'I could see this coming'. Although, at the time she gave up work, none of her elderly relatives was in immediate need of care, Mrs Green fully expected that her services could be called upon at any time. This was because she seemed to be the only woman in the immediate kin network of both her parents-in-law and her mother since both Mr and Mrs Green had been only children.

Mrs Green's resignation from work had also coincided with a period of illness from which she knew she would need some time to recover. This seems to me to be rather important especially because a similar story emerged from Mrs Jackson. Given that many women in their fifties do experience quite severe health problems they may think that they will find caring less of a strain on their health than paid work. However, giving up work in favour of unpaid caring on health grounds may not be entirely voluntary. Given that so many women are in *part-time* paid work, their rights to remain in a job, especially those employed less than sixteen hours a week, are not fully protected under the Employment Protection legislation. They are neither protected from dismissal should they need to take time off work over a long period on grounds of sickness, nor are they eligible for sick pay under the National Insurance scheme. Moreover, even if they are eligible under that scheme, the fact that employers are now responsible for the first six weeks of sick pay means that there are also considerable incentives on employers to dismiss their eligible employees if they possibly can. Thus women in their middle fifties who became ill are particularly vulnerable to 'persuasion' or even enforcement to leave their jobs altogether, just at the point in their life course when they are likely to have elderly kin becoming increasingly frail. Assuming that their husbands continue to work until the men's retirement age of sixty-five, these women will have approximately fifteen years in which they have nothing to do but keep a largely empty house. The opportunity to care for an elderly relative may indeed appear as something of a godsend since it both legitimizes their apparent 'idleness', provides an occupation for their time, and may also, at least initially, offer some companionship in what would otherwise be a rather isolated and potentially boring life.

But before leaping to the conclusion that illness in middle age drives many women to caring it is also important to remember that, just as with women who take on caring to postpone the 'empty nest syndrome' so there may well be class and income dimensions to these women's willingness to care. Morbidity is not a fixed or finite state and it is highly likely that many middle-aged women who need the money for themselves and their households will continue to struggle into paid work when their bodies are crying out in protest and against their own (and others') better judgement.

Caring in addition to paid work

Mrs Jackson and Mrs Green, both of whom had ostensibly given up work to care for an elderly relative, were, however, somewhat unusual women. Most women continue to work even when they have an elderly relative to care for. According to Martin and Roberts, amongst women up to age fifty-nine who were caring for an elderly relative, 58 per cent were still economically active, of whom just over half were working part-time (Martin and Roberts 1984: Table 8.35). Unfortunately, Martin and Roberts do not break their employment and caring data down by age or life course stage, but given that they also found that in their sample of women aged up to fifty-nine, the majority of carers (70 per cent) were over forty years old (Martin and Roberts 1984: Table 8.91) we have to assume that the majority of women in their sample who were caring, but whose children had left home, were still in paid work of some kind. On page 197, where the women who had remained in work at the time they took on caring despite also having quite young children were under discussion, I suggested that these women probably stayed in work because they and their families particularly needed their financial contribution and also because their paid work was important to them as a source of independence and sense of self. And on page 201 I suggested that there may be rather special reasons why women without the care of children give up paid work apparently in order to care for an elderly person. Those reasons, I suggested, probably have a considerable amount to do with their own health, their attitude towards their health and paid work, and their rights to remain in a particular job despite needing a long period of convalescence.

However, most women in their fifties are in active and good health, and even if they are not, they continue to work. Thus it would have been extremely surprising if, even in this unrepresentative sample, there were not some women who continued to work, especially among those women whose children had left home.

There were, in fact, two women who had no children living at home at the time they started caring and who were still in paid work at the time of the interview. These were Mrs Hall and Miss Nicholson, who had one important thing in common. Both of them had organized their lives in such a way that of all the carers, they, and one other, were the ones that had sufficiently extensive help to suggest that they should be considered as 'joint carers' with one other person without whom it would have been out of the question for either of them to continue in paid work. Moreover, both of them had particularly pressing reasons for wanting to stay in paid work. In Miss Nicholson's case her determination probably reflected the fact that she particularly needed that continuity in her life in order to maintain her self-identity. In Mrs Hall's case, it is interesting to note that she struggled into work despite the fact that she was quite severely disabled with arthritis. Indeed, her 'joint caring' arrangement had really only got going when she had had to go into hospital for an operation on her knee and she had decided that, rather than leave her mother entirely in her husband's care, she needed the further help of her friend and neighbour. Her household was dependent on her earnings from her thirty hour-a-week job, and in recently purchasing their council house had incurred a considerable debt at an age when most owner-occupiers would be about to finish paying their mortgage. Although I have no hard and fast data to indicate as much, I suspect that the Halls were in no position to become a single-earner household with the additional expense of caring for Mrs Hall's mother.

Given that I have suggested that both these carers were completely dependent on the services of the 'joint carer' in their lives to allow them to continue in paid work, it is also important to note the corollary to this arrangement: if either of these joint caring arrangements breaks down, then neither of these carers will be able to carry on working. A parallel situation exists for those women carers who first take on caring while they are still in paid work and who are unable to find someone else with whom to share the caring work. For them there must eventually come a point when the needs of the person they are caring for are such that they feel that they can no longer remain in paid work and have to give it up in order to care for their dependants full time. In this sample two women had found themselves in that position: Mrs Mitchell had given up work to care for her husband and Mrs Evans had eventually reluctantly given up work to care for her mother.

CONCLUSIONS

In this chapter I began by distinguishing between the life courses of men and women carers and suggested that the importance of full-time paid work in men's life courses was enough to 'blot out' any other calls upon their time. Women, on the other hand, experience life as a conglomeration of continuous demands, emanating from different sources. Hence it is not surprising that women carers in this sample started caring at a variety of points in their personal life courses. This is not to say that the other demands on women's time, namely child-care and paid work, are not important in determining whether or not, at a particular point in her life, a woman will become available or decide to become available for the caring task. But a woman will, if possible, combine these roles as mother, paid worker, and carer or, at the very least, juggle them together in order to maximize the servicing that she can adequately provide for members of her family.

At the start of the discussion of the life course position of women carers, I distinguished between the women carers' life course position at the time of the interview with their life course position at the time when they began caring. In so doing two things became clear: first, the women carers may well have been feeling particularly frustrated with their caring at the time of the interview since almost all of them had finished caring for their children or were well within sight of that goal, and hence caring was increasingly incongruent with the rest of their lives. But second, by looking at the point in the life course when these women took on caring it was possible to see that some had initiated caring at a point in their life courses when the tasks of caring were particularly compatible with other domestic parts of their lives. It was for this reason I suggested that, where caring occurs between generations rather than between spouses it seems to fit in with particular life course stages, and there seems to be an element of 'voluntariness' about the initiation of the caring relationship. Given the other two calls on women's time – namely, child-care and paid work – I suggest that these two factors might be the crucial variables in analysing the decision to care.

Ideally an analysis of the decision to care should include an analysis of the decision not to care.If that were possible then one might see more clearly how far some people do 'volunteer' to care and what are the particular circumstances under which they make that decision. But in a study of carers only, the best one can do is to look at the particular variables that one thinks may affect that decision and how far those variables seem to tell a sensible and internally consistent story. It is this largely inductive method that I have used to draw up a typology of the decision by women to take on caring for someone other than their husbands. In that typology I assumed that life course position and position in the labour market (both actual and potential) were crucial variables and analysed the interviews within that framework. For that typology I devised the following categories:

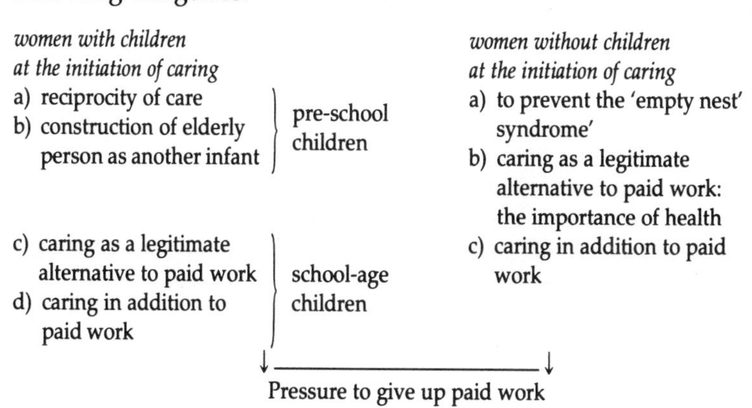

For each category in this typology I discussed cases that seemed to demonstrate some of the reasons why women, at those particular points in their lives, should apparently 'choose' to take on caring.

I am quite certain this typology is not complete. For one thing it has taken account of the circumstances only of married and never married women and excludes the circumstances of divorced and separated women simply because they did not occur in this small sample. The typology is only an interpretation of the circumstances of the women carers whom I interviewed and as such it should be treated as a research tool rather than a research finding. There is one more extremely important proviso to make about it: I have referred throughout this particular discussion to the element of 'voluntariness' in the motivation to care; but this is to lose the sense in which *no* woman is a 'volunteer'. By this I mean that women, in contrast to men, are subject to considerable ideological and material pressure to be the carers of the last resort largely irrespective of their personal circumstances, and whether or not on an individual basis they would rather spend their time in paid work or caring more completely for their children. (I have discussed these issues elsewhere [Ungerson 1983] and so will not go into great detail about them at this juncture.) Although this sample cannot be used to draw any inference about the general incidence of caring between the sexes, it is in my opinion important and significant that there was not a single man in this sample who was caring for someone other than his wife. In other words, only women are apparently the appropriate people to combine caring with paid work and child-care and to care for dependants of a different generation from themselves. But within the general group of women as a whole, there is usually some choice as to which particular woman should take on caring when it is called for. There were at least some women in this sample who did not seem to be the most obvious candidates to care for the particular elderly person for whom they had assumed responsibility. Some of the reasons why they apparently 'volunteered' have been outlined in the discussion in this chapter; other reasons, more concerned with individual feelings than with labour market position or life course point, will be discussed elsewhere (Ungerson forthcoming).

Finally, it is important to point out that there are both considerable parallels with the care of children, while, at the same time, there are also interesting contrasts. In the first place, neither the care of small children nor the care of elderly dependants is compatible with full-time work unless some alternative form of supplementary care can be found from within the kin or marital network, from the public sector, or from private sources. But pressures to work and the availability of time to work increase as children grow older while in contrast, as the elderly age even further, there are considerable pressures on the carer to reduce working hours or to give it up altogether. However, just as with child-care, the care of the elderly and women's position in the labour market are inextricably linked. Lower wages and lack of protection for periods off work, linked to part-time working, all combine to make women rather than men the likely carers should it become necessary to care for a relative at home. Similarly caring may in itself weaken women's labour market position because of the need to take time off work when crises occur. Moreover, where women expect to have to take on the full-time care of an elderly person at some time in the future this may well stop those women from pursuing goals related to their position in the labour market.

Finally, however, caring for an elderly dependant is *unlike* child-care in one important respect. Children only have one mother; elderly people generally have more than one child and children-in-law. In other words, the network of obligations and pressures on mothers to care for their children are rather different from the comparable pressures on children to care for their parents or parents-in-law. Mothers are spot-lighted. Children, and especially daughters and daughters-in-law, are simply lit; their position in their personal life course provides the stage backdrop.

REFERENCES

Briggs, A. and Oliver, J. (1985) *Caring: Experiences of Looking After Disabled Relatives*. London: Routledge & Kegan Paul.

Bulmer, M. (1986) *Neighbours: The work of Philip Abrams*. Cambridge: Cambridge University Press.

Central Statistical Office (1984) *Social Trends 14*. London: HMSO.

Cmnd. 9517 (1985) *Reform of Social Security*. London: HMSO.

Martin, J. and Roberts, C. (1984) *Women and Employment: A Lifetime Perspective*. London: HMSO.

Nissel, M. and Bonnerjea, L. (1982) *Family Care of the Handicapped Elderly: Who Pays?* No. 602. London: Policy Studies Institute.

Office of Population Censuses and Surveys (1984) *The General Household Survey 1983*. London: HMSO.

Pahl, R.E. (1984) *Divisions of Labour*. Oxford: Blackwell.

Thatcher, M. (1981) Facing the Now Challenge. In C. Ungerson (ed.) (1985) *Women and Social Policy, a Reader*. London: Macmillan.

Ungerson, C. (1981) *Gender Divisions and Community Care*. End of Award Report to the ESRC, lodged in British Library Lending Division.

Ungerson, C. (forthcoming) *Nursing for Nothing: Sex, Gender, and Informal Care*. London: Tavistock.

9
Social change and the family cycle

Muriel Nissel

THE SIGNIFICANCE OF GENERATIONAL CHANGE

Introduction

'All the world's a stage . . .
And one man in his time plays many parts
His acts being seven ages . . .
. . . Last scene of all,
That ends this strange eventful history,
Is second childishness and mere oblivion,
Sans teeth, sans eyes, sans taste, sans everything.'
(Shakespeare, *As You Like It*)

In each of Shakespeare's seven ages, the life course is determined both by the biological fact of ageing and by the historical circumstances and the cultural norm of the time in which it is lived. Many of the seventh age today may be confused, but with teeth, with eyes, and with a great deal else besides. Life style, at any particular stage of the life cycle or life course, depends very much on what a person brings into it and what kind of human capital in its broadest sense he or she has amassed during that lifetime. People are born with inherent characteristics and the circumstances in which they grow up determine the extent to which they can fulfil their potential. Some people are inherently more gifted, stronger, and healthier, both mentally and physically, than others. But, whatever these innate characteristics, the environment into which they are born, particularly the parents they have and the love and affection as well as the material advantages they receive, will powerfully influence the kind of human beings they become.

As an illustration of the influence of environment on development, the author of the present chapter introduces in the paragraphs below a brief biographical note comparing certain aspects of her own life with those of her mother. She then contrasts this with the changing background which has affected the life course of her daughter. The second part of the chapter reviews the main demographic changes which have been taking place during the past century, particularly those which have affected family structure. The third part of the chapter discusses some of the economic changes, mainly employment and income, which have led to differing family life styles. Finally, it sums up the impact of some of these social and political changes on the various generations who have lived through them, thus linking the chapter back to the experiences of the author's own family.

Family history

My mother was in many ways typical of the middle class of her generation living in rural England. She was born shortly before the turn of the century, the second of eight children, two of whom died shortly after birth. One of the babies who died, the third child, was a boy, and it was my mother's firm belief that the grief her mother felt at the loss of this much-prized first male child was reflected in resentment towards her second child, my mother, who was still a very demanding baby. The father of the family died at the age of thirty-two, leaving his widow to bring up single-handed six children, the eldest of whom was twelve. This young family thus lost its male breadwinner but, compared with most such 'lone parent' families in our present society, they had certain advantages. The family owned a modest-sized mixed farm which the widow, as well as bringing up her six children, successfully managed. They were not rich but they had enough to eat and were not deprived in the way they might be today. The children walked to school, three miles there and three miles back, and the three boys were put through engineering apprenticeships before taking up farming themselves or, in the case of the eldest, being killed in the First World War. My mother's younger sister married a farmer and emigrated to Canada: her elder sister also married a farmer and settled next to the family farm.

My mother herself came to London. Her family had rejected her when she became pregnant by a young man who (so the story goes) had the effrontery to be drowned at sea before he could make an honest woman of her and she thus sought the anonymity which the big city could give. She managed to survive with the help of religious and charitable organizations but her health suffered under the strain and she had a prolapse after the birth of the baby. She eventually took a job as a governess looking after other people's children but she also tried to keep contact with her own child by fostering her – and even driving a motor bike so she could visit her – but the struggle was too great and the little girl was eventually adopted by a couple who were unable to have children of their own.

At the end of the First World War, when she was aged twenty-nine, my mother married a thirty-five-year-old Welshman whose parents came to London from Wales towards the end of the nineteenth century. His mother, as was the custom of the time, had been sent to London to be 'put into service' and she met her future husband at the Welsh Tabernacle in King's Cross. The family genealogy on my grandfather's side, written on the fly leaf of the family Bible as was the tradition in Wales, is a microcosm of family experiences of births and deaths in the nineteenth century. During the fifteen years from 1836 to 1850 my great grandparents bore six live children, only three of whom survived beyond their teens. My paternal grandfather lived until the age of forty-eight and, like my mother's father, when he died he left a widow and young children. She was able to bring them up by continuing the family business (an 'oil' shop in Islington). She herself lived until she was eighty-four and, unlike my father who was born after his grandparents had died, I remember my grandmother well.

My father died of a heart attack when he was sixty-four and my mother was fifty-nine. She was still an attractive and much-sought-after woman but, as she cynically and uncharacteristically remarked to me, those who wooed her were principally in search of a housekeeper to succour them in their old age and she could enjoy their company without having to marry them. Thus for the next twenty-four years my mother was a widow, almost as long as the thirty years she had been married. She spent the last seven years of her life in a 'granny' flat in our house and finally died of pneumonia at the age of eighty-three with her body otherwise healthy and her mind still lively but without her teeth, with failing eyesight, and very hard of hearing.

My own history has been differently shaped. The times in which I have lived and the circumstances surrounding me have inevitably compelled me to lead a very different life.

I was born in 1921, the year of the post-war 'baby boom', and grew up in the 1920s and 1930s. The fact that I was an only child was due, not to my parents' choice, but to my mother's health and miscarriages following the birth of her earlier child, something that the better maternity care and health services of today could have prevented.

Unlike my mother, who was born into a rural agricultural community and moved to London only to avoid the stigma of bearing an illegitimate child in a small close-knit society, I was born and grew up in London and its suburbs. With the help of money inherited from my mother's eldest brother who died in the First World War we bought a house in the country some fifteen miles from the centre of the city and we moved there when I was still a small child.

Money was not plentiful but my father, who was a middle-grade civil servant, was never unemployed like so many others during the depression years of the 1930s. It would never have occurred to my mother to try to supplement the family income by working for money. Not only would it not have been socially acceptable, but also she was happy and contented with her life as it was.

At one point we ran into debt and various pieces of furniture were sold; the reason for this is unclear but it could have been high medical costs when both my mother and father were ill.

Though his comparatively low salary would have entitled him to it, my father never became what was then known as a 'panel' patient and the family doctor, complete with yellow waistcoat and grey topper, always called at the house. We never went to his surgery which was some three miles distant; our minor ailments we discussed with the local pharmacist who, unusually for the time, was a woman.

My education was a problem. Class barriers inhibited any possibility of going to the local state primary school, or 'Board' school as it was still known from the days of the school boards set up under the Education Act, 1870. So I went to a 'dame' school. Secondary school was more difficult. The nearest grammar school was in a different county and would not accept me and, from the age of ten, I travelled ten miles to school by train. At the age of twelve I won a scholarship to a girls' public school where I became a boarder: it did not cover the whole cost and I was always acutely conscious of the strain it imposed on my parents.

University was something which few girls and their parents aspired to and, for the most part, my fellow pupils at school regarded their education as a way of 'finishing' them in acquiring the social skills and preparing them for marriage. But a group of us, stimulated by our university-trained teachers, perceived that we could widen our horizons and greatly increase our earning capacity if we went on to study further. The importance which my father's Welsh background put on education and the timely benefit of a small inheritance from my paternal grandmother (originally stemming from money sent to her by her oil-rich brothers who had emigrated to North America in the latter half of the nineteenth century) combined to make it a possibility. I studied history, French, and music in my sixth-form years; mathematics, which would have been my natural choice, was ruled out because my school was not able to teach it. At the beginning of the Second World War, with the help of a small grant from the local authority, I went to Oxford to study philosophy, politics, and economics. This was unique in our little neighbourhood and immensely raised our family status in the local street.

After university I became a temporary civil servant, this being regarded as a suitable alternative to being drafted into the armed forces or other forms of war work. At the end of the war, as men

– and women – returned from the forces, it was they who were regarded as the heroes and whose jobs and careers were given preference. People who had been in civilian employment, who were predominantly women, had to take a back seat. In many jobs, for example, those who had been in the services were allowed to count the whole of their war service towards their pensions whereas my work in government service was only allowed to reckon as half. Moreover I was not able to compete for the permanent Civil Service because there was a bar to the acceptance of married women and I, misguidedly, had already married. The bar was lifted in 1946 and, after taking the entrance examination, I became an established civil servant at the beginning of 1948.

My marriage was preceded by a period of living together with my husband-to-be, a civil engineer from South Africa. This unmarried state struck horror and consternation into my parents. The subsequent rift with them was such that, when I later wished for a divorce, pride prevented me from leaving my husband until my father died. The decision to marry, following this period of living together, was prompted partly by the fact that it was still socially difficult and a continual nuisance to have to explain why we were not married and also by our own wish to tie our union legally when my husband left England to work abroad.

My second marriage was to a musician who came to this country from Austria in 1939. We married in 1957 and my first child, a daughter, was born a year later. I remained at work until a few weeks before she was born. This was still not entirely acceptable in certain quarters and, on the occasions when I needed to go there for meetings, the Bank of England made it clear that an obviously pregnant woman, even as an emissary of Her Majesty's Treasury, was not welcome.

My second child, a son, was born in 1962 and, for the next five years, I continued to work at home, looking after the children and taking part in various local activities. I became a magistrate and for a short while also worked on a research project, rather to the envy of many of my academically qualified 'housewife' neighbours with growing children who were by this time beginning to wonder what the future held for them.

The two main problems most of us faced were, first the lack of retraining opportunities which could give the confidence needed to return to a regular job and, second, how to get the money to pay for child-care and settle the children before we actually left to work outside the home. The money might be there once the job had been secured and started but it was often difficult to tide over the transition.

I was fortunate in having Civil Service colleagues who encouraged me to rejoin them and enough money to employ resident child-care. I also had, as a statistician, certain specialist qualifications which were in demand and this helped me to go back into the Civil Service, in a temporary capacity, at the same level on the salary scale as when I left nine years earlier; the usual practice at this time was to have to start all over again at the bottom level.

The re-entry was traumatic. My erstwhile contemporaries were all very senior and high-ranking. I was working four days a week (plus another half day as a magistrate) but none the less tended to be regarded as 'that part-time woman'. Of equal importance was the lack of retraining. During my spell working at home the approach to statistics had been revolutionalized by the introduction of computers and there was no way I could find a suitable course to give me the type of updating that was so much needed.

I subsequently became re-established in the permanent Civil Service and can now benefit from an occupational pension. I did however leave before retiring age to start a new career in research. I had the advantage of a high-earning husband and, as is the case with so many other women, the flexibility and lesser responsibility of this type of academic work was attractive. It also had the great advantage of enabling me to retire, or semi-retire, in stages by gradually reducing the number of hours worked.

My own daughter has experienced, directly or indirectly, neither the poverty of the depression years in the 1930s nor the levelling effect of the war years in the 1940s. She spent her early childhood in the 'never had it so good' material prosperity of the 1960s, when there was still a mood of optimism, before the welfare state began to be dismantled and before unemployment and inflation dominated people's attitudes. Throughout her life she has had available to her free health and education services and her middle-class environment gave her every encouragement to go on to some form of further education.

She has been able to take advantage of the greater freedom of choice which less rigid class distinctions now make possible for the younger generations. Her friends come from varied backgrounds and have very different types of jobs. Her experience has also been greatly enriched by the growth of communications which have enabled her to travel the world in a way it would never have been possible or permitted for me to do. She has benefited in particular from the more equal opportunities and much greater freedom which women now have with men. The 'pill' and other factors have fundamentally changed the attitude of the sexes towards one another. A woman is no longer dependent on a man in the way she was even a generation ago. Though she is still disadvantaged compared with a man, she is in a better position to earn her own living, and the decision whether or not to have a child can be her own.

This changed relationship, enabling men and women to regard each other more equally as friends and companions, has inevitably affected attitudes to marriage. To the extent that marriage becomes less of a career and a financial investment, the man-hunt which precedes it is directed more at companionship and fatherhood. Indeed the marriage bond as a legal contract becomes less important and its meaning and substance more so. Cohabiting in a continuing relationship is now accepted and my daughter's first common-law union provoked no raised eyebrows either from her parents or their friends.

She too lives in London, not out of choice but because for her that is where the jobs and career opportunities lie. The shadow of unemployment and, at the same time, a better appreciation of the fact that work and a career are not ends in themselves, are two of the factors which differentiate my daughter's generation from my own. Whereas I was able (though not without difficulty) to return to paid work after a period at home caring for children, the prospects of re-entering the labour market and finding a well paid job are now much worse.

I have described this little family history of grandmother, mother, and daughter at some length to emphasize the importance of generational change. Certain features of my parents' and my children's background are significantly different from my own because of the time in which they lived and are living and the circumstances surrounding me and my family have inevitably compelled us to follow very different paths. Some of these more general issues will be discussed in the rest of the chapter. The section which follows considers the demographic changes.

DEMOGRAPHIC TRENDS

Table 3 Demographic changes: population, age structures, and household size, Great Britain[1]

life cycle stages	*birth years*	*population (millions)*	*age structure (percentages)*				*persons per household*
			under 15	*15–44*	*45–59*	*60 and over*	
children and adolescents	1984	55	19	43	17	21	2.6
	1981–83	54	20	42	18	20	2.7
	1971–80	54	24	39	18	19	2.9
young adults	1961–70	52	23	40	20	17	3.1
	1951–60	49	22	43	19	16	3.2
middle aged	1941–50	47	21	47	18	14	n.a.
	1931–40	45	24	47	17	12	3.7
	1921–30	43	28	47	16	9	4.1
elderly	1911–20	41	31	48	13	8	4.4
	1901–10	37	33	48	12	7	4.6
	[1851	21	36	46	11	7	n.a.]

Note: [1]Up to 1931 Census enumerated population; from 1941 to 1971 total population; after 1981 resident population. Figures relate to beginning of each period.

Sources: Report of the Population Panel (1973).
Census Reports.

Tables 3 and 4 show some of the demographic factors over the last century which set the background to the lives of successive generations. The left side of *Table 3*, indicates, for those who are alive today in 1986, the birth years of those in four main stages of the life cycle: children and adolescents (aged seventeen and under), young adults (aged eighteen to twenty-nine), those in the middle phase of life (aged thirty to sixty-four), and those who are elderly (aged sixty-five and over). Thus those who are children and adolescents were born in 1968 or later, young adults were born between 1956 and 1967, the middle-aged between 1921 and 1955, and the elderly before 1921.

Table 4 *Demographic changes: births, marriages, and divorce, Great Britain*

year	*birth-rates per 1000 women 15–44*[1]	*illegit-imate births as per cent of total births*[1]	*total period fertility rate*[2,5]	*sex ratio: males per 100 women 15–44 (UK)*[2]	*women aged 30: per cent ever married (E&W)*[2]	*median age of marriage of spinsters (E&W)*[1]	*persons divorcing per 100 married population (E&W)*[1]
1984	60	17[3]	1.8	102	n.a.	22.6	12.0
1981–83	61	14	1.8	103	89	22.1	12.0
1971–80	66	10	2.4	103	91	21.5	9.8
1961–70	90	7	2.8	101	89	21.3	3.2
1951–60	78	5	2.2	99	82	22.1	2.3
1941–50	75	6		97	75	22.9	2.4
1931–40	62	5		91	70	24.2	0.5
1921–30	76	5		88		24.3	0.4
1911–20	89	5		93		24.5	0.2
1901–10	110	4		92		25.0	0.1
1891–1900	123	4[3]		92			
1881–90	139	5[3]					
1871–80	154	5[3]		92			
1861–70	152	6[3]					
1851–60	146	7[3]		93[4]			

Notes: 1 average for period
2 beginning of period
3 England and Wales
4 aged 15–49
5 average number of children which would be born per woman if women experienced the age-specific fertility rates of the period in question throughout their child-bearing span.

Sources: Report of the Population Panel (1973). Census reports and other publications of the Office of Population Censuses and Surveys.

These stages have been somewhat arbitrarily selected and relate mainly to biological development. They correspond only very broadly to other events in the life course, such as births, marriages, employment, education, housing, and so on. Most people marry and bear children during the 'young adult' phase but many do not. Some never marry or never have children. A few may already have married or have borne children by the time they are aged eighteen whereas others may wait until they are thirty or more. Similarly in the middle and later phases of life there is no 'average' or representative life course and many different patterns emerge (Murphy 1983: Tables 2 and 3).

The choice of life cycle phases, moreover, is coloured by changing social attitudes over time, or what is known as the cohort effect. Someone who is considered a child or an old person today would certainly have been differently regarded, not only at the beginning of the century but even a generation ago. For example, the age of majority, which carries with it the right to vote and to marry without parental consent, was lowered in 1969 from twenty-one to eighteen. Not only were young people legally adults, independent of their parents and individuals in their own right, at this younger age, but the change also reflected a variety of social and other factors, such as earlier physical maturity, the higher level of education, and the greater economic independence of young people, leading to their earlier acceptance as adults. Similarly at the turn of the century people were regarded as old at a much younger age, if only because there were relatively fewer of them: those aged sixty and over made up only 7 per cent of the population compared with 20 per cent today. Moreover people born in the nineteenth century grew up against a background of poverty, hard work, and poor housing and when health and educational levels and expectations from life generally were lower. These circumstances inevitably coloured the way their lives subsequently developed.

Population

The population of Britain more than doubled from 1851 to 1951 when it reached 49 million. Since then the growth has slowed and the number is not expected to reach more than 55 million by the end of the present century. *Figure 3* shows that the number of deaths, despite the increase in the total population, have increased only very gradually during the present century. Births, on the other hand, have fluctuated widely with high numbers in a particular period tending to set up cyclical fluctuations as the girl babies become fertile a generation later.

Figure 3 Population changes and projections, United Kingdom

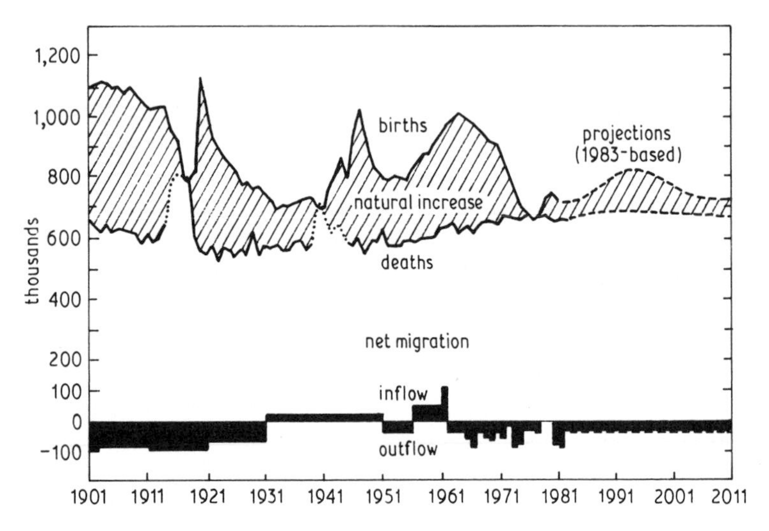

Source: Central Statistical Office (1985): Chart 1.6.

Figure 4 Population age structure, Great Britain

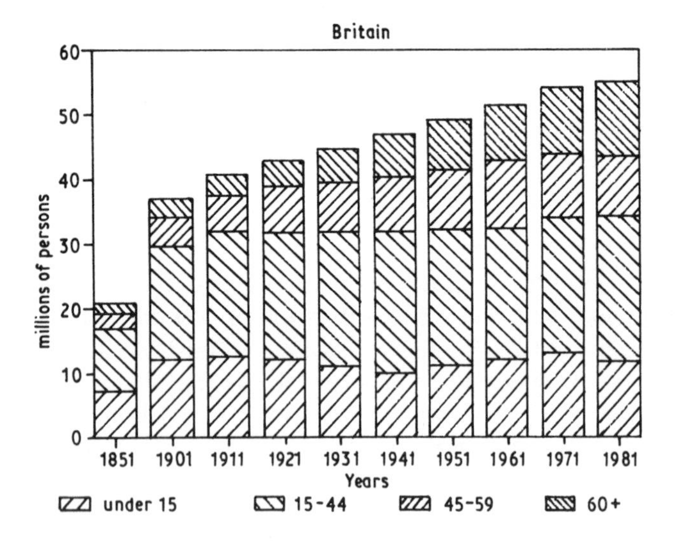

One of the big changes since the mid-1950s has been the influx of people of different ethnic origins bringing with them different life styles and cultural patterns. This has changed the ethnic balance of the population and it is estimated that some 6 per cent are now of non-white origin. About half of these are of West Indian, Guyanese, Indian, or Pakistani ethnic origin. Nearly three-fifths of the West Indian or Guyanese and over two-fifths of the Indian population live in Greater London. The population of Pakistani ethnic origin live predominantly in Greater London and in the West Midlands and West Yorkshire metropolitan counties (Central Statistical Office 1985: 23).

Figure 4 shows the age structure of the population. The interesting feature of the chart is the extent to which almost the whole of the increase in population has been in the age group forty-five and over. The actual number of children is very much the same today as it was at the beginning of the century but there are relatively fewer of them. This has important implications for family and household structure. There has been a marked decrease in household size during the present century and, in the last thirty years, it has been largely concentrated amongst the one- and two-person households: indeed, since 1951, the whole of the increase of 5 million in the total number of households has been accounted for by these small households. This in turn can be largely attributed to the ageing structure of the population and the fact that old people, even at the beginning of the century, tend to live separately from their children. The change is thus not primarily due to different living patterns but to the different population structure.

Unjustified conclusions about radical changes in the way we live are often drawn from statistics showing increases in the number of small households because the data are analysed at one point in time and the longitudinal aspect is overlooked. For example, it is often noted that only 13 per cent of families consist of the so-called 'representative' two adults and two children. This is merely a snapshot on a particular date and, during the life course, nearly all of us go through the phase of living with at least one parent and most of us with two (Murphy 1983: Figure 1).

There are however other factors underlying the increasing number of small households which do reflect changes in the way we live. These include earlier separation of young people from their parents before marriage; increased numbers of one-parent families; separation and divorce; and the earlier impact of the 'empty nest' stage when children have left home (Kiernan 1985). Some of these issues are discussed in later paragraphs.

Expectation of life

Figure 5 Expectation of life, Great Britain

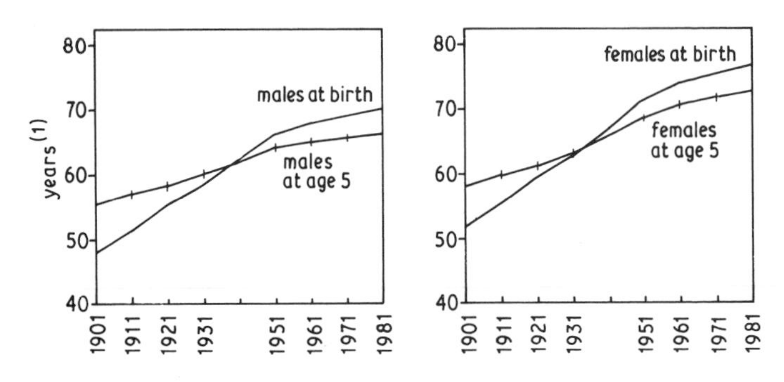

Note: [1] Further number of years which a person can expect to live
Sources: Report of the Population Panel (1973). CSO (1985) *Social Trends 16*. London: HMSO.

Figure 5 shows changes in the expectation of life. A boy baby born in the middle of the last century could not on average expect to live beyond the age of forty; a girl baby could expect to live two years longer. Today the expectation of life for men has increased to seventy years and for women to seventy-six. This has resulted mainly from the steep decline in infant mortality and in the deaths of young children from infectious diseases. Once they reached the age of twenty, even in the middle of the last century, men could expect to live another thirty-nine years and women another forty. Today the figures are fifty-one and fifty-seven years respectively. Death nevertheless (as was the case for both the author's grandfathers) brought single parenthood to many families much earlier than it does today and, unless they separate, couples who marry can expect to share a longer life together. This factor, although only one amongst many, has played a part in changing attitudes towards divorce and separation in the second half of the present century. Just as the untimely death of a loved partner is less likely to be feared today, so death will less frequently bring release from an unhappy marriage. The importance of death at the beginning of the century as a factor in breaking up marriages and creating one-parent families through widow(er)hood has given way in the latter part to increased numbers of such families arising from divorce and separation. The changed situation is well illustrated by Martin Anderson in *Figure 6*, showing the percentage of marriages broken by death and divorce for different marriage cohorts (Anderson 1983; Schoen and Baj 1984).

Figure 6 Percentage of marriages broken by marriage cohort, England and Wales

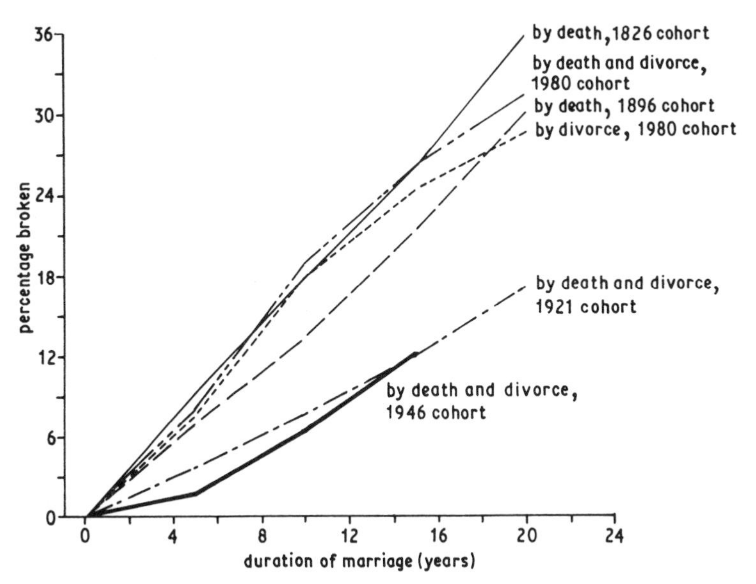

Source: Anderson (1983).

Another consequence of the longer expectation of life is the number of children who can now expect to know not only their grandparents but also their great grandparents. This has important implications for family care and the mutual support which can be given by the different generations. This too has been described by Martin Anderson and is summarized

Figure 7 Life courses of women by birth cohort (medians), England and Wales[1]

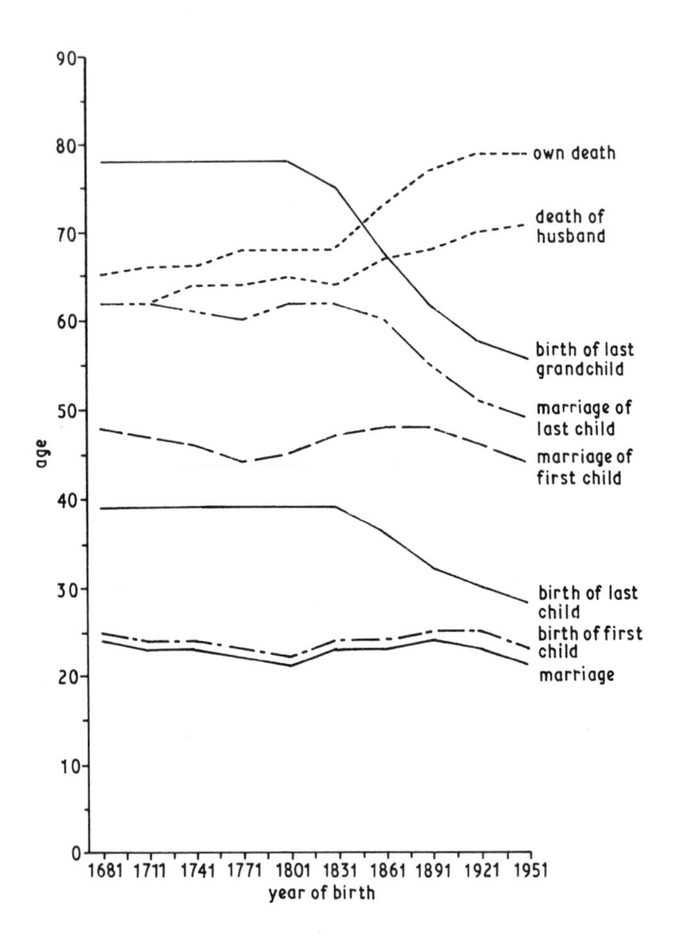

Note: [1] 'The data are based on estimates of the life course of individuals whose vital events (and those of their children and grandchildren) took place at the median age for the cohorts to which they respectively belonged. It is assumed the first and last children survived to marriage and married and that husbands survived at least to the birth of the last child.

Source: Anderson (1983).

in *Figure 7*. Whereas women born in 1946 will 'typically' have some seventeen years between the birth of the last child and the birth of the first grandchild, in 1831 the period was only nine years. In earlier generations it was thus possible for women to spend their whole lives caring first for their own children and then helping in the care of their children's children. Women growing old in the later nineteenth and early twentieth century did so at a period while their own children were child-bearing and there was the very real possibility of reciprocity of grandchild care by grandparents and parent care by children. This has now changed. As Martin Anderson writes:

> 'Increasingly in the 1960s and 1970s women, free of their own childcare responsibilities by their forties, returned to work – and worked right through the period when their grandchildren were born. And now that they themselves are entering old age, with around twenty more years to live, they find that their own children have in turn had their families and returned to work.'
>
> (Anderson 1983: 8)

Moreover (as Ungerson points out in Chapter 8) increasing longevity combined with the smaller number of children imposes additional responsibilities on the surviving children for those of their parents who may need care.

A further consequence of longevity, and of the shrinking gap between generations discussed above, is their impact on inheritance. On the assumption that the children do not inherit until their mother dies – this usually being later than the death of the father – the ages at which they can expect to inherit are a function of the mother's age at their birth and of her expectation of life at that time. Thus the steadily increasing expectation of life over the past century and the more recent falls in the average age at which mothers give birth have combined to delay the age at which wealth is passed from one generation to the next. Today the average age at which women have children is about twenty-seven, an age at which they can expect, at present mortality rates, to live another fifty-one years. Their children will thus be well into middle age and beyond the stage at which inherited capital might have helped in bringing them up, or helping them establish their own children. Although the expectation of life of those who own property is likely to be higher than average, the age at which they have children tends to be rather later, so that the age at which these children inherit is probably not markedly different from that of other social classes. One consequence of these changes, already apparent today, is for grandparents to lend or otherwise distribute their wealth to their grandchildren rather than their children.

Births and family size

Table 5 *Distribution of family size in Great Britain (percentages)*

<table>
<tr><th rowspan="2">number of children live-born in first marriage</th><th colspan="6">women married in period</th></tr>
<tr><th>mainly around 1860</th><th>1900–09</th><th>1920–24</th><th>1935–39</th><th>1956–60 (part estimated)</th><th>1961–65</th></tr>
<tr><td>0</td><td>9</td><td>10</td><td>16</td><td>15</td><td>10</td><td>8</td></tr>
<tr><td>1</td><td>5</td><td>14</td><td>24</td><td>26</td><td>17</td><td>21</td></tr>
<tr><td>2</td><td>6</td><td>18</td><td>24</td><td>29</td><td>39</td><td>41</td></tr>
<tr><td>3</td><td>8</td><td>16</td><td>14</td><td>15</td><td>22</td><td>23</td></tr>
<tr><td>4</td><td>9</td><td>12</td><td>8</td><td>7</td><td rowspan="2">12</td><td rowspan="2">7</td></tr>
<tr><td>5 or more</td><td>63</td><td>30</td><td>14</td><td>8</td></tr>
<tr><td></td><td>100</td><td>100</td><td>100</td><td>100</td><td>100</td><td>100</td></tr>
<tr><td>average number of children</td><td>5.7</td><td>3.5</td><td>2.4</td><td>2.1</td><td>(2.2)</td><td>(2.0)</td></tr>
</table>

Source: Office of Population Censuses and Surveys (1985).

The increase in life expectation has been matched during the present century by a steady decline in birth-rates and family size. The birth-rate is now below the level necessary for long-term replacement of the population. *Table 5* shows the increasing tendency for families to be limited to two children, with a big drop in the number of families with four or more children. The last two columns of the table are necessarily tentative as many of the women concerned are still of child-bearing age. The table also omits births in second and subsequent marriages (8 per cent of all legitimate births in 1984) and those births occurring outside marriage (17 per cent of all births in 1984). Changes in fertility are notoriously difficult to predict but recent trends suggest that an increasing number of couples are either delaying births until they are older or will not have children at all.

A particular feature of the change in family size is the extent to which there is now much greater uniformity across social classes, although fathers in manual occupations still have somewhat larger families than those in non-manual occupations (Central Statistical Office 1980: Table 2.18). Fertility is highest amongst semi- and unskilled manual workers and declines for skilled manual workers. It falls still further for junior non-manual workers and then begins to rise again for managerial and professional groups (Heath 1985).

The fertility rates of mothers born in the New Commonwealth, particularly mothers coming from the Indian sub-continent, are higher than of those born in the United Kingdom. During the ten years from 1971 to 1981, however, there were marked falls as families began to be more assimilated into the prevailing culture in the United Kingdom: the fall was especially noticeable amongst mothers from the Caribbean where the rate at the end of the period was only slightly higher than for mothers born in this country.

The reduction in family size shown in *Table 5* has been accompanied by a shortening of the period during which women build their families. Until the early 1970s the average age at which women were having their babies was steadily declining but, possibly for economic and career reasons and also because of a fall in births to teenaged mothers, it has risen in recent years by about a year and is now twenty-seven (Rimmer 1981: Table 5). These changes in family building, which are in part a result of women's employment, also enable those who wish to, to take a shorter spell out of the labour force. A further consequence of this earlier completion of families combined with longer life expectation is that a couple can expect to live together for a longer time after their children have left home.

Illegitimacy rates (17 per cent of all births in 1984 in England and Wales) have risen sharply in recent years as have total conceptions outside marriage. Between 1971 and 1983 the proportion of live-born babies conceived outside marriage rose from 17 to 22 per cent. However, the proportion of babies conceived outside but born within eight months of marriage has fallen and this suggests that, to an increasing extent, single women who become pregnant, particularly those aged under twenty, are tending not to get married before the birth of the child. Over the past decade there has also been an increase in the proportion of illegitimate births registered jointly by both parents, the implication being that, although single women who become pregnant may not get married before the birth of the child, they are increasingly likely to have maintained a stable relationship with the father at least up to the birth of the child (Central Statistical Office 1985: Chart 2.22).

Unlike the situation even a couple of generations ago far more lone parents are willing and able to support their children themselves rather than have them adopted. One child in eight now lives in a one-parent family (Central Statistical Office 1985: Chart 2.25).

Marriage and divorce

Table 6 *Women aged 18–49: de facto marital condition by age, Great Britain*

women aged 18–49[1] *de facto marital condition*	*age* 18–19 %	20–24 %	25–29 %	30–34 %	35–39 %	40–44 %	45–49 %	total %
					Great Britain: 1981 and 1982 combined			
cohabiting	4	7	5	3	2	2	2	4
married:								
first marriage	9	44	69	76	76	75	75	65
second or subsequent marriage	nil	1	4	8	9	10	8	6
single	86	45	14	7	5	4	5	19
widowed	nil	0	0	1	1	2	4	1
divorced	0	1	5	4	5	6	5	4
separated	1	2	2	2	2	2	2	2
Base = 100%	854	1,913	1,928	2,102	1,973	1,696	1,554	12,020

Note: [1] Except if the woman was cohabiting, marital status is that originally given to the interviewer. [0 = less than ½]
Source: General Household Survey (1982) London: HMSO.

The diminished stigma of illegitimacy and the greater social acceptance of cohabitation mark two of the most radical changes in family living patterns in the present century. Inevitably these two factors have affected and been affected by changing attitudes towards marriage and divorce. Indeed marriage has necessarily acquired a new meaning and purpose beyond its limited legal form (see Clark, Chapter 5). Although these trends have not as yet led to any substantial decline in the proportion of people who marry, the figures for the most recent years in *Table 6* suggest that the trend is now downward, in contrast to the steadily upward trend in the rest of the post-war period. It reached its peak in the late 1970s when more than nine out of ten women had married by the time they were aged thirty compared with only seven out of ten in the 1930s.

Until recent years, because of the higher mortality rates of boys at birth, there has always been a greater proportion of women than of men at the marriageable ages. By the 1950s however the number of men aged fifteen to forty-five was about equal to the number of women and today it is rather higher, one reason perhaps why young men are more fashion conscious than they used to be. The low proportion of women married in the inter-war years was partly the result of the unusually large imbalance brought about by the slaughter of young men during the First World War and also the comparatively high rates of emigration during the immediate post-war years. For many women therefore the family cycle never included marriage and children. Often it meant a life of caring for other people and other people's children and employment in the many occupations which, partly because of the availability of these single women, maintained a strict ban on employment of married women. For example, it is strange today to imagine a teaching profession almost wholly staffed by men and single women.

The proportion of marriages where one or both partners have been married before now accounts for one-third of all marriages. A generation ago, in the 1950s, it was about one in six and, if present trends continue, one marriage in three can be expected to end in divorce (Haskey 1982: 5). It is interesting to note that, even after taking account of the age variable, there is a strong social class gradient amongst divorcees, with the professional and managerial occupations having much lower rates than those in unskilled occupations (Haskey 1984: 425–26).

With the substantial increase in marriage breakdown, the number of children affected has risen dramatically. Six out of ten couples who divorced in 1982 had children under sixteen and, if present trends continue, one child in five can expect to see their parents divorce before they reach sixteen (Haskey 1983: 25). Most children from broken marriages spend part of their lives in a one-parent family. If that parent remarries they grow up in step-families: in 1979 one child in twenty lived with their natual mother and a step-father. It is however important not to exaggerate the situation and to remember that by far the majority of children, 84 per cent, live with both their natural parents.

Demographic trends and the life course

Today one in ten people do not marry and one in ten married couples do not have children. Many couples cohabit and may never marry. Others separate and divorce. Some may be lone parents for a while and then remarry and also become step-parents. Statistics to illustrate numbers of families at different stages of the life course and with different living patterns are very limited. *Table 7* gives a general indication only. It subdivides households into three broad groups: the elderly, young and middle-aged households without children (but including, in the three or more adult households, grown-up children still living at home with their parents), and households with children aged under sixteen. Each type of household makes up about one-third of the total.

Table 7 *Household types, Great Britain, 1984*

	as % of all households
one adult aged 16–59	8
two adults aged 16–59	13
three or more adults	12
youngest person aged 0–4	14
youngest person aged 5–15	19
two adults, one or both aged 60 or over	17
one adult aged 60 or over	16
all households	100

Source: General Household Survey. London: HMSO.

SOCIAL CHANGE: WORK, EMPLOYMENT, AND INCOMES

Work and employment

The section which follows looks at some of the economic changes, particularly in work, employment, and incomes, which have affected the living patterns of families during the course of their lives. Inevitably, because of its impact on the family, much of the discussion is concerned with the changing status of women.

At the time of the first population census in 1801, a question relating to the occupation of the head of the household made little sense to those who had to answer it. Households were accustomed to thinking of themselves as a collective entity carrying out a variety of tasks rather than as a collection of individuals with separate occupations. The question was therefore modified in the succeeding two censuses and it was not until 1841 onwards that the definition of occupation and economic activity became narrower and more precise. According to Catherine Hakim, however, the census still included unpaid household work in the definition of economic activity from 1851 to 1871: it was not until 1881 onwards that it was excluded, 'as the primary concern with work done for pay or profit began to emerge' (Hakim 1980: 88).

Since that time, the continuing growth of manufacturing industry, the institutionalization of the education of children in schools and the increasing segregation of home and work-place have all combined to destroy the concept of the household as an economic unit where tasks are shared. Women, especially those in the aspiring middle classes, suffered from this change in attitude. Women's work became associated with home and child-care: the man's world, by contrast, lay outside the home in the market-place.

In the immediate post-war years there was some recognition of the part which women played during the war and moves were made towards greater equality with men in employment and education. Equal opportunity however was slow to gain impetus. For the most part, particularly in social security and tax legislation, women, above all married women, were regarded as dependants of men.

A number of factors combined to modify the attitude towards women's employment. The shortening of the child-rearing span has already been described in earlier paragraphs, and technical changes lightened the burden of housework. Technical changes were also altering the structure of the British economy and the growing service industries were anxious to recruit women on both a full- and a part-time basis. Women themselves, as a consequence of free access to secondary education and to health services, were becoming more articulate and healthier. An increasing proportion acquired some kind of marketable qualification and those born in the 1950s started catching up with the educational attainments of men. Many more thus began to take paid work, irrespective of social class (Joshi 1985: 66–7). *Table 8*, relating to married women, shows the very marked growth in activity rates, particularly amongst the older age groups. Although much of the work which women undertake is part-time, low-paid, non-career work the very fact of going outside the home and taking paid employment has significantly altered family attitudes to the economic role which women can play in the household (see Burgoyne, Chapter 2).

Table 8 *Economic activity rates for married women (percentages), Great Britain*

age	*1951*	*1961*	*1971*	*1981*	*1984*
16–19	38	41	42	49	n.a.
20–24	36	41	46	57	53[1]
25–44	25	34	46	59	61
45–54	21	36	57	69	67
55–59		26	46	54	53
60 plus	5	7	14	12	8

Note: [1] 18–24: the corresponding figure for 1981 is 52 per cent.
Source: General Household Survey. London: HMSO, various issues.

The implications of these changes for women's life courses have been far reaching. *Figure 8* summarizes for all women, both married and unmarried, the type of employment pattern which prevailed in 1980 at different ages. It is now the birth of the first child rather than marriage which leads to a break in employment. Many however return soon after the birth of their children. In the period 1982–84, 21 per cent of married women with a youngest child under five were working part-time and 6 per cent full-time. Of those with a youngest dependent child aged five or over, 44 per cent were working part time and 20 per cent full time (Office of Population Censuses and Surveys 1985: Table 14).

Figure 8 Economic activity by age: all women except full-time students, Great Britain (1980)

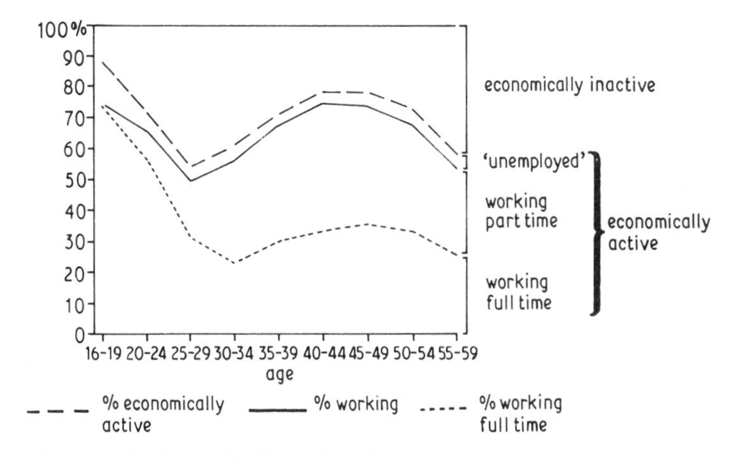

Source: Martin and Roberts (1984).

The life course for men follows a different pattern. Not only is it unbroken by childbirth but, during the time when the family are young and could most benefit from their father's presence at home, men's earnings are much needed and they tend to work longer hours than at any other period in their lives. Unemployment, however, has resulted in many of them retiring earlier than they otherwise would have done and, in some cases, using redundancy payments to embark on new careers.

One of the big social changes affecting the employment of both men and women has been the decline in agriculture, mining, and manufacturing industries and the growth of the service industries. This has brought with it a shift from manual to non-manual occupations, particularly to professional and managerial occupations. There has thus been a general upward social-class mobility from 'working' to middle-class occupations and many parents have seen their children adopt the different values which this change in social class may involve (Heath 1985).

Unemployment

Not only has there been a long-term relative decline in manual occupations but, at the present time, unemployment is particularly severe amongst semi- and unskilled manual workers. A high proportion of immigrants and their families look for employment in this type of work and they have thus been seriously affected. Unemployment has also had a bigger impact on the young and the elderly than those of other ages. The implications for these two groups have been explored by Coffield (Chapter 4) and Phillipson (Chapter 7). The rapidly accumulating evidence of the effect of unemployment on health, marriage, and crime makes abundantly clear the social consequences of the present situation. It is also worth noting that, as early as the spring of 1981, 8 per cent or about 1 million children lived in families where the head was unemployed: were later figures available they would show an even more distressing picture.

It is difficult to estimate how many women are unemployed because many do not register as such, there being no apparent advantage in doing so, but it would seem that fewer have been affected than might have been expected. One reason is that employers may prefer the flexibility of a labour force which is less protected by statutory regulations and more easily sackable. There has, for example, been a small switch from full- to part-time working amongst women: part-time employees for the most part fall outside protective employment legislation. However, whereas in many industries technological change has tended to affect craft skills and hence men's jobs rather than women's, as the introduction of electronics into the service industries begins to penetrate more deeply women too are likely to be substantially affected.

Attitudes towards work are changing and unemployment no longer carries with it the stamp of 'loafing' which characterized it in earlier generations. There is now a greater questioning of the value and meaning of work and recognition that it is a means of making a living rather than an end in itself. As Ray Pahl has written in a recent book emphasizing the importance of the household rather than the individual as the basic economic unit, work is 'a necessary and pragmatic activity essential to getting by' and the much lauded political objective of the 'right to work' might now, perhaps, 'be formulated more cautiously as the right to some minimum level of subsistence' (Pahl 1984: 84). Indeed the lessened stigma attached to the receipt of Supplementary Benefit, regarding it as a right and not a charitable hand-out, is a symptom of this changed attitude, particularly amongst young people searching for jobs and trying to establish careers (Hedges and Hyatt 1985).

Incomes

Most women work mainly for money although the satisfaction and esteem they obtain from it are as great, if not greater, than for men. Apart from the exceptional period during the inter-war years, women have tradionally earned money to help support the family and the household, either by taking outside employment or by making goods for sale within their homes. Ordinary households have not normally expected to rely on the earnings of only one (male) worker to support them. Today, wives in families with no children contribute about 30 per cent of household income and those with children some 25 per cent (Department of Employment 1984: Table 21).

Figure 9 shows how household incomes vary over the life course and how taxes and benefits affect these incomes: final income represents the combined effect on original income of taxes, cash benefits, and the estimated value of benefits in kind, such as education and health. One of the difficult phases is when a couple first marry and they have young children under the age of five. There are, on average, four mouths to feed and, in many cases, only one earner instead of two. Data from the Family Expenditure Survey show a drop in the number of economically active persons to 1.2 per household compared with 1.8 during the earlier phase before the family had children. Child Benefit and the National Health Service (for which an imputed value is included in 'final' income in *Figure 9*) are particularly valuable during this stage. At the next stage, when the youngest child is aged over five, things seem to improve a little. More mothers take up employment so the household has 1.6 economically active people and incomes are marginally higher, but the children are growing and becoming more costly to feed and clothe and both parents at work mean higher expenses generally.

Education benefits now join Child Benefit and the NHS as major items of support and, as might be expected, become particularly important when the family reaches the stage when it contains young adults who are still receiving full-time education.

Figure 9 The effect of taxes and benefits by life course categories of households, United Kingdom (1983)

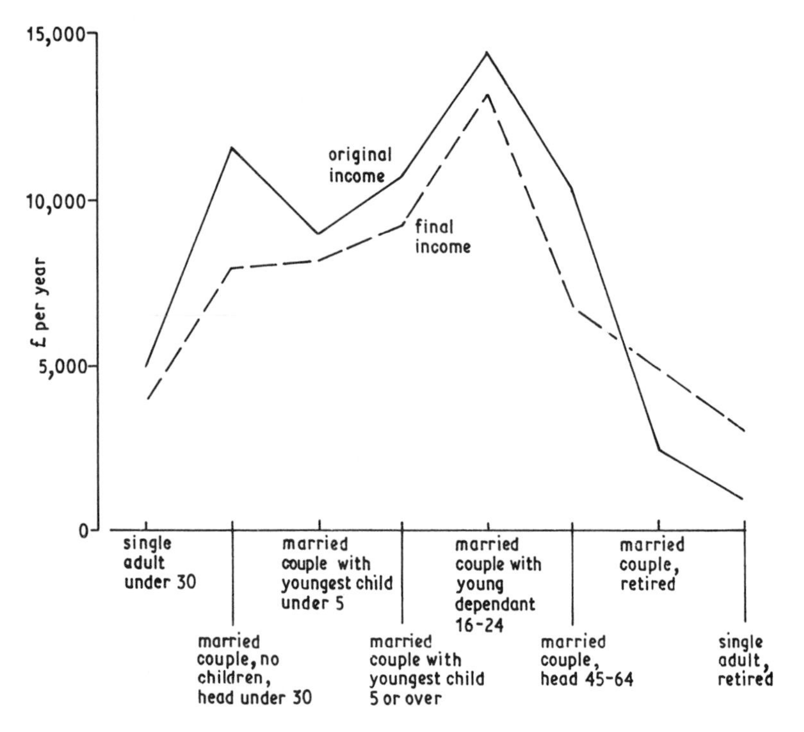

Source: Central Statistical Office (1984b).

The varying number of persons of different ages in a household makes it difficult to interpret the household income figures. One way of allowing for this in a very rough and ready way is to use 'adult equivalent' scales and this approach is used in *Figure 9* to convert total disposable income per household to income per person unit. Various scales have been devised in recent years but different methods of construction tend to give broadly similar results (Central Statistical Office 1981: 12). The scales used in the chart are as follows:

Married couple = 1.6
Single adult = 1.0
Child = 0.4
Young dependant = 0.6

Figure 10 Average disposable income, United Kingdom (1983)

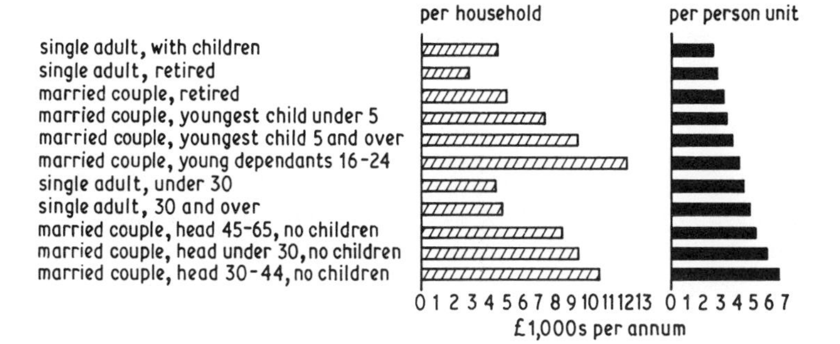

Source: Central Statistical Office (1984b).

Whatever the shortcomings of the estimates presented in *Figure 10*, it is obvious that the retired and those with children have less cash to spend than single and married people without children. Benefits in kind, however, particularly education and health services, go disproportionately to children and the elderly.

Evidence prepared in 1978 for the Royal Commission on the Distribution of Income and Wealth concluded that almost three-quarters of elderly people live in or on the margins of poverty and that the typical low-income elderly household consists of a woman in her mid-seventies living alone (Layard, Piachaud, and Stewart 1978). The mix of household types in the bottom quintile group of income has however changed considerably in recent years. In 1975, 80 per cent of these households were retired, compared with 65 per cent in 1983. Many of the retired have begun to benefit from occupational pensions which have helped to push their incomes into the higher quintile groups whereas, in contrast, there have been increasing numbers of households with children in the lowest income group because of unemployment. If the State Earnings Related Pensions Scheme (SERPS) is retained women too might in future be expected to benefit in their retirement. A further important factor affecting the future of many of the elderly, both men and women, is the growth in house ownership and the prospect of mortgage-free tenure in old age. There is thus the possibility that, at least for the fortunate minority, the closing years of the life course may be less dominated by poverty than it was in past generations. As Ungerson points out in Chapter 8, however, these trends will tend to accentuate and perpetuate into old age the division between the 'haves' and the 'have-nots'.

CONCLUSION

The social changes affecting the family cycle described in the preceding two sections have been reflected in the author's own family history outlined in the first section.

The demographic, migratory, and occupational background of my grandparents were in many ways typical of the time in which they lived. They had comparatively large numbers of children, many of whom did not live to maturity. Neither grandfather lived to see his grandchildren and they both died leaving young widows to bring up children single-handed. Farming was the main occupation, and the household as a whole the economic unit. The gradual contraction of agriculture led various family members to migrate, either to big cities such as London or to countries overseas.

My parents lived in a very different age and their life courses were shaped accordingly. Like many other couples who started married life in the centre of London, they later moved out to the suburbs and bought their own newly built house with the help of a mortgage. Money was often tight but it was generally accepted that middle-class mothers did not take paid work to supplement the family income.

It was a period when families were small and, along with many others of my generation, I was an only child with no siblings for support. As a young adult I bearded the still strong social disapproval of the time to live together with my future husband before marriage. When I separated from him at the end of the 1940s it was still difficult to get a divorce for it was not until 1970 that the law was reformed. Unlike the great majority of women of my generation I had the benefit of a university education. This helped me to get a well-paid job which I kept until the birth of my first child. The prosperity of the 1960s and the demand for trained employees enabled me to return to it after the birth of my children, something which was still difficult for many women of my generation.

During my childhood, health services, for the most part, had to be paid for and priority often had to be given to the man, who was the bread-winner. Later, in the post-war period, both my husband and I benefited during the middle years of our lives from medical advances and free health services: new drugs enabled me to survive tuberculosis, and open heart surgery has made it possible for him to hope for a longer life than my father, who died at the age of sixty-four shortly after a heart attack.

My two children have grown up in a world where rapid technical developments have changed the face of the environment. In the first place, it looks a different society in that it now includes far more people of different races and religions. In many respects the quality of life has improved but other trends have brought evil as well as good. Material standards of living are much higher and social security provides some kind of safety net, particularly for those impoverished by age, sickness, and unemployment. Houses are warmer and better equipped and the air outside is less polluted. Better diet and improved medical services have enabled people to be healthier and look younger, if only because they have better teeth, better hearing aids, contact lenses rather than spectacles. Life expectation is longer and few babies die in the first year of life. Mothers devote a shorter span of years to child-bearing and, in their middle years, have both the time and the health to follow other paths. Education is universally available and information spread by radio and television has opened the windows on the world at large in a way it would have been impossible to imagine at the end of the last century. Families are more geographically spread but cars, telephones, and even aeroplanes can keep them in regular touch with each other. At the same time motor vehicles have brought with them danger on the roads and, along with the cities and suburbs they have fostered, they have helped to destroy the countryside.

One of the biggest changes, which would certainly have raised eyebrows amongst the middle-class Victorians who expected their children to be seen and not heard, is the much greater independence and respect accorded to children and young people. This in its turn may make it more difficult for them to face extended periods of dependency resulting from prolonged periods of unemployment (Coffield, Chapter 4). The willingness to treat people more as individuals has likewise been reflected in one of the most important transformations in our society in the present century – the improved status of women. The greater equality between the sexes has altered the nature of marriage and, at the same time, brought a more tolerant attitude towards cohabitation and illegitimate children. This change in the way many people live, along with the prevalence of divorce, would scarcely have been approved by the Victorians.

War was a phenomenon familiar to the Victorians but they did not live beneath the shadow of a possible nuclear holocaust. Nor was there such widespread pessimism about the future of the country and its economy. The belief in progress has not been one to prevail through the life course of those who have lived in the present century.

NOTE

1 I would like to acknowledge the helpful comments on this chapter which I received from Jackie Morris of the Central Statistical Office and from Margaret Lane and John Haskey in the Office of Population Censuses and Surveys.

REFERENCES

Anderson, M. (1983) What is New about the Modern Family: An Historical Perspective. In *The Family*. British Society for Population Studies conference papers, University of Bath. OPCS Occasional Paper 31. London: Office of Population Censuses and Surveys.

Central Statistical Office (1980) *Social Trends 10*. London: HMSO.

Central Statistical Office (1981) The Effect of Taxes and Benefits on Household Incomes. *Economic Trends 1981*. London: HMSO.

Central Statistical Office (1984a) *Social Trends 14*. London: HMSO.

Central Statistical Office (1984b) The Effect of Taxes and Benefits on Household Incomes. *Economic Trends 374* December 1984. London: HMSO.

Central Statistical Office (1985a) *Social Trends 15*. London: HMSO.

Central Statistical Office (1985b) *Social Trends 16*. London: HMSO.

Department of Employment (1984) *Family Expenditure Survey Report for 1983*. London: HMSO.

Hakim, C. (1980) Social Aspects of Employment: Data for Policy Research. *Journal of Social Policy* 1. London: Cambridge University Press.

Haskey, J. (1982) The Proportion of Marriages Ending in Divorce. *Population Trends 27*. London: HMSO.

Haskey, J. (1983) Children of Divorcing Couples. *Population Trends 31*. London: HMSO.

Haskey, J. (1984) Social Class and Socio-Economic Differentials in Divorce in England and Wales. *Population Studies 38*. London: Cambridge University Press.

Heath, A. (1985) Social Mobility and Fertility. In *Measuring Socio-Demographic Change*. British Society of Population Studies conference papers, University of Sussex. OPCS Occasional Paper 34. London: Office of Population Censuses and Surveys.

Hedges, A. and Hyatt, J. (1985) *Attitudes of Beneficiaries to Child Benefit and Benefits for Young People*. London: Social and Community Planning Research.

Joshi, H. (1985) Motherhood and Employment: Change and Continuity in Post-War Britain. In *Measuring Socio-Demographic Change*. British Society of Population Studies conference papers, University of Sussex. OPCS Occasional Paper 34. London: Office of Population Censuses and Surveys.

Kiernan, K. (1985) The Departure of Children: The Timing of Leaving Home Over the Life-Cycles of Parents and Children. *Centre for Population Studies Research Paper 85–3*. University of London.

Layard, R., Piachaud, D., and Stewart, M. (1978) *The Causes of Poverty: Background Paper for the Royal Commission on the Distribution of Income and Wealth*. London: HMSO.

Martin, J. and Roberts, C. (1984) *Women and Employment: A Lifetime Perspective*. London: HMSO.

Murphy, M. (1983) The Life Course of Individuals in the Family. In *The Family*. British Society for Population Studies conference papers, University of Bath. OPCS Occasional Paper 31. London: Office of Population Censuses and Surveys.

Office of Population Censuses and Surveys. *General Household Survey*. Various reports. London: HMSO.

Office of Population Censuses and Surveys (1985) *General Household Survey: Preliminary Results for 1984*. OPCS Monitor GHS 85/1. London: OPCS.

Pahl, R.E. (1984) *Divisions of Labour*. Oxford: Blackwell.

Report of the Population Panel (1973) Cmnd 5258. London: HMSO.

Rimmer, L. (1981) *Families in Focus – Marriage, Divorce and Family Patterns*. Occasional Paper 6. London: Study Commission on the Family.

Schoen, R. and Baj. J. (1984) Twentieth-century Cohort Marriage and Divorce in England and Wales. *Population Studies 38*. London: Cambridge University Press.

Name index

Subject index